THE
PROFESSIONAL
PASTRY CHEF

THE
PROFESSIONAL
PASTRY CHEF

* *

Bo Friberg

A CBI BOOK

Published by Van Nostrand Reinhold Company

New York

A CBI Book
(CBI is an imprint of Van Nostrand Reinhold Company Inc.)
Copyright © 1985 by Van Nostrand Reinhold Company Inc.
Library of Congress Catalog Card Number 84-2214
ISBN 0-442-22635-7

Printed in the United States of America

Designed by Sheila Lynch

Published by Van Nostrand Reinhold Company Inc.
135 West 50th Street
New York, New York 10020

Van Nostrand Reinhold Company Limited
Molly Millars Lane
Wokingham, Berkshire RG11 2PY, England

Van Nostrand Reinhold
480 La Trobe Street
Melbourne, Victoria 3000, Australia

Macmillan of Canada
Division of Gage Publishing Limited
164 Commander Boulevard
Agincourt, Ontario M1S 3C7, Canada

16 15 14 13 12 11 10 9 8 7 6 5 4 3 2 1

Library of Congress Cataloging in Publication Data

Friberg, Bo, 1940-
    The professional pastry chef.

    "A CBI book."
    Includes index.
    1. Pastry. I. Title.
TX773.F75   1984   641.8'65   84-2214
ISBN 0-442-22635-7

Contents

*To two great Swedish confectioners who not only had
the patience and craft to teach me what they knew about their
profession, but also taught me a lot about life!*
  JOHN HAKANSON AND KURT ANDERSON

*To the management of the California Culinary Academy for
providing the opportunity and to the students for
helping in testing all these recipes in the course of their learning.*

Foreword

Europeans have long been distinguished as the finest-trained chefs in the world. The California Culinary Academy was modeled after the European system of education to meet an ever-increasing need for professional chef training in the United States.

Six years ago pastry chef Bo Inge Friberg joined the Academy's staff of European chefs devoted to teaching the culinary arts to American student chefs. Since his arrival, hundreds of students have completed their studies at the academy and have departed with a solid foundation in the methods and techniques of the discipline and a repertoire of recipes as a result of his dedicated tutelage. As culinary generalists, they entered the industry with a fine sense of the pastry-baking specialization. Students who demonstrated unique talents in the art of pastry and baking were selected to work exclusively with Chef Friberg. Those select students now work as pastry and baking specialists in fine restaurants, bakeshops, clubs, resorts, and aboard cruise ships—from New York to Hawaii.

This extensive collection is the culmination of Chef Friberg's years of training, experience in Sweden, operation of a successful bakeshop, and years as a chef/instructor at the California Culinary Academy. Each recipe was developed, tested, refined, and retested by Chef Friberg.

I congratulate Chef Friberg not only on this wonderful book, but also on the refined sense of professionalism he has imparted to generations of students.

DANIELLE CARLISLE, PRESIDENT
CALIFORNIA CULINARY ACADEMY

Introduction

All of these recipes have two things in common: They have been written so that any person with a basic knowledge of cooking will be able to understand them, and they have all been proven by my students, who were in different stages of development, from sophomores to seniors. This book was started several years ago when I came back from a trip to Europe, full of inspirations and new ideas. It is a little different from an ordinary cookbook because it tells you both what to do and what not to do. Some selections are classical recipes made my way. Some date back to when I was an apprentice. A few I have "borrowed" from restaurants and pastry shops around Europe, where I would order something that looked interesting, pick it apart, literally and mentally, and then try to duplicate it or even improve it. Many of the recipes have been developed through knowing what goes well together and what the American customer likes.

Pastry is very different from other cooking because you cannot stick your finger in for a taste and add a pinch of this and a pinch of that: most ingredients must be measured precisely. To be a good pastry chef, you need to be a perfectionist. You must pay attention to details. You must have some artistic talent, a sense of coordination and taste, and a steady hand. You must also earn the respect of the people who are working with you. You must be able to solve problems and hire the right people. A good chef must be born with a little of these talents, but a keen interest and a lot of practice will improve him or her over the years.

A good chef's most important asset is common sense. It is the one thing that cannot be taught. If you believe in yourself and believe that you can do the job, you will give anything your best effort. If the result is less than perfect, at least you have learned something and the next time you will try a little harder.

When I was a fifteen-year-old apprentice in Sweden, my first six months were spent practicing the three Ls—listening, looking, and learning. While I was helping a little here and cleaning up over there, I saw the breads and pastries being made. I had helped in making the dough for rye bread, but I had not done it on my own from start to finish. One morning when I arrived at work, my master said, "Bo! We are shorthanded today. Make up the rye bread!" I was startled and said, "I can't do that." My master angrily replied, "Do not ever use that word here again! You can do anything you want to do if you want to do it badly enough. The least you can do is to give it your very best try." I have always remembered that and tried to live by those words. It is one of the philosophies that I try to relate to all of my students.

My first experiment with cooking happened in my mother's kitchen when I was eleven years old. Coming home from school and finding the house empty, I attempted some kind of candy I guess. I do not remember exactly what it was supposed to be, but I do remember my poor mother had great difficulty cleaning up the sticky pots and pans. We both learned something from this: my mom, to time her trips to the grocery store better; and I, to clean up my messes.

After graduating from school at fourteen, I started as an apprentice at one of the local bakeries—quite small, three bakers and myself. I was lucky—without knowing it then, I happened to pick the best: my master and teacher for the next five years was a dedicated and skillful craftsman. He slowly and surely taught me the tricks of the trade, as well as a lot about life. When I began I was, of course, a young boy who knew everything already. However, I soon found out about the real world—how to take constructive criticism and to learn by my mistakes. I remember his words, "One mistake is no mistake. But two mistakes are two mistakes too many." I also developed my own tricks of the trade.

After I had become a regular on the rye bread, the retired owner of the bakery used to come down to check me out. (Bakeries in Sweden were always in the cellar with small windows level with the street, so when the bakers looked out all they could see were shoes.) After a few lectures about "not too perfectly formed loaves," I learned that he would walk in a straight line from the door to the shelves where the breads cooled and pick up a loaf to examine. After I started placing the almost-perfect loaves on the shelf he would always walk to, I could practice and improve in peace. In the end, my "yes-I-know-that" attitude must have improved too, for my master named his first and only son Bo, which I claimed as an ultimate victory. He assured me, however, that it had nothing to do with a certain apprentice.

What I learned during those first five years were the basics and the discipline—"if it's worth doing, do it so you can be proud of it." As I gradually picked up speed and ability, I moved up from rye breads to cookies. But if I happened to pay too much attention to those shoes outside the windows, I used to hear, from across the room, "Bo, throw some sheet pans on the floor. I cannot see you doing anything, so let me at least hear you."

Unfortunately, very few restaurants or pastry shops these days can afford to completely train an apprentice; it costs too much in both time and materials. Schools such as the California Culinary Academy are now providing the training the small businesses cannot. Now an employer can hire a graduate with at least sixteen months of basic training.

Once the basic methods are mastered, you can start to create, improve, and put a little bit of yourself and your own style into dishes. I think what our industry lacks today, especially in the dessert menus in most restaurants, is creativity and that "bit of self." Too often the menu offers a basic chocolate cake with too much sponge and not enough filling, a basic custard, and an overbaked (to be sure it is firm in the middle) cheesecake. The worst offender is plain vanilla or chocolate ice cream, sometimes creatively put together in one dish. Most of the time these desserts are not even made on the premises, so that they are a few days old and dry, in addition to being boring.

The first and last impressions of a meal are very important. I do not expect anything of a meal if the kitchen cannot make a decent salad or serve the soup hot. However, even if the meal is mediocre, a great-looking and tasting dessert will give a positive last impression. I have noted with pleasure a rebirth of interest in great desserts. Especially rewarding for me is when I realize by a look at a dessert menu in a restaurant or a taste of a certain dessert that there is, or has been, a former student in the kitchen.

This book is about making pastries and cakes good and exciting. It is not meant to impress or to set any particular standards. The methods described and used in the recipes are not the only way or necessarily the best way. There are different ways to form a loaf of bread, to frost a cake, or to hold a decorating bag. One way is better for one person, the other way for another.

In this book I have tried to give the best of my knowledge, as I give it to my students at the academy. It is my hope that this knowledge will be passed on to you as you seek to better yourself in our creative and honorable profession.

Ingredients and Equipment

Alcoholic Flavorings

Amaretto is an Italian liqueur flavored for the most part with almonds, sweet and bitter.

Arrack is the fermented and distilled product of palm juice, raisins, and dates. It has a very strong and particular aroma and is used in desserts and candies.

Brandy, which is distilled from wine, is classified by these labels: E-extra special, F-fine, M-mellow, O-old, P-pale, S-superior, V-very, X-extra. V.S.O.P. means very superior old pale.

Calvados is brandy made from apples. It is very strong and originated in the Normandy region of France.

Chambord is a liqueur made of black raspberries, other fruits, herbs, and honey.

Cognac is a type of brandy made in the area of Cognac, a town in the Charente region of France.

Cointreau is a colorless French liqueur flavored with the peel of Curacao oranges and other oranges. For baking, it is interchangeable with Grand Marnier.

Crème de cacao is a French liqueur flavored with chocolate.

Frangelico is an Italian liqueur derived primarily from hazelnuts but is flavored with other berries and flowers as well.

Grand Marnier is a French liqueur made with oranges and aged Cognac.

Kirschwasser, or kirsch, is a colorless brandy distilled from the juice of a small black cherry found in the southern part of Germany.

Madeira is a fortified sweet wine from the island of Madeira.

Maraschino, a liqueur made from the *marasca* cherry, can be substituted for Kirschwasser.

Marsala is an Italian dessert wine originating from the Sicilian town Marsala.

Raspberry brandy is a very strong, colorless brandy made from raspberries.

Rum is made from the fermented juice of the sugarcane and is available light or dark in strengths up to 150 proof. The dark rum has the stronger flavor.

Butter, Margarine, and Lard

Butter should be no more than 15% water and at least 80% fat. The remaining 5% is mineral matter, such as salt, and milk solids. Because of its low melting point and wonderful aroma, butter is indispensable in making quality pastries, especially buttercream and puff paste. In hot climates, a small amount of margarine must be added to the butter to make it workable. There are three kinds of butter used in cooking and baking: salted butter, sweet butter, and clarified butter, which is melted butter with the milk solids removed. All the recipes in this book use sweet butter, but salted butter can be substituted if the salt in the recipe is reduced by approximately ⅕ ounce (6 g) for every 1 pound (455 g) of butter. You cannot use salted butter, however, if there is little salt in the recipe or if the main ingredient in the recipe is butter.

Clarifying butter makes it possible to lightly sauté or fry with butter without overbrowning or splitting off the fat. To clarify butter, melt butter over low heat. Let it stand for a few minutes, skim off all the milk solids on top, and carefully spoon or pour the clear butterfat into a clean container. Discard any residue in the bottom of the pan.

Lard is almost 100% refined pork fat. The highest quality lard is pork leaf fat; lard from other sources must be labeled "rendered pork fat." It is excellent for frying and is unbeatable in making flaky pie dough because of its elasticity and shortening power. It can be kept for months if stored covered in the refrigerator.

Margarine is about 80% fat, 18% skim milk, and 2% salt, unless it is unsalted. There are two types of margarine: oleo margarine, which is made from beef and veal fat with vegetable and/or other oils added, and vegetable margarine, which was generated to substitute for butter. Oleo margarine is made primarily for the baking industry and has been developed to meet various demands of baking professionals. Some margarines are purposely made tough and with a high melting point; others cream well and are best in baked goods. If kept for a long time, margarine should be stored in a dark, dry place that is below 70° F (21° C).

Eggs

Although assumed to be from the domestic hen, eggs from turkeys, ostriches, and ducks can also be used in baking; they are bigger but the composition is the same. Eggs are the one of two structural materials in baking (flour is the other). When combined with flour, eggs create a framework that supports and traps the air in cake batters. If you are lucky enough to have a source for fresh eggs, save them for your breakfast. A mature egg that has been stored under the proper conditions for a few weeks is much better to use in baking. Because the shell is porous, an egg loses a fraction of its water content every day. You can check the freshness of an egg by placing it in water mixed with 12% salt. If the egg is no more than a few days old, it will sink to the bottom. If the egg floats on the top, it is bad.

An average egg weighs about 2 ounces (55 g); the white is 1 ounce (28 g), the yolk is ⅔ ounce (20 g), and the shell ¼ ounce (7 g). Eggs should be weighed instead of counted in any recipe. By far the most common way eggs are sold is in the shell. The only reason for not buying eggs this way is the time it takes to crack and empty the shell in a busy bakery. For this reason eggs are sold freshly cracked in many countries. Once cracked, the egg loses its quality and whipping power very quickly. If cracked and separated, the yolks will form a skin on top within a minute if left standing uncovered.

Bad eggs are very rare these days due to improved methods of storing and checking them, but it is still a good idea when cracking a large number of eggs to crack a half dozen or so in a small container before emptying them into the big batch. In this way, should you encounter a rotten egg, the entire batch will not be wasted; a small amount of rotten egg will spoil many. An egg that is merely sour can be used as long as it is to be baked, although it will not contribute as much to the volume. The smell and taste of the sour egg disappears with heat.

Frozen eggs are an excellent substitute for fresh and are very convenient to use. They must be thawed slowly at a temperature below 100° F (38° C) the day before they are to be used, although they can be placed under cold running water in an emergency. It is also important to stir the eggs thoroughly before using. Frozen egg whites and yolks can also be purchased.

Dehydrated eggs have had their water content removed. Although the dehydrated egg is used by cake-mix and candy manufacturers, it is not practical for use in batters that need volume, such as yeast doughs, cakes, and some pastries. Dehydrated eggs are reconstituted by adding one part egg powder to three parts water by weight. Add the water slowly to the powder. Dried egg whites are widely used in the pastry shop with excellent results. They are especially useful when mixed with sugar and preservatives to make meringue powder. Dried egg yolks are useful in making egg wash for baked goods.

Except for those that will be used that day, eggs, especially cracked eggs, should always be refrigerated.

Flour

Flour is the other of the two structural materials used in baking (eggs are the first). Most of the flour used in the bakery today is wheat flour. It is grown all over the world in various quantities and qualities. The wheat kernel has three parts: endosperm (85%), germ or embryo (2%), and bran (13%). White flour comes from the endosperm in various degrees of quality and strength.

All flour absorbs a certain amount of water. Newly milled cake flour will absorb less water because its water content is higher than aged flours, which absorb more. You can increase any flour's absorption of water by scalding the flour; that is, boiling part of the water and mixing it into part of the flour and letting it stand for several hours or overnight.

Bread flour, or high-gluten flour, is milled from wheats rich in protein and grown in areas which have the right amount of rainfall, and a soil rich in nitrogen. It is pale yellow when first milled and turns off-white with aging. Bread flour is very easy to dust into a thin film; it is ideal for rolling out and working with doughs.

Cake flour is milled very finely from wheat of good quality. The flour is then chlorinated to break down the strength of the gluten. It is whiter in color than high-gluten flour and is also harder to dust with because it tends to cake.

Whole-wheat flour is milled from the whole kernel, including the germ and the bran. It is very nutritious and ranks next to white flour in gluten strength. Whole-wheat bread is slightly heavier than bread made solely from white flour, but the dough takes less time to mix and rise.

Graham flour is whole-wheat flour milled very finely, which makes the bran less distinguishable in the finished product.

Rye flour is one of the best-tasting flours for bread making. Although there are light, medium, and dark rye flours, medium is the most commonly used. Because of the poor gluten content in rye, it is mixed with bread flour when making bread. A small amount of vinegar helps bring out the rye flavor.

Pumpernickel flour is dark rye flour with a higher proportion of the bran added and a small amount of whole-wheat flour mixed in. If this flour is not used with a high-gluten flour, it will barely rise at all.

Rolled-wheat flour looks almost like rolled oats and is added to breads in small amounts to give the loaf a distinctive taste and texture.

There are in addition a variety of mixed and whole-grain flours, as well as flours other than wheat, such as potato flour, corn flour (which is not the same as cornstarch), barley flour, oat flour, and buckwheat flour.

Jellying Agents

Agar-agar, a vegetable substance extracted from Japanese seaweed, is available in both powder and strips. Agar-agar is odorless, colorless, and eight times stronger than gelatin. It is used when a very strong thickening agent is needed, as for special meringues, pastries, and some ice creams.

Gelatin is derived from the bones and skins of animals. It is used in puddings, cakes, and creams. Although it can be purchased in flavors, unflavored gelatin is the only kind used in the pastry kitchen. Gelatin is available in sheet or powdered form. Sheet gelatin is more expensive but much easier to use. Sheet gelatin is first placed in cold water for a few minutes to soften. In the process it will absorb enough water to melt. Approximately 1½ ounces (4½ cl) of water is absorbed for every ⅓ ounce (10 g) of gelatin. The sheet must be removed without squeezing out any of the absorbed water. Powdered gelatin is first dissolved in the amount of cold water a particular recipe calls for. If no amount is specified and the gelatin manufacturer has not provided instructions, use 1½ ounces (4½ cl) for every ⅓ ounce of gelatin. Both sheet and powdered gelatin must be heated to 150° F (65° C) in order to gel the mixture when it cools, but it should never be boiled because boiling reduces the strength of the gelatin and also causes a skin to form on top. Sheet gelatin can be substituted for powder in equal weight. If a recipe calls for a larger amount of water than is called for in the ratio above, the extra water has to be added. For instance, if a recipe instructs you to dissolve ⅓ ounce (10 g) gelatin powder in 2 ounces (6 cl) water, you must add another ½ ounce (1½ cl) to the softened sheet gelatin.

Pectin is naturally present in varying amounts in all kinds of fruits. Pectin is the ingredient that thickens marmalades, jams, and jellies. Commercial pectin is usually extracted from apples and can be purchased in a powder or liquid form.

A glaze made with apricot jam is frequently substituted in this country for pectin glaze, which is not yet commercially available. Pectin glaze is especially good when brushed on pastries and tarts because it does not soak into the fruit but gives the surface an attractive gloss. See index for recipe.

Leavening Agents

Ammonium carbonate is also called hartshorn because it originally was produced from the hart's horns and hooves. Presently made chemically, it is used mainly in cookies and short doughs but can also be used in *páte à choux* to give it an extra puff. It reacts only to heat and has a very strong odor that totally disappears above 140° F (60° C). Always store ammonium carbonate in an airtight container.

Baking powder is composed of one part sodium bicarbonate and two parts baking acid, generally cream of tartar, with a small amount of starch added to keep it from caking. When baking powder comes in contact with liquid and heat, it releases carbon dioxide gas, which causes a cake to expand and rise. If the right amount has been added, baking powder will leave no aftertaste and will leave only small holes inside the baked dessert. Generally speaking, the softer or more fluid the batter is, the more the baking powder will react.

Cream of tartar is made from tartaric acid; starch is added to dilute its strength. It can be substituted for tartaric acid and is found in baking powder and ammonium carbonate. It is most often used to stiffen egg whites for meringues.

Potash produces carbon dioxide when in contact with acid. An uncommon leavening agent, it is used mostly in cookies with spices and honey.

Sodium bicarbonate, or baking soda as it is commonly called, is used alone or in combination with baking powder in some cakes and cookies. In addition to acting as a leavening agent, bicarbonate will darken the texture of baked cakes and cookies, which is an advantage when making gingerbread. It will leave a strong alkaline aroma if too much is used, but in the case of gingerbread, the aroma is overshadowed by the strong spices.

Yeast is one of the most important ingredients for the bread baker. It is a living microorganism, actually a fungus, which multiplies very quickly in the right temperature (78° to 82° F, 26° to 28° C). The ferments it produces convert sugars and starch into carbon dioxide and alcohol. Fresh, or compressed, yeast should have a pleasant smell, almost like apple, a cakey consistency, and should break easily. Fresh yeast can be kept up to two weeks in the refrigerator before it starts to lose its strength. To test yeast, dissolve a small amount in a mixture of ½ cup (1 dl, 2 cl) water, 2 teaspoons (10 g) of sugar, and 1 ounce (30 g) flour. If the yeast is good, it will expand and foam within 10 minutes. Fresh yeast that is too old will be dry and crumbly; older yeast will break down into a sticky, foul-smelling substance. Yeast can be frozen, but it will lose about 5% of its strength. Frozen yeast must be thawed slowly and then used as soon as possible. Some of the yeast cells will die at temperatures above 115° F (46° C). Temperatures above 140° F (60° C) will kill all the yeast cells. Mixing yeast directly into a large amount of sugar or salt will also damage it.

There are three basic kinds of yeast: fresh (compressed), dry, and brewer's. Of these, only fresh and dry yeast are used in bread making. When substituting dry yeast for fresh, reduce the amount by half.

Nuts

Almonds are of two basic kinds: bitter, which are used for flavorings and extracts, and sweet, which are eaten fresh or used for cooking. To remove the skin from the almond, blanch in hot water and squeeze off the skin before it dries.

Chestnuts are used in purées and syrups and are eaten raw or roasted. The skin is removed by piercing the nut and then blanching for a short while or by roasting the nuts in the oven with water on the baking pan.

Hazelnuts are called filberts when grown commercially, but there is no difference between the two. To remove the skin, roast them and rub the skin off between your hands, or blanch them in hot water with a small amount of baking soda added. Removing all of the skin from the nuts by hand is difficult and sometimes takes an inordinate amount of time.

Hazelnut paste, made of roasted hazelnuts and sugar worked to a paste, is sold to the professional baker by the Swiss Carma and Felchlin companies, but it can be made very easily. To make the paste, remove as much of the skins as possible by one of the methods described above. Process in a food processor, adding 4 ounces (1 dl, 21) of Simple Syrup (see Index) for every pound (455 g) of roasted hazelnuts. Store in an airtight container and use as needed.

Macadamia nuts are slightly bigger than hazelnuts when they are shelled, which is the way they are sold.

Pecans are usually sold shelled in halves or in broken pieces.

Pine nuts are the edible nuts of certain pine trees. The domestic and European nuts are slightly bigger than a lemon seed, but the pine nuts of South America grow up to two inches (5 cm) in length.

Pistachios have two shells. The outer shell is usually dyed light red on nuts that are imported; the almond-shaped inner shell is thin and fragile. The small seeds are green in color. The skins are removed by blanching the nuts in hot water with some salt added, which brings out the green color as well, and then squeezing off the skins.

Walnuts should only be used if the meat is white and crisp. If the meat is soft and grayish, the nuts are past their prime. Because the walnut is rich in oil, it turns rancid very quickly. Store the nuts in a dry cool place or, if they must be kept for a long time, in an airtight container in the refrigerator. Walnuts are difficult to crush or grind without ending up with a mash because of the oil in them; they should be chopped instead.

Sweeteners

AA confectioners' sugar is a granulated sugar with big crystals and few impurities. It is frequently used in decorating and in cakes and pastries and is excellent for boiling and caramelizing sugar.

Brown or golden sugar is sugar that is not fully refined. It has a distinctive taste and comes in a range of color from light to dark brown. The darker sugars are more bitter. The most common is golden brown sugar, which has a honeylike taste. Brown sugar is very wet and must be stored in an airtight container to keep it from hardening.

Castor sugar is granulated sugar ground finer but not as fine as powdered sugar. If a sugar that dissolves faster than granulated is needed, castor sugar is used.

Corn syrup is made from starch. Light corn syrup is the most common, but dark is also available. Corn syrup is somewhat more fluid than glucose, but the two are interchangeable.

Fondant, a combination of very fine sugar crystals and invert sugar syrup, is used as the base for many icings. Although it can be made by the baker, it is usually bought ready-made to save time. It gives a very special shine and appearance to many fancy pastries.

Glucose, a mixture of dextrose and gum, is a thick syrup made from starch. Also called heavy or thick corn syrup, it is not as sweet as sugar. It is used in icing and in marzipan to improve elasticity.

Golden syrup is a by-product of sugar manufacture that is more refined than molasses. When the sugar, after many boilings, stops yielding crystals, the remaining syrup is filtered and reduced. Golden syrup is composed of sucrose, dextrose, levulose, and a small amount of water. It is used in breads, cookies, and cakes.

Granulated sugar is the most widely used and is what is meant when a recipe simply calls for sugar. The granules are the right size for incorporating the proper amount of air in cake batters. It also melts and dissolves at the right speed and temperature in cakes during baking.

Honey is an invert sugar from a natural source. It will, in addition to having the sugar taste, have the aroma of the different flowers from which it was obtained. It is not as sweet as sugar and crystallizes very quickly when it is stored. It gives a soft and chewy texture to specialty cakes and cookies, such as gingerbread.

Invert sugar is a chemically processed heavy syrup, sweeter than sugar, that will not crystallize. Today it is used mostly in icings and flavorings.

Loaf and cube sugar is made by pressing damp granulated sugar, drying it, and then cutting it into sizes. Loaf sugar is needed to make sugar sculptures. Both loaf and cube sugar are perfect for sugar boiling.

Malt sugar or syrup caramelizes at low temperatures and has a very distinctive taste. Excellent for retaining moisture, it is used in many yeast breads.

Maple syrup is used mainly for flavoring. It will turn dark when stored but this will not affect the flavor. Maple syrup should be refrigerated after opening.

Molasses is produced in the first stages of refining raw sugar. Used in breads and cakes, it adds a distinctive flavor. It comes in various grades and shades of brown; the lighter color is the sweeter and is most commonly used.

Powdered sugar is ground even finer than castor sugar. Starch is added to prevent it from caking or lumping. It is used mostly for uncooked icings, decorating, and some meringues.

Tartaric Acid

Some tartaric acid is found in most fruits, but the commercial product is extracted from grapes. Despite the somewhat poisonous-sounding name, tartaric acid is used for a number of things in cooking. Cream of tartar is made from it, and it is found in baking powder and ammonium carbonate. When used in sorbets and fruit desserts, it brings out the fruit flavor. It can be used whenever acidulated water or citric acid (when the citrus flavor is not necessary) is called for. Although not usually available in grocery stores, tartaric acid can be bought or ordered from a drugstore. It is quite inexpensive and lasts a very long time. It also acts as the catalyst for pectin glaze (see Index). To make it into a liquid, mix 4 ounces (1 dl, 2 cl) hot water and 4 ounces (115 g) tartaric acid until all the granules are dissolved. Pour the liquid into a drop bottle and store it with the other spices.

Thickeners

Cornstarch is one of the most commonly used thickening agents. It must be dissolved in cold water before being added to any hot mixture to keep it from lumping. Cornstarch gelatinizes at temperatures above 170° F (77° C), and it will leave an unpleasant taste if not cooked long enough. In sponge and cake batters, it is used to dilute the gluten strength of flour because it is close to 100% starch.

Potato starch, or potato flour, can be substituted for cornstarch, often with better results. It gelatinizes at 176° F (81° C), leaves no unpleasant taste, and when used as a thickener, will not break down and get watery the next day, as cornstarch tends to do. It also is used to reduce the gluten strength of flour.

Tapioca starch digests well and is used as a thickener as well as an ingredient in desserts.

Vanilla

The vanilla bean is a thin black bean about 8 inches (20 cm) long. Once picked, it is cured by dipping in boiling water and drying slowly. Vanilla beans are quite expensive, but each bean can be used 3 or 4 times. Place them in glass jars filled with granulated sugar to store them and make vanilla sugar at the same time. Pure vanilla extract is a more practical and less expensive way of getting vanilla flavor. The uses of vanilla bean and extract in the pastry kitchen are endless because their taste will mix with almost any other flavor and improve many of them.

Equipment

Adjustable frame: a 2-inch-high (5-cm) frame usually placed around a baking pan. It adjusts to different widths and lengths.

Adjustable ring: a 2-inch-high (5-cm) ring that adjusts from 8 inches (20 cm) to 16 inches (40 cm) in diameter. It is used to hold a filling while it sets and is useful for making odd-size cakes.

Balloon whisk: a whisk with a round (balloon) shape at the end. It is especially useful for incorporating the maximum amount of air into a batter.

Cake rack or cake cooler: This rack looks like a grill and is designed so that air can circulate under as well as around cooling breads or cakes. It is handy for icing pastry as well if a sheet is placed under the rack to collect the runoff.

Chinois: a cone-shaped strainer with a fine mesh also known as a China cap.

Comb scraper: a plastic or metal scraper with a fluted or serrated edge. It is used to make a pattern on the surface of cakes or pastries.

Dipping fork: a small fork, also known as a tempering fork, with 2 to 4 prongs. It is used for dipping pastries and candies into chocolate or icing.

Docker or pricker: a tool that has spikes to prick doughs, eliminating air bubbles and preventing them from rising too much during baking.

False-bottom tart pan: a tart pan with a side 1 inch (25 mm) high and a removable bottom. It is used for quiches and fruit tarts.

Flan ring: a thin metal circle about 1 inch high (25 mm) that comes in various sizes. It is used to bake open tarts.

Hotel pan: a stainless-steel pan that comes in different sizes and depths. The pan has a lip all around so that it can be placed on top of a basin of hot water (bain-marie) to keep the food warm. Hotel pans are also useful for marinating and storing food and for baking custards and soufflés in a water bath.

Mazarin form: a small, round baking form with slanted sides, typically 2½ inches (64 mm) in diameter on top, 1½ inches (30 mm) on the bottom, and 1 inch (25 mm) high.

Multiple pastry wheel: a tool with 4 or 5 pastry wheels connected so that multiple strips of dough can be cut quickly. The wheels are adjustable.

Parchment paper: also called parchment baking paper, baking paper, or silicon-coated paper. It is a specially treated nonstick paper that is used extensively in pastry and cake baking. It is available in thick or thin; the thick paper can be used more than once.

Pastry bag: a cone-shaped plastic, nylon, or cloth bag that comes in lengths from 7 inches (17.5 cm) to over 20 inches (50 cm). When connected to a piping tip, it is used to pipe out batters or doughs. Fill the bag no more than two-thirds full; fold the upper third over the rest of the bag and tightly seal it to prevent batter from coming out the top as you work.

Pastry wheel: a sharp round disk attached to a handle so that it can roll. Also known as a pizza cutter, it comes fluted or plain and is used to cut dough.

Pincers: a small hand tool with two flat, springy arms of different widths and shapes that have a fluted pattern on the edges. It is used for decorating the edges of pies or to pinch a design on marzipan.

Piping bag: a small, approximately 5-inch (12.5-cm) paper cone. It is used for precise and delicate decorations and is held by the fingers only. To make the cones: Cut a standard full-sheet (24 × 16 inches, 60 × 40 cm) parchment paper into six 8-inch squares. Fold each square diagonally and cut into 2 triangles. Make the cone by holding the triangle horizontally, in such a way that the longest side is in front of you. Fold into a cone shape so that the long side becomes the tip and the point of the triangle (opposite the long side) becomes the opening of the cone. Fold the top into the cone to secure the shape. Fill the cone only halfway. Close the top securely and cut the tip into the desired opening.

Piping tip: a small, metal or plastic, hollow cone that is fitted onto a pastry bag. The tips come in many shapes and sizes.

Proof box: a cabinet or room with a controlled amount of heat and humidity to create the correct environment for a yeast dough to proof.

Ramekin: individual, shallow, earthenware dish in which food is baked and served, such as individual soufflés.

Salamander: a broiler with the heat source at the top or a hot metal plate that is used to brown or caramelize food.

Savarin form: a small, doughnut-shaped baking form. Its sizes vary, but a useful one to use is 3½ inches (89 mm) in diameter, 1 inch (25 cm) deep, with a 1¼-inch (31-mm) hole. It is used for making individual servings of savarins, as the name suggests, but can also be used for many other pastries and desserts.

Sheet pan: a metal baking sheet used in professional kitchens. Its sides are 1 inch (25 mm) high, and it measures 24 × 16 inches (60 × 40 cm). Half-sheet pans are 16 × 12 inches (40 × 30 cm) and will fit the home oven.

Skimmer: a flat, finely meshed (or with small holes) strainer fixed to a handle. It is used to remove dirt or scum from a boiling liquid, to poach, and to deep fry.

Springform pan: a baking pan with a removable rim. A clamp tightens the rim around the bottom. It is used mostly for baking cheesecakes.

Tartlet pans: pans used for making small, individual tarts that are usually filled with fruit or custard.

Waffle roller: a small, pipelike tool, about 13 inches (32½ cm) long and 1 inch (25 mm) in diameter. Its surface resembles a waffle iron, so that, when rolled over dough, it will create a decorative waffle pattern.

2

Pastries and Tarts

Short Dough

Short dough is a name that will make sense only if one realizes that "short" refers to the crumbly quality of the dough produced by the shortening in it when baked. To be worked fast and efficiently, the dough must be somewhat elastic so it will not break too easily as it is molded and fit into pans and molds, but it cannot be too soft. When combining the ingredients, use the dough hook at low speed, and mix just until combined. Overmixing will incorporate too much air, making the dough difficult to work. Although the flavor of a dough made with all butter cannot be beat, such a dough is hard to manage because the butter will be either rock hard if stored in the refrigerator or too soft if left at room temperature. The span of time when the butter's consistency is just right is not very long. A short dough made with good vegetable margarine is easier to handle. In cold climates a combination of margarine and butter can be used.

An efficient pastry kitchen will always have a supply of short dough, cool and ready to use, in the refrigerator. Aside from the typical uses of lining form and tart pans and providing the bases for numerous cakes and pastries, short dough is irreplaceable for preparing what I call "arriving-in-the-morning-with-nothing-left-in-the-showcase cookies." With one basic dough, you can make up many different pastries and cookies speedily and efficiently

Before you roll out short dough, knead it with your hands until it is smooth and elastic, which will minimize the cracking around the edges when you roll it out and prevent the dough from breaking if you line tarts or forms. Do not use more bread flour than is necessary to keep the dough from sticking because too much flour will make the dough dry and crumbly. As you need more dough, add new dough, cold and firm from the refrigerator, to the batch you are working. The dough, before or after it is shaped, can be stored covered in the refrigerator or freezer for a few days. Short dough can be baked at any temperature between 325° and 425° F (165° and 220° C), but 375° F (190° C) is normal. When the short dough starts to show a golden brown color, you can be sure it is done, if you are using the recipes and procedures in this book.

How to Make Short-Dough Bottoms

Work a piece of short dough smooth with your hands, shaping it into a thick circle in the process. Roll to ⅛ inch (3 mm) thick and slightly larger than the size you need. Sprinkle just enough bread flour on the board to keep it from sticking. Keep moving and turning the dough over—first with your hands and then, as the dough gets thinner, by rolling it up on the dowel. If only the edge of the dough is moving and not the middle as you are rolling it out, the middle of the dough is sticking to the table. Try to roll the dough into the general shape of what you plan to make. Cut off the ragged edge that always develops when the dough starts to get thin because that edge often tears from the dough when you are picking it up or rolling it. When the short dough is ⅛ inch (3 mm) thick, roll it up on a dowel (never a rolling pin) and place it on a sheet pan lined with parchment paper. Place an adjustable cake ring or a template on top of the short dough; cut around the ring or template and remove the leftover dough. If the dough bottom is cut before it is transferred to the pan, you will probably stretch the dough when moving it, resulting in an oval instead of a circle. Prick the dough lightly on top to ensure that any trapped air can escape. Bake at 375° F (190° C) for about 10 minutes.

How to Line Large Tart Pans

Prepare and roll out the dough the same way as for making short-dough bottoms. Roll the dough into a ⅛-inch-thick (3-mm) circle, 1 to 2 inches (2.5 to 5 cm) larger than the pan. Roll it up on a dowel (remember, not the rolling pin, if that is what you are using to roll out the dough). Place the tart pan in front of the dough, and, working as quickly as you can, roll out the dough over the pan. Pick up the edge of the dough all around, and gently press it against the side and bottom of the pan. Take care not to stretch the dough when lining the pan; it should still be ⅛ inch (3 mm) thick when you have finished. To make sure trapped air can escape, prick the dough lightly.

If the tart shell must be prebaked, line the bottom only with a piece of paper, fill with dried beans or pie weights, and bake as indicated by your recipe. The use of pie weights is not necessary if it does not matter that the side will settle (not shrink) slightly as it bakes. The dough settles because it is so thin and the side of the form so straight; lining the forms with a thicker layer of dough would prevent the settling but would also take away from the taste. A short dough that is made correctly will not shrink or puff up if the dough has been pricked and does not need to rest before it is baked.

How to Line Small Individual Forms

Prepare and roll out short dough the same way as for short dough bottoms, rolling the dough into a rectangle. If the forms you are lining are very small, roll the dough slightly thinner than usual so that there is room in the forms for filling. Stagger the forms, 1 to 2 inches (2.5 to 5 cm) apart, in the approximate shape of the dough. The taller the forms are, the more space they need between them. Roll the dough up on a dowel, roll out over the forms, and push the forms together with your hands so that there is enough slack for the insides of the forms without overstretching and breaking the dough. Dust the dough lightly with bread flour and, using a piece of dough that is shaped to fit the form, pound the dough gently in place.

When all the air pockets are eliminated, roll the rolling pin over the edges of the forms to cut off the excess dough. You can also press down on the forms with the palm of your hand to do the same thing. Place the finished forms on a sheet pan.

How to Cut Short-Dough Cookies

Prepare the short dough as for short-dough bottoms, and roll it ⅛ inch (3 mm) thick into a rectangle, making sure the dough is not sticking to the board. Using a plain or fluted cutter, with your hand next to the dough, cut and, at the same time, flip the cookie in a smooth motion into your hand. When you have six or so in your hand, place them on a sheet pan lined with parchment paper, and continue cutting and flipping. Stagger the cutting and placing of the cookies for the least amount of wasted dough and space. Bake the cookies at 375° F (190° C) until golden brown, 10 to 12 minutes, depending on the size. The smaller cookies are easiest to flip up with the cutter. With a little practice the method will work well with sizes up to 3½ inches (8.75 cm). If you are doing this for a living, you simply have to learn this method to save time.

SHORT DOUGH
19 pounds, 8 ounces (8 kg, 870 g) dough

>   7 pounds (3 kg, 185 g) butter or margarine
>   3 pounds (1 kg, 356 g) sugar
>   1 pound (4 dl, 8 cl) eggs
>   1 teaspoon (2 g) ammonium carbonate
>   2 teaspoons (6 g) vanilla extract
> 8½ pounds (3 kg, 865 g) bread flour

¼ **recipe**

4 pounds, 14 ounces (2 kg, 220 g) of dough (will line about 95 2½-inch/6.2-cm tartlets or 7 11-inch/27.5-cm tarts)

> 1¾ pounds (795 g) butter or margarine
>   12 ounces (340 g) sugar
>   ¼ cup (6 cl) eggs
>   1 pinch ammonium carbonate
>   ½ teaspoon (2 g) vanilla extract
>   2 pounds, 2 ounces (970 g) bread flour

Place all ingredients except flour in a mixing bowl; mix with the dough hook just until combined. Add the flour and mix until the dough is smooth. If overmixed, the dough will be much harder to roll out. If you use all butter or a large proportion of butter, you must take care that the dough is not too soft for efficient work.

Place the dough as flat as possible on a paper-lined sheet pan so that the dough takes up less space and cools down quickly. Cover and refrigerate.

COCOA SHORT DOUGH
3 pounds, 12 ounces (1 kg, 705 g) dough

>   8 ounces (225 g) sugar
> 1¾ pounds (795 g) butter or margarine
>   4 ounces (1 dl, 2 cl) eggs
>   ½ teaspoon (1½ g) vanilla extract
> 2¼ pounds (1 kg, 30 g) bread flour
>   1 ounce (30 g) cocoa powder
>   1 pinch ammonium carbonate

Combine sugar, butter, eggs, and vanilla in a mixing bowl with dough hook for 1 minute or less. Sift flour, cocoa powder, and ammonium carbonate together; add to first mixture. Mix just until dough is smooth. Cover and refrigerate.

RASPBERRY TURNOVERS
color photograph, p. C-1

> Short Dough (see p. 19)
> raspberry jam (2 ounces (55 g) for every 24 turnovers)
> egg wash
> AA confectioners' sugar
> crushed sliced almonds

Use Short Dough that has not been rolled out too many times before because the dough will break if too much flour has been mixed into it. Roll out the dough ⅛ inch (3 mm) thick; cut out 3-inch (7.5-cm) cookies with a fluted cookie cutter. Pipe raspberry jam onto each circle slightly off center and toward yourself. The jam, with or without seeds, can be straight from the container if it has the consistency of a purée. Brush egg wash on the lower edge; fold the top over the jam and onto the lower half; press the edges together with your fingers. Combine equal parts of sugar and almonds. Brush the tops of the turnovers with egg wash and invert them into the sugar mixture. Be sure not to get any egg wash or sugar on the bottoms of the turnovers as it will burn. Place them right side up on sheet pans. Bake at 375° F (190° C) until golden, about 10 minutes.

Because raspberry jam gets rubbery after one day, the turnovers should be served as soon as possible after baking. They can be made up in big batches, stored in the refrigerator or freezer, and baked as needed.

KIWI TART
one 11-inch (27.5-cm) tart   *photograph, p. 54*

> Short Dough (see p. 19)
> Cointreau Custard (recipe follows)
> 2 kiwis, peeled, sliced crosswise
> about 10 medium-size strawberries, cut in half
> Apricot Glaze (see p. 239)

Line an 11-inch (27.5-cm) false-bottom tart pan with Short Dough; bake weighted at 375° F (190° C) to a light golden, about 12 minutes. When the shells have cooled, remove paper and weights.

Make Cointreau Custard and pour it into the tart shell. Bake at 325° F (165° C) until the custard is set, 30 to 35 minutes.

When the tart is cool to the touch, remove it from the pan. Arrange sliced kiwis in the center and the strawberries around the edge. Brush with Apricot Glaze. Cut into slices.

Cointreau Custard
3¼ cups (7 dl, 8 cl) custard

> 8 egg yolks
> 6½ ounces (185 g) granulated sugar
> 3⅓ cups (8 dl) heavy cream
> 1½ ounces (4½ cl) Cointreau

Beat egg yolks and sugar for a few seconds by hand, just enough to combine. Mix in cream and Cointreau thoroughly.

RASPBERRY-LEMON TART
two 11-inch (27.5-cm) tarts   *photograph, p. 54*

> **Short Dough** (see p. 19)
> **Lemon Cream** (see p. 261)
> **fresh raspberries**
> **whipped cream**

Line two 11-inch (27.5-cm) false-bottom tart pans with Short Dough. Bake weighted at 375° F (190° C) to a light golden, not brown, color, about 12 minutes.

While crust is baking, make Lemon Cream. When the tart shells are cool enough to handle, remove the paper and weights. Divide the Lemon Cream evenly between the shells. Bake at 375° F (190° C) until the filling is set, about 15 minutes. The filling sets a little more as it cools.

When the tarts are cool enough to handle, remove them from the pans and slide them onto cardboards (or cardboards covered with doilies). Cut or mark the tarts into desired pieces; then cover the surface of each slice with raspberries so that the raspberries are not cut when the tart is sliced. To keep the natural satin look of the raspberries, do not rinse or glaze them.

If the pieces are being served on separate plates, pipe whipped cream on the plate next to the tart using a no. 3 (6-mm) star tube. If the pieces remain on a serving platter, leave a ½-inch (12-mm) space at the edge of each slice and pipe the whipped cream there, being careful not to cover any of the raspberries. These tarts may also be served without whipped cream.

WALNUT-CARAMEL TART

three 11-inch (27.5-cm) tarts   photograph, p. 54

> **Short Dough (see p. 19)**
> **Caramel Filling (recipe follows)**
> **egg wash**
> 15 ounces (430 g) **Ganache (see p. 247)**
> 8 ounces (225 g) **roasted hazelnuts, skins removed**
> **whipped cream (optional)**

Line three 11-inch (27.5-cm), 1-inch-deep (25-mm) tart pans with Short Dough (these do not have to be false-bottom pans). Bake weighted at 375° F (190° C) until half done, about 10 minutes, and set aside.

Make Caramel Filling. Remove weights and papers from shells; divide the filling evenly among the shells. Roll out more Short Dough ⅛ inch (3 mm) thick. Brush the edge of each tart with egg wash, cover with the dough, and trim. Prick the dough lightly to let the air escape. Bake tarts at 375° F (190° C) until golden brown, about 30 minutes. If the pastry bubbles, press it down with the bottom of a cake pan or any other flat object while the tart is still hot from the oven. Cool to room temperature.

Remove the tarts from the pans. Crush the hazelnuts to the size of small peas. Sift to remove the powder that results (use powder for other recipes, such as Swedish Hazelnut Tarts or Rumballs—see Index). Warm the Ganache to a soft, but not runny, consistency; it should have a nice shine. Spread a thin even layer of warm Ganache on top of each tart. Place a 5- to 6-inch (12.5- to 15-cm) plain cookie cutter (or anything with a rim around so it will not damage the Ganache) in the middle of one tart. Sprinkle the hazelnuts on the outside rim of the tart before the Ganache hardens, taking care not to spill in the middle. Remove the cookie cutter and refrigerate the tart to set the Ganache. Repeat with the remaining tarts.

Cut into the desired number of slices with a sharp knife dipped into hot water. If you wish, pipe a rosette of whipped cream at the edge of each slice. Walnut-Caramel Tart must be served at room temperature because the caramelized sugar is very hard when cold.

Caramel Filling

    3 pounds (1 kg, 356 g) sugar
       juice of ½ lemon
1½ cups (3 dl, 6 cl) heavy cream, room temperature
  14 ounces (400 g) butter
1½ pounds (680 g) walnuts, coarsely chopped

Caramelize the sugar with the lemon juice in a heavy-bottomed saucepan, stirring constantly with a wooden spoon, to a light brown color, 335° F (168° C) on a candy thermometer. Remove from heat; quickly add the cream, swirl it around to mix. Stir in butter. Finally, stir in the walnuts.

LEMON-ALMOND TARTLETS
approximately 90 tartlets   *photograph, p. 54*

       Short Dough (see p. 19)
       Kirschwasser Filling (recipe follows)
       sugar
½ recipe Lemon Curd (see p. 261)
       Apricot Glaze (see p. 239)
       crushed roasted almonds

Line individual tart pans or mazarin pans (see Index) with Short Dough. Make the Kirschwasser Filling; pipe it into the pans, filling each two-thirds full. Bake at 400° F (205° C) until golden brown, about 12 minutes. Dust lightly with sugar, and turn them upside down immediately to make the tops flat and even. Be careful: if the skin is damaged, it will show in the finished product. When the tartlets have cooled, they can be stored in the freezer or finished immediately.

To finish: Make the Lemon Curd. Brush the tops with Apricot Glaze. Dip tartlets into the almonds to coat. Cut out the center of each tartlet with a plain 1-inch (25-mm) cookie cutter and reserve. Fill the holes with Lemon Curd. Place the cutouts on top of the Lemon Curd. These tartlets should be finished fresh every day, which is easy if they are stored in the freezer and finished as needed.

Kirschwasser Filling

        13 ounces (370 g) butter
         7 ounces (200 g) sugar
         1 pound, 6½ ounces (640 g) almond paste
            pinch of salt
         6 eggs
         1 ounce (3 cl) Kirschwasser
         6 ounces (170 g) flour
         1 teaspoon (3 g) baking powder

Slowly mix butter into sugar, almond paste, and salt; mix until smooth, but do not overmix. Mix in eggs, two at a time; mix in Kirschwasser. Sift the flour and the baking powder, and fold in. Again, do not incorporate too much air into the batter by overmixing.

COINTREAU TART WITH APPLE, PEAR, OR RHUBARB

two 11-inch (27.5-cm) tarts   *photograph, p. 54*

        1½ pounds (680 g) Short Dough (see p. 19)
            Cointreau Custard (see p. 21)
            apples, pears, or rhubarb
            cinnamon sugar for apple and pear or sugar for rhubarb
            Pectin or Apricot Glaze (see pp. 237, 239)
            whipped cream, optional

Line two 11-inch (27.5-cm) false-bottom tart pans with Short Dough. Prick the dough lightly with a fork. Bake weighted at 375° F (190° C) just until light golden, about 12 minutes. Let cool; remove the paper and weights.

Make the Cointreau Custard; divide it evenly between the two shells (it should fill each shell halfway.)

Peel and core the apples or pears, and place them in acidulated water. If the apples or pears are too unripe, poach them for a few minutes to soften them up. Slice them when you are ready to assemble the tarts. Cut each apple or pear lengthwise in half; cut each half crosswise into thin slices. Fan the thin slices out evenly in circles starting at the outside edge. Sprinkle with cinnamon sugar over two or three circles only. Bake at 325° to 350° F (165° to 175° C) until the custard is set, about

30 minutes. When the tarts are cool enough so that they will not break when you handle them, remove them from the pans and glaze them with Pectin or Apricot Glaze. Slice and serve at room temperature. If you like, pipe whipped cream at the edge of the slice.

For a fresh rhubarb tart, cut the stalks into 2- × ½-inch (5-cm × 12-mm) pieces. Place them in a stainless-steel or other noncorrosive pan, and sprinkle granulated sugar on top to draw out some of the juice; steam covered at 375° F (190° C) until slightly softened, about 8 minutes. If overcooked, the rhubarb will be a purée. Proceed as described for the apple or pear tart but use sugar instead of cinnamon sugar.

FRUIT TARTLETS

thirty 2½-inch (6.25-cm) tartlets   color photograph, p. C-1

      Short Dough (see p. 19)
      melted dark chocolate
1 **pound (455 g) Bavarian Cream (see p. 261)**
      fresh fruit
      Apricot or Pectin Glaze (see pp. 237, 239)

Line 2½-inch (6.25-cm) tartlet pans with Short Dough. Prick dough lightly with a fork. Bake at 375° (190° C) until light golden brown. Unmold while still warm and cool shells completely. Coat the inside of each shell with Apricot Glaze or brush with dark chocolate so that the filling cannot soften the shell.

Make Bavarian Cream. Pipe into each shell up to the rim in a nice mound. Decorate tartlets with the fruit that is in season. Use small fruits if possible, such as raspberries, blackberries, strawberries, kiwis, figs, plums, and, not to be forgotten, wonderful blueberries. Leave the skin on when it is edible and adds to the appearance (figs and plums, for example). Slice the fruits in thin slices to make it look more appealing. A whole or half strawberry may look good on a large tart, but on a small tartlet it looks clumsy; if you slice a half strawberry thinly and fan it out as you place it on the tartlet, it will look elegant. The whole top should be covered with fruit in a simple and elegant pattern; do not get too complicated.

Finally, glaze the fruit with Apricot or Pectin Glaze, and place the tartlets in decorative cups. Use these tarts the day they are made; they usually look a bit wilted the day after.

SWEDISH HAZELNUT TARTS

three 11-inch (27.5-cm) tarts   color photograph, p. C-1

>   Short Dough (see p. 19)
> 7½ ounces (215 g) Apricot Jam (see p. 239)
>   1 pound, 1½ ounces (500 g) shelled hazelnuts
>   7 ounces (200 g) candied orange peel
>   1 pound, 1½ ounces (500 g) sugar
>   1 pound, 1½ ounces (500 g) butter
>   4 whole eggs (200 g)
>   6 egg yolks (120 g)
>   2 teaspoons (6 g) vanilla extract
>   powdered sugar
>   Ganache (see p. 247)
>   fresh orange slices for decoration

Line three 11-inch (27.5-cm) tart pans, false bottom or solid, with Short Dough. Place lined pans in the refrigerator or freezer to firm the dough. While the dough is chilling, make sure the jam has a soft consistency; if it does not, work it until it is free of lumps. Spread 2½ ounces (70 g) jam in a thin film on the bottom of each tart. Refrigerate.

Grind hazelnuts, orange peel, and half the sugar very finely until almost a paste. Cream butter with the remaining sugar; gradually mix in whole eggs, extra yolks, vanilla, and the nut mixture carefully. Do not overmix; if too much air is incorporated, the filling will puff up too much in baking and then fall in the center, making the tart look unshapely and taste dry. Mix in vanilla to taste.

Divide the hazelnut filling evenly among the 3 pans, and spread it out, mounding it slightly higher in the middle. Bake at 350° F (175° C) until the filling is firm in the middle and the shell is golden brown, about 50 minutes. Unmold the tarts when completely cool.

Make a template ½ inch (12 mm) smaller than the tart with a circle 3½ to 4 inches (8.5 to 10 cm) cut out of the center. Place the template on the tart and sift powdered sugar over it. To get a precise and sharp contrast, use a plain cookie cutter as a guide for the center circle when you cut your template; then place the cutter in the opening to act as a seal when you sift the powdered sugar. Slice the tarts.

Work and warm Ganache until it develops a slight shine; if overworked, it will turn light in color because too much air has been worked in. Using a no. 4 (8-mm) plain tube, pipe a heart design of Ganache at the edge of each slice. Decorate each slice with a small slice of fresh orange. Unfortunately the oranges will look fresh for only 6 to 8 hours, but they are very easy to replace.

APPLE MAZARINS
about 35 mazarins *photograph, p. 54*

> Short Dough (see p. 19)
> 1 pound (455 g) Mazarin Filling (see p. 262)
> ⅓ recipe Apple Filling (see p. 262)
> 1½ pounds (680 g) Streusel (see p. 263)
> powdered sugar

Line mazarin forms (a plain oval form about 2½ × 1¾ inches/6 × 4.5 cm and 1½ inches/4 cm high) with Short Dough ⅛ inch (3 mm) thick. Pipe in the Apple Filling, filling the forms halfway. Cover with Mazarin Filling to about ⅛ inch (3 mm) below the rim of the form. Put Streusel on top in a small mound. It is a good idea to prepare the mazarins on one sheet pan and then transfer them to another because it is impossible not to spill Streusel around the forms. Bake at 360° F (180° C) until golden brown, about 45 minutes (make sure the bottoms are done).

When the pastries have cooled to room temperature, unmold each one carefully by cupping your hand over the Streusel to hold it in place. Sift powdered sugar very lightly over the tops.

TOSCA
75 pastries *photograph, p. 54*

> Short Dough (see p. 19)
> 4½ ounces (130 g) strawberry jam
> 4 pounds, 10 ounces (1 kg, 200 g) Mazarin Filling (see p. 262)
> ⅓ recipe Florentina I or ¼ recipe Florentina II (see p. 176)
> melted dark chocolate

This is one of many Scandinavian pastries made with almond paste or hazelnuts. Because Italy cultivates and exports a lot of hazelnuts, almonds, and oranges, this pastry was named Tosca for the Italian opera.

Line the bottom of a half-sheet pan, 16 × 12 inches (40 × 30 cm), with parchment paper; then line with Short Dough, ⅛ inch (3 mm) thick. Spread the jam in a thin layer on the dough, and cover with Mazarin Filling almost to the top of the pan. Bake at 375° F (190° C) about 50 minutes. Do not overbake because it will go back in the oven.

When the mazarin sheet is cold (preferably the day after baking), cut off the skin but keep the mazarin sheet in the pan. If using Florentina I, heat Florentina base to boiling; then stir in slightly crushed sliced almonds and oats but omit the flour. Spread Florentina I or II just to cover the mazarin, using a spatula dipped into hot water to make it slide more easily. Place the mazarin sheet (still in its original pan) onto a second pan the same size. This is called double-panning in the industry and is done to prevent the bottom from getting too dark or overdone. Bake at 425° F (220° C) until the topping begins to bubble and turn golden brown, about 5 minutes. Let cool to room temperature.

Cut the sheet loose from the sides of the pan, turn upside down on cardboard, and refrigerate until cool and hard. While still upside down, cut it lengthwise into five strips; then cut each strip individually into 15 pieces, holding the knife at a 90° angle. Dip the bottom and sides but not the tops of each piece into dark chocolate. Do not refrigerate after dipping because the topping will get soggy.

CITRONS

55 barquettes   *photograph, p. 54*

> Short Dough (see p. 19)
> 4 ounces (115 g) strawberry jam
> 1 pound, 2 ounces (510 g) Mazarin Filling (see p. 262)
> sugar
> 14 ounces (400 g) Buttercream (see p. 239)
> 3½ ounces (100 g) Lemon Cream (see p. 261)
> melted dark chocolate
> Marzipan (see p. 255), colored yellow
> chocolate for piping (see p. 244)

Line barquette forms, 3½ × 1½ inches (9 × 4 cm), with Short Dough. Pipe a ribbon of strawberry jam on each bottom, and fill each two-thirds full with Mazarin Filling. Bake at 400° F (205° C) to a golden brown, about 10 minutes. When they have cooled, sprinkle tops very lightly with sugar, turn upside down, and remove molds.

Flavor Buttercream with Lemon Cream. Turn barquettes right side up and pipe a ribbon of Buttercream on top. With a small spatula, spread both sides into a ridge in the middle about ½ inch (12 mm) high. Refrigerate until the Buttercream is firm.

Dip the tops of the barquettes, the buttercream part, into dark chocolate. Roll out yellow Marzipan very thinly; cut out strips, 1¾ × ⅜ inch (45 × 9 mm). With dark piping chocolate write "Citron" on each strip. Pipe a thin diagonal line of chocolate on each pastry, and place a marzipan strip on top. Do not refrigerate.

GREEN TRIANGLES
55 pastries   photograph, p. 55

>   Short Dough (see p. 19)
> 4½ ounces (130 g) strawberry jam
>   4 pounds, 10 ounces (2 kg, 100 g) Mazarin Filling (see p. 262)
>   Buttercream (see Index)
>   Marzipan, colored green (see p. 255)
>   melted dark chocolate

Line a paper-lined half-sheet pan, 16 × 12 inches (40 × 30 cm), with Short Dough. Spread strawberry jam in a thin layer on the Short Dough. Top with Mazarin Filling, and spread it evenly. Bake at 375° F (190° C) until baked through, about 55 minutes.

When the pastry has cooled, preferably the next day, cut the skin off the top. This is easier if done before unmolding because the edge of the pan will serve as a guide for your knife. Cut the sheet evenly. Cut around the edges and unmold. If the bottom of the sheet does not come away from the pan, do not force it; place a hot sheet pan underneath for a few seconds to soften the butter around the Short Dough, and try again. Once unmolded, turn it right side up again.

Spread Buttercream in a thin film on top of the filling. Roll out green Marzipan ⅛ inch (3 mm) thick. Mark it with a waffle roller, and arrange it on top of the pastry. Turn the pastry upside down and cut off excess Marzipan. Refrigerate until thoroughly chilled but no longer than a few hours, to prevent the Marzipan from getting soggy. Keeping the pastry upside down, cut it into 5 lengthwise strips, holding the knife at a 90° angle. A serrated knife or the very tip of a sharp chef's knife works best. Cut each strip into 11 triangles, saving the scraps for rum balls. Dip triangles into dark chocolate so both the bottom and sides are coated up to the marzipan.

If more than a half-sheet is needed, make 1 full sheet rather than 2 halves so that there are fewer scraps when you cut them. These will stay fresh for 4 to 5 days but should not be refrigerated.

TRIER SQUARES

fifty-four 1½-inch (37-mm) squares   *photograph, p. 55*

> Short Dough (see p. 19)
> 4½ ounces (130 g) Apricot Jam (see p. 238)
> Trier Filling (recipe follows)
> egg wash

Line a half-sheet pan, 16 × 12 inches (40 × 30 cm), with Short Dough. Refrigerate the pan briefly to stiffen the dough. In the meantime, if the jam is not soft, work it free of lumps. Spread jam in a thin layer on the Short Dough. Spread Trier Filling evenly over the jam.

Roll out more Short Dough, and place it on a piece of cardboard or on the bottom of a pan (so the sides of the pan will not be in your way). Refrigerate it briefly to make it easier to work with. Cut the dough into ¼-inch-wide (6-mm) strips with a fluted or plain pastry wheel. Brush the top of the filling with egg wash; arrange the dough strips diagonally ¼ inch (6 mm) apart over the filling; then arrange the strips in the other direction so that they make a diamond pattern. Press them lightly with your hand as you go along to make sure they stick. Brush the strips with egg wash.

Bake at 375° F (190° C) until golden brown and baked through, about 40 minutes. Let the pastry cool completely before cutting. Unmold the sheet, cut the edges clean, and measure and cut into the 1½-inch (37-mm) squares, using a ruler as a guide.

Trier Filling

> 15 ounces (430 g) almonds, sliced or coarsely crushed
> 14 ounces (400 g) sugar
> 5 ounces (1 dl, 5 cl) milk
> 5 ounces (140 g) butter
> 6 ounces (170 g) golden raisins
> 2 ounces (6 cl) lemon juice
>   grated zest of 1 lemon
> 1 tablespoon (7 g) ground cinnamon

Combine almonds, sugar, and milk. Heat the butter in a skillet slightly past the almond-colored stage, and mix it into the almond mixture. Mix in the raisins, lemon juice and zest, and cinnamon.

PIE DOUGH
four 10-inch (25-cm) shells

> 1 pound, 9 ounces (710 g) bread flour
> 1 ounce (30 g) salt
> 1 pound (455 g) butter, cold
> 5 ounces (140 g) lard, cold
> 5 ounces (1 dl, 5 cl) ice water

Pie dough should always be mixed by hand because it is almost certain to be overmixed if you use a machine. Measure the flour and salt into a bowl. Add the firm butter and lard into the flour; then pinch it down to the size of hazelnuts. Add the ice water, and mix just until the dough comes together. The butter should still be lumpy. Overmixing or using butter that is too soft will make a creamy dough that not only tends to shrink but also becomes mealy. Flatten the dough, and let it rest covered for at least 30 minutes.

The pie dough should also rest for about 30 minutes after it has been rolled out, to prevent shrinking when baked. The scraps should never be kneaded together but placed on top of each other and then pressed together. This prevents them from becoming rubbery and hard to work with.

CREAM-CHEESE PIE DOUGH
two 11-inch (27.5-cm) shells

> 7 ounces (200 g) cream cheese, room temperature
> 9 ounces (255 g) butter, room temperature
> ½ ounce (15 g) salt
>   few drops lemon juice
> 9 ounces (255 g) bread flour

This is a fast and uncomplicated pie dough that sacrifices flakiness, but makes up for it in time gained. The cream cheese and butter must be soft to prevent lumps. Combine butter gradually with the cream cheese. Add salt, lemon juices, and flour; mix just until combined. Refrigerate covered, and use as regular pie dough.

ALMOND TART
two 11-inch (27.5-cm) tarts   *photograph, p. 55*

> ½ recipe Pie Dough (see p. 31)
> 5 ounces (140 g) Apricot Jam (see p. 238)
> 3 pounds (1 kg, 365 g) Mazarin Filling (see p. 262)
> 2 ounces (55 g) sliced almonds
> Short Dough (see p. 19)
> egg wash
> powdered sugar

Line two 11-inch (27.5-cm) tart pans (they need not be false-bottom) with Pie Dough ⅛ inch (3 mm) thick. Place a paper in the bottom, fill with beans or pie weights, and let rest for at least 30 minutes. Bake them at 375° F (190° C) for about 10 minutes. Cool shells until they can be handled; then remove paper and beans.

Spread jam in a thin layer on the bottom of each shell. Using a no. 6 (12-mm) plain tube, pipe half of the Mazarin Filling into each tart. Sprinkle sliced almonds evenly on top of both fillings.

Roll out Short Dough ⅛ inch (3 mm) thick. Chill, to make it easier to handle. Cut ¼-inch-wide (6-mm) strips with a fluted pastry wheel, and arrange them ½ inch (12 mm) apart in a diamond pattern on top of each tart. Push them down so they stick to each other. Carefully brush strips with egg wash. Bake at 375° F (190° C) until golden brown, about 45 minutes.

When the tarts have cooled to room temperature, remove from pans, slice, and sift powdered sugar lightly over the tops.

PECAN TARTS
two 11-inch (27.5-cm) tarts   *photograph, p. 55*

> ½ recipe Pie Dough (see p. 31)
> 1 pound (455 g) granulated sugar
> 1 pint (4 dl, 8 cl) light corn syrup
> 8 eggs
> 2 ounces (55 g) melted butter
> ½ teaspoon (3 g) vanilla extract
> 12 ounces (340 g) pecans, whole or pieces
> whipped cream, optional

Roll out Pie Dough ⅛ inch (3 mm) thick. Line two 11-inch (27.5-cm) tart pans with Pie Dough. Mix sugar, syrup, eggs, butter, and vanilla to taste. Stir in the pecans. Pour the filling into the pans. Bake at 360° F (180° C) about 35 minutes. Cover the tops with pieces of parchment paper; bake until the shells are browned and fillings set, 10 to 15 minutes.

When tarts have cooled, cut into slices and serve plain or with whipped cream.

Puff Paste

For a light and flaky puff paste, the dough must be well made or the end result will be a disappointment. It is most important that the basic dough is made properly. If you add too much flour or do not work the dough long enough, it will be glutenous and rubbery, hard to work with, and will shrink when it is baked. Even if the basic dough is correct, great care still must be taken when rolling in the fat for the optimum rise or puff in the dough.

Puff paste freezes very well both as a dough or made up and ready to be baked. It should be kept in the refrigerator as little as possible. The ideal procedures are to make up all of the dough the day after you rolled it, freeze the apple turnovers, fleurons, or what have you, and take these out and bake as needed; or to divide the dough into suitably sized pieces, freeze, and take them out as needed. Puff paste must be covered at all times, especially in the freezer, to prevent the top from drying and forming a skin.

Scraps from puff paste dough or any other dough, such as Danish, pie, and croissant, will not be as good rolled out the second time, but they should be saved nevertheless. Puff paste scraps are better than fresh dough for pastries that should not puff up as much. By "fresh dough," I mean puff paste that has not been rolled out before. In both cases the dough should not be more than a few days old. Scrap pieces can be frozen until needed or added to fresh dough, saving part of the fresh dough for other use. Scrap puff-paste dough can also be used for Butter-wheat Bread (see Index).

Fleurons

Roll out puff paste ⅛ inch (3 mm) thick, and prick the dough lightly. If you are making a lot of these garnishes and you are not quite sure about the dough, make a few samples and adjust the thickness of the dough if necessary. Place the dough on a cardboard or on an upside-down sheet pan. Brush with egg wash. Using the back of a chef's knife, make a diamond pattern in the egg wash. Refrigerate or freeze until firm; the egg wash will dry slightly. Then cut out the crescents, using a fluted or plain cookie cutter that is dipped occasionally into oil. Brushing with egg wash and marking before you cut is much easier than trying to do it one at a time.

Fleurons can be frozen; bake directly from the freezer at 400° F (205° C) about 12 minutes. As a general rule all puff paste should rest at least 30 minutes after you have rolled it out and before baking to keep from shrinking.

Vol-au-Vent and Bouchée

You could say that a *vol-au-vent* is a big *bouchée* or, to put it another way, a *bouchée* is a small *vol-au-vent*; in principle, they are the same thing. A *vol-au-vent* is a large shell, from 5 to 10 inches (12.5 to 25 cm) in diameter, that serves 5 to 12 people; if you need one bigger than that, it is best to make 2 smaller ones.

Roll out scrap dough ⅛ inch (3 mm) thick (fresh dough slightly thinner), large enough so that you can cut from it 2 circles the size of the *vol-au-vent* you are planning (bottom and lid). Do not cut out the circles now. Prick the dough and refrigerate it.

Roll out fresh dough slightly larger than the planned *vol-au-vent*, ¼ to ¾ inch (6 to 20 mm) thick, depending on the quality of the dough. If you are not sure, bake a small piece of the dough to see how high it rises. Refrigerate the dough until firm. Place a ring or a template of the appropriate size on top; with a sharp knife, cut along the outside edge of the template, making sure you are cutting at a 90° angle to prevent the *vol-au-vent* from falling to one side as it puffs up. Place a 2-inch (5-cm) smaller ring or template in the middle and cut again so the dough is a doughnut-shaped circle 1 inch (25 mm) wide all around. Place in the refrigerator. Take out the thin prerolled sheet and cut half of it into a bottom, using the larger of the templates. Place the bottom on an even sheet pan, brush the outer 1 inch (25 mm) with egg wash, place the ring on top so that it sticks to the egg wash, and adjust it so that the *vol-au-vent* is perfectly round. With the back side of a knife, mark the *vol-au-vent* every 1½ inches (37 mm) around the outside, holding the knife vertically, marking from the bottom to the top, and pushing in just a little bit for a scallop pattern. Prick and brush the top of the ring lightly with egg wash. (If egg wash runs down the side, the puff paste will not rise evenly.) Cut a lid out of the remaining half of the dough, using the smaller of the templates, and place it on the sheet pan next to the *vol-au-vent*. Brush it with egg wash and make a diamond pattern with the backside of a chef's knife. Bake double-panned to prevent the bottom from getting too dark, at 400° F (205° C) until puffed, about 15 minutes. Reduce heat to 375° F (190° C); bake until dry and golden, 30 to 35 minutes, depending on the size. If the top is getting too dark, cover it with a piece of paper or aluminum foil. Of course, the lid will be finished long before the case of the *vol-au-vent*.

One of the best ways to keep the sides from falling in as it puffs up (the best way, of course, is to work carefully with a perfectly rolled piece of puff paste) is to arrange a cake cooler above the *vol-au-vent* on baking forms or coffee cups at the corners of the baking pan at a height slightly below the point you expect, or want, the *vol-au-vent* to puff. This acts as a mold, preventing the *vol-au-vent* from puffing too high and keeping its sides straight. If it is a big *vol-au-vent* and a powerful dough, you should place a few 1-pound (455-g) weights on top to ensure that the *vol-au-vent* does not take the cake cooler with it as it puffs up.

Bouchées

Bouchées are individual patty shells, usually made in 2- to 4-inch (5- to 10-cm) sizes. There are two basic ways to make them: the production method and the classic method. Using the production method, they won't get quite as high, and you will have some wasted dough, but they can be made very quickly. With the classic method, you will get a higher and more elegant *bouchée,* but they take a little longer to finish, and you will have more scrap dough left.

To make the production *bouchée:* Roll out puff paste ¼ to ½ inch (6 mm to 12 mm) thick, depending on the quality of your dough. Again, if you are not sure, you would be wise to make a test. The dough must be firm (cool) while you are working with it; for the best result, refrigerate when necessary. Dip the edge of a cookie cutter (plain or fluted) the size of the *bouchée* you want in oil, and push the cutter straight into the dough to cut them out. Stagger the cut for minimal waste of puff paste. Place them on sheet pans, also staggered, about ¾ inch (20 mm) from each other, to help them puff up straight. Then, using a cutter about 1 inch (25 mm) smaller, partially dipped in oil, cut the center of each puff-paste circle almost to the bottom of the dough. Prick the inside thoroughly to prevent it from puffing; if you wish, brush them with egg wash very carefully so that none runs into the cuts or down the outsides. Bake at 400° F (205° C) until puffed, about 10 minutes; reduce heat to 375° F (190° C); bake until they dry enough to hold their shapes, about 30 minutes. (You might have to use a second pan underneath to prevent the bottoms from getting too dark, and remove the *bouchées* on the edges of the pan if they are done before those in the middle.) When they have cooled somewhat, lift off the lids and scrape out the unbaked puff paste inside with a fork. If necessary, put them back in the oven to dry some more.

To make the classic *bouchée:* Roll out scrap dough ⅛ inch (3 mm) thick, or roll fresh dough slightly thinner and prick it well. If you are not sure how high the dough will rise, make a test with a small piece of the dough (do not forget to let it rest). Place the rolled-out dough on a sheet pan in the refrigerator; roll out another piece ¼ to ½ inch (6 to 12 mm) thick. Using 2 cookie cutters, one about 1 inch (25 mm) smaller than the other, dip the edges in oil and cut out ½-inch-wide (12-mm) rings. Place the rings in the refrigerator. Take out the prerolled sheet and brush the entire surface with egg wash. With the larger cutter, cut out the bottoms and place them fairly close to each other on a sheet pan. Cut out the lids, using the smaller of the cutters, and place them on another sheet pan. If you want a pattern on the lids, mark it with the back of your knife. If you are making only a few *bouchées,* they can be placed on the same sheet pan, but the lids will be done before the bottoms. Before the egg wash dries, place the rings on the bottoms, brush with egg wash, and prick them lightly. Bake at 400° F (205° C) until puffed, about 10 minutes. Reduce heat to 375° F (190° C); bake until golden and completely dry, about 25 minutes. You may need a second pan underneath to protect the bottoms from overbrowning and/or parchment paper on top to prevent them from getting too dark.

There are many tricks to keeping the sides of the *bouchées* from falling or puffing up unevenly. The best one is to work with a perfectly made and rolled puff paste that has not been allowed to warm and get too soft. If you think your pastry needs some help, you can bake the *bouchées* with greased parchment paper on top, but in this case, do not brush them with egg wash. Another trick is to rig a cake cooler at a point slightly below the height you expect them to puff up to or at the point you would like them to stop; the *bouchées* will puff to the cake cooler, stop, and stay straight.

CLASSIC (FRENCH) PUFF PASTE

    4 pounds, 6 ounces (1 kg, 990 g) butter, cold
      juice of 1 lemon
      pinch salt
17½ ounces (500 g) bread flour
    1 quart (9 dl, 6 cl) water
    2 ounces (55 g) salt
   14 ounces (400 g) cake flour
    2 pounds, 10 ounces (1 kg, 195 g) bread flour, approximately
    7 ounces (200 g) soft butter

Make the butter block first: Work cold butter into the proper consistency with the warmth of your hand, adding lemon juice, pinch of salt, and 17½ ounces (500 g) bread flour. Shape into a 12-inch (30-cm) square; refrigerate until firm. The butter should not be so soft that it is hard to handle. You should be able to transfer the finished block from one hand to another without breaking it. It should not be so firm that it cracks or breaks if you press on it. Ideally, the dough and the butter block should have the same consistency. A dough that is softer than the butter will be forced to the sides by the firmer butter; a dough that is too firm will force the butter out on the sides. Either will result in a poor-quality puff paste. Do not make the dough before the butter block is ready.

To make the dough: Mix water, 2 ounces (55 g) salt, cake flour, 7 ounces soft butter, and enough of the remaining bread flour to make a soft elastic dough. If you add too much flour, the dough will be too glutenous and rubbery. Keep mixing until the dough is elastic enough to be easily pulled (about 6 to 8 minutes at medium speed). Shape the dough into a tight ball, and cut a cross halfway down with a sharp knife. Let rest covered 5 minutes.

Push the corners of the cuts out to make the dough square shaped. Roll the dough out to a square slightly larger than the butter block, and place the butter block crosswise on it so there are 4 triangles around the sides. Fold these dough triangles into the middle, forming an envelope. Seal in the butter block; roll out the dough into a rectangle, ½ inch (12 mm) thick. Do not roll the dough wider than a sheet pan is long. Give the dough 4 double turns (instructions follow), refrigerating it for a minimum of 30 minutes between each turn. Make sure the dough is well covered at all times.

After the last turn, roll the puff paste out ½ inch (12 mm) thick, cut into halves, place the 2 pieces on a sheet pan with paper between them, and cover. Refrigerate or freeze. Remember that puff paste should not be kept in the refrigerator for more than a few days.

Single turn: Roll the dough out to a rectangle 30 × 20 inches (75 × 50 cm) as carefully and evenly as possible. Divide the rectangle into three sections by sight alone or mark the dough lightly with the edge of your hand. Fold one-third of the dough over the middle one-third section and the last one-third over both of them, brushing away excess flour. Now the dough will have one single turn. Carefully position the dough so the long side runs horizontally. Roll the dough out to the same size and give it the second single turn, only this time make the first fold from the opposite direction of the first turn. Let the dough rest covered in the refrigerator in between each turn for at least 30 minutes.

Double turn: Mark the middle, fold both ends of the dough to this mark, and fold once more, as if you were closing a book. Do not forget to brush away excess flour. You will now have a dough with one double turn. Carefully place the dough on a sheet pan. Cover the dough and place in the refrigerator for 30 minutes.

QUICK PUFF PASTE

If there is not enough time to make the Classic Puff Paste, Quick Puff Paste is a fast compromise. You will not get the height of the French version, but this one can easily be made "from scale to baked" in 2 hours. It is perfect to use for lining tarts and making *fleurons* and Napoleons, when the dough must not puff up too much.

    5 pounds (2 kg, 275 g) butter, cold
    5 pounds (2 kg, 275 g) flour
    2 ounces (55 g) salt
       cold water

Cut the butter (it must be firm but not hard) into 2-inch (5-cm) pieces; mix it with the flour, being careful not to knead. Add the salt, and mix in just enough water so that the dough can be handled. Mix carefully so that the lumps of butter are not broken up. The dough should look like well-made pie dough. Shape the dough into a square; roll 2 single and 2 double turns alternately. This dough does not rest between turns; it is ready to use immediately after the last turn. After the dough has been rolled, however, it must rest 20 to 30 minutes before baking to keep it from shrinking.

CHOUX SURPRISE
color photograph, p. C-1

    Classic Puff Paste (recipe precedes)
    Pâte à Choux (see p. 256)
    AA confectioners' sugar
    crushed sliced almonds
    egg wash
    Pastry Cream (see p. 242)
    Simple Syrup (see p. 233)
    Fondant (see p. 249)

Roll out puff paste $\frac{3}{16}$ inch (5 mm) thick; cut into $3\frac{1}{2}$-inch (8.5-cm) squares or desired size. Pipe a small mound of Pâte à Choux, about the size of a prune for a $3\frac{1}{2}$-inch (8.5-cm) square, in the center of each square. Brush the sides of the square with egg wash; fold the points up to meet in the middle like an envelope. With your thumb press the spot where the points come together right to the bottom. Mix equal amounts of sugar and almonds. As each square is folded and pressed, brush with egg wash, invert onto the sugar mixture and place it right side up on a baking pan. Pipe a small amount of Pastry Cream in the impression left by your thumb. The impression must be deep so that the cream is not pushed onto the pan. Bake double-panned at 375° F (190° C) about 40 minutes. If the Pâte à Choux is not thoroughly baked, it will fall. Brush the pastries with Simple Syrup as soon as they come out of the oven. When cool, spread some white Fondant on top.

APPLE TURNOVERS
photograph, p. 55

> Classic Puff Paste (see p. 36)
> egg wash
> Apple Filling (see p. 262) (1 pound (455 g) filling for
>   every 24 turnovers)
> cinnamon sugar
> AA confectioners' sugar
> crushed sliced almonds
> Simple Syrup (see p. 233)

Roll out puff paste $\frac{1}{8}$ inch (3 mm) thick; let it stand 5 to 10 minutes to relax; cut into $4\frac{1}{4}$-inch (10.5-cm) squares. If the puff paste gets too soft, refrigerate it for a few minutes and work on another piece. Brush the 2 adjoining edges of one square with egg wash, pipe a mound of Apple Filling in the middle, and sprinkle cinnamon sugar on top. Fold the upper part of the square onto the part brushed with egg wash so that it makes a triangle. Make sure no Apple Filling gets on the egg wash. Mix equal amounts sugar and almonds. Press the edges of the triangle together with your fingers, brush the top lightly with more egg wash, and invert it onto the sugar mixture. Place turnovers sugar side up on sheet pans, no more than 16 to a full-size pan, 24 × 16 inches (60 × 40 cm). Make a small cut in the middle of each turnover. Bake at 350° F (180° C) until golden and completely done, about 30 minutes. You may need a second pan underneath and/or parchment paper on top to prevent them from overbrowning. Brush lightly with Simple Syrup as soon as they come out of the oven. Apple Turnovers are excellent to make up ahead of time and freeze; when needed, bake them directly from the freezer.

Cherry filling is an excellent substitute for the apple.

APPLE CROSS-OVER STRIP
color photograph, p. C-1

> **Classic Puff Paste (see p. 36)**
> 12 **ounces (340 g) Apple Filling per strip (see p. 262)**
> 1 **ounce (30 g) cinnamon sugar per strip**
> **sugar**
> **crushed sliced almonds**
> **Simple Syrup (see p. 233)**
> **Fondant (see p. 249)**

Roll out puff paste ⅛ inch (3 mm) thick, and 23 inches (57.5 cm) long, and 8 inches (20 cm) wide. If you are making many of these, it is faster to roll out the puff paste to 23 inches (57.5 cm) wide and as long as needed; then cut the dough into 8-inch-wide (20-cm) strips.

Fold the strip over a 1-inch-wide (25-mm) dowel so that the long cut edges meet and are pointing towards you. The dough should be firm for easy handling; if you are making more than one, place a strip in the refrigerator while working with another. Using the back of a chef's knife, you can lightly mark, but do not cut, a line about 2 inches (5 cm) away from the cut edges and parallel to them. With the sharp edge of the chef's knife, cut ¼-inch (6-mm) strips up to the line along the entire length, leaving the folded edge of the strip uncut. With the aid of the dowel, place the strip of dough on an inverted sheet pan lined with baking paper. Two strips will fit on one pan. Remove the dowel carefully and separate the fringed edges so that the dough lies open and flat.

Using a no. 8 (16-mm) plain tube, pipe Apple Filling down the uncut center. If needed, spread it out with a spatula. Sprinkle with cinnamon sugar. Fold the left and right cut strips alternately over the middle, using both your hands in an even rhythm. Make sure the left one is folded on top of the right one, the right one on top of the left one, and so on, so that they lock each other in place. Place the dowel in the middle and press down hard enough to be sure the strips will not unfold in the oven.

Mix equal amounts of sugar and almonds. Brush the pastry lightly with water, and sprinkle with the sugar mixture. Bake double-panned at 360° F (180° C) about 35 minutes. You may also need to protect the top from overbrowning with parchment paper to give the dough time to bake completely.

Brush with Simple Syrup immediately when taken out of the oven. When cool, ice with Fondant.

Cherry filling can be substituted for the apple. Pastry strip freezes very well; bake as needed directly from the freezer.

GÂTEAU SAINT-HONORÉ
two 11-inch (27.5-cm) cakes   photograph, p. 55

Classic Puff Paste (see p. 36)
½ **recipe Pâte à Choux (see p. 47)**
Bavarian Cream for Saint-Honoré (recipe follows)
Caramel (see p. 233)
strawberries
whipped cream

Roll out puff paste ⅛ inch (3 mm) thick, 23 inches (57.5 cm) long, and 12 inches (30 cm) wide, and place on a sheet pan lined with baking paper. Refrigerate covered at least 20 minutes. Meanwhile, make the Pâte à Choux and put it in a pastry bag fitted with a no. 6 (12-mm) plain tip.

Cut two 11-inch (27.5-cm) circles from the sheet of puff paste and remove the scraps. Prick the circles lightly. Starting about ¼ inch (6 mm) from the edge of one circle, pipe 4 concentric circles of Pâte à Choux with 1-inch (25-mm) spaces between them. Place a no. 3 (6-mm) plain tip on top of the no. 6 (12-mm) and hold on to it. On a separate sheet pan lined with baking paper, pipe 35 to 40 Pâte à Choux profiteroles the size of Bing cherries, if you plan to cut the cake into 16 pieces for a buffet. For regular servings, you do not need as many profiteroles, but they should be a little bigger. Bake at 400° F (205° C) until the Pâte à Choux has puffed up, about 10 minutes; reduce heat to 375° F (190° C). Bake until Pâte à Choux dries out enough to hold its shape, about 35 minutes. Bake the profiteroles about 18 minutes. If these are to be frozen, it is best to freeze them unbaked, and bake them directly from the freezer.

Make the Bavarian Cream (not before you are ready to use it), reserve some to fill the profiteroles, and divide the rest equally between the 2 cakes, spreading it into a dome shape. Refrigerate the cakes for at least 2 hours to set the cream.

Meanwhile, fill the profiteroles with the rest of the cream, and dip them into hot Caramel. The Caramel must be hot so that it goes on in a thin layer. Reheat it if necessary, but do not get any cream mixed into it because the sugar will crystallize.

Slice the cakes, decorate with strawberries and whipped cream, and place a profiterole at the end of each piece.

Bavarian Cream for Saint Honoré

    ½ ounce (15 g) unflavored gelatin
    3 ounces (9 cl) water
    1½ ounces (4.5 cl) rum
    1 pound (455 g) whipped cream
    1 pound (455 g) Pastry Cream (see p. 242)

Dissolve gelatin in the water, add the rum, and heat to 150° F (65° C). Mix the whipped cream with the Pastry Cream. Transfer a small amount to a separate bowl and fold in the gelatin. Then add the remaining cream.

FRUIT WAFFLES
color photograph, p. C-1

    Classic Puff Paste (see p. 36)
    flour
    sugar
    Pastry Cream (see p. 242)
    fresh or frozen cooking apples, cut into small wedges
    cinnamon sugar
    Apricot or Pectin Glaze (see pp. 237, 239)

Roll out puff pastry ¼ inch (6 mm) thick, and cut out circles, using a 1½-inch (37-mm) fluted cookie cutter for buffet servings or a 2- to 2¼-inch (5- to 6-cm) cutter, for regular servings. Place 4 or 5 pastry circles on top of each other, and cover the top so they do not dry out; if necessary, place them in the refrigerator to get firm. If you are right-handed, place some flour in a pie tin on your left, granulated sugar directly onto the table in front of you, and a sheet pan on your right. Place a dozen or so of the circles on top of the flour; then invert them (flour side up), one at a time, onto the sugar, and roll each one with a dowel to an oval about 4 inches (10 cm) long for the small size and 6 inches (15 cm) long for the larger. If they stick to the dowel, turn them over in the flour as many times as needed. Do not get sugar on the top side (which will be the bottom when baking) when you roll them out because it will burn when they are baked.

Place the pastries, sugar side up, on sheet pans. With a no. 3 (6 mm) plain tip, pipe a small oval of Pastry Cream on top of each one. Do not pipe all the way to the ends because you want the puff paste to bake up around the cream. Arrange 4 or 5 small apple wedges, less for the smaller waffles, at an angle in the Pastry Cream, and finish with a sprinkle of cinnamon sugar. Frozen apples will work fine here; if using fresh apples, first poach them lightly. Bake at 400° F (205° C) just until the sugar caramelizes, about 20 minutes. Cool completely.

When waffles have cooled to room temperature, glaze with Apricot or Pectin Glaze. These will be soggy if not served the day they are made.

The waffles can also be baked only with Pastry Cream; reduce baking time to 15 minutes. Decorate with fresh fruit in season; apricots and figs are especially tasty with puff paste.

Because these waffles, like all puff-paste goods, should be fresh every day, it is a good idea to make a large number. You can stack 6 layers of waffles on papers on one sheet pan; freeze them and bake as needed.

Variation: Pariser Waffles
photograph, p. 55
Follow directions for fruit waffles but omit Pastry Cream and apples. Instead make three ¼-inch (6-mm) cuts at an angle on top. Let pastries rest for at least 30 minutes. Bake ovals at 425° F (220° C) until they are golden and the sugar on top begins to caramelize, about 12 minutes. When they have cooled, turn half of them upside down, reserving the best-looking ones for the tops. Flavor enough Buttercream with arrack or rum to pipe a border around each bottom waffle with a no. 4 (8-mm) plain tip. Pipe a small ribbon of strawberry jam down the middle. Press the reserved waffles on top lightly into the Buttercream so that they stick.

PUFF-PASTE CUTS WITH FRESH FRUIT
photograph, p. 55

    Classic Puff Paste (see p. 36)
    egg wash
    Pastry Cream (see p. 242)
    fresh fruit, thinly sliced
    cinnamon sugar
    Apricot or Pectin Glaze (see pp. 237, 239)

If using scrap dough, roll out puff paste the length of a sheet pan and ⅛ inch (3 mm) thick; if using fresh dough, roll it a little thinner. Prick well. Cut out 3-inch-wide (7.5-cm) strips for buffet servings or 4-inch-wide (10-

cm) strips for regular servings. Place no more than 3 strips on a pan. Roll out fresh (not scrap) puff paste the same length as the first, ⅛ inch (3 mm) thick. Place this strip on a cardboard or on the back of a sheet pan; refrigerate all the dough until firm.

With a sharp knife, cut ½-inch-wide (12-mm) strips from the uncut puff paste. Brush both long edges of the large strips with egg wash; place a ½-inch (12-mm) strip evenly on each edge. This is easy to do if the dough is chilled as recommended. Prick the small strips just a few times on top to prevent air bubbles from forming. Brush with egg wash.

Using a no. 2 (4-mm) plain tip, pipe a ⅛-inch (3-mm) layer of Pastry Cream in the middle of the strip. The pastries can be frozen at this point and baked as needed.

Bake the strips at 400° F (205° C) until puffed, about 10 minutes; reduce heat to 375° F (190° C). Bake until cooked through, about 10 minutes. If the strips have been frozen, they should be baked directly from the freezer; the baking time will increase slightly.

When the strips have cooled, thinly slice fresh fruit, and arrange it in between the small puffed-up strips. Finally, glaze the fruit with Apricot or Pectin Glaze, and cut into serving slices. As with all puff paste, these should be eaten the same day.

Variation: Baked Apple Puff-paste Cuts
Peel and core apples, and keep them in acidulated water to prevent browning. Cut the apples in half, and thinly slice. Fan slices out on top of the Pastry Cream, and sprinkle with cinnamon sugar. Bake at 375° F (190° C) about 40 minutes. When cooled to room temperature, glaze with Apricot or Pectin Glaze. You can substitute pears for the apples to make Baked Pear Puff-paste Cuts.

PUFF-PASTE DIAMONDS
photograph, p. 56

> Classic Puff Paste (see p. 36)
> egg wash
> Pastry Cream (see p. 242)
> pears or apples
> cinnamon sugar
> Apricot Glaze (see p. 239)
> whipped cream (optional)

Roll out puff paste ⅛ inch (3 mm) thick and chill. With a sharp knife, cut out 3- or 4-inch (7.5- or 10-cm) squares. Again, with a sharp knife and chilled firm dough, fold the square into a triangle. Making sure that the dough is still firm, place the triangle in front of you, with the fold toward you. Cut a strip into the left and right sides ¼ inch (6 mm) from each edge. Be careful not to cut all the way to the upper tip of the triangle. Unfold the triangle. The square will now have two L shapes on each side. Brush egg wash onto the square. Cross the left L to the right side and the right L to the left to make the frame. Brush egg wash lightly on top of this frame but not on the sides.

Using a no. 2 (4-mm) plain tip, pipe Pastry Cream on the inside of the frame. Peel, core, and slice fruit; arrange on top of the Pastry Cream. Sprinkle lightly with cinnamon sugar. Bake at 400° F (205° C) about 20 minutes. When cool, brush with Apricot Glaze. If used as dessert, serve with a rosette of whipped cream.

Puff-paste Diamonds can be made with any fruit. If you wish to use fruit that does not have to be baked, such as strawberry, fig, or raspberry, bake the pastry blind first. This pastry can also be prepared up to the point of baking; freeze and bake as needed.

CREAM HORNS
photograph, p. 56

> **Classic Puff Paste (see p. 36)**
> **granulated sugar**
> **strawberry jam**
> **whipped cream**
> **strawberries**
> **powdered sugar**

Roll out puff paste ⅛ inch (3 mm) thick. Cut ¾-inch-wide (20-mm) strips. The length depends on the size horn you are using. Brush strips with water. Roll them on to horn molds, water-brushed side facing the mold, starting at the bottom and overlapping strips halfway. Brush pastry with water, invert the tops of the horns in sugar, and freeze at least 30 minutes.

Bake horns at 390° F (200° C) about 45 minutes. When the horns are almost done, take the forms out and finish baking.

When the horns have cooled, fill with strawberry jam and as much whipped cream as can be forced into the hollow. Decorate with strawberries and sift very lightly with powdered sugar.

SWEDISH NAPOLEONS
15 pastries   photograph, p. 56

> Quick Puff Paste (see p. 38)
> 4½ ounces (130 g) strawberry jam
> 3 ounces (85 g) Fondant (see p. 249)
> Simple Syrup (see p. 233)
> 2 pounds (910 g) whipped cream

This is a good recipe for using up scrap dough, but, if you do so, do not knead the pieces together; rather layer them on each other and press them together. If using scrap dough, roll out the length of a sheet pan, 24 inches (60 cm), and ⅛ inch (3 mm) thick; prick well. If using fresh dough, roll it a bit thinner. If you are making puff paste only for Napoleons, make Quick Puff Paste. Let dough rest at least 30 minutes in the refrigerator; then bake at 375° F (190° C) about 25 minutes.

When the pastry sheet is baked and cooled, cut it into 3 strips the length of the pan, 4 inches (10 cm) wide each for regular servings or 3 inches (7.5 cm) wide for buffet servings. Select the nicest strip for the top, and turn it upside down. Spread a very thin layer of strawberry jam, just enough to color it, on the top strip. Spread a slightly thicker layer of jam on the bottom strip. Spread a thin layer of Fondant, thinned to a spreadable consistency with simple syrup (a little thinner than for *petits fours*) on the top strip, blending it gently with the jam. Set top strip aside for about 30 minutes or place in a warm oven for 30 seconds to set Fondant.

Place the middle strip on the bottom strip. With a large plain tip, pipe the whipped cream on the strip in a 1-inch (25-mm) layer. Cut the top layer into 1½-inch (37-mm) pieces; then place on top of the whipped cream. Using the top pieces as a guide, cut through the other layers. Napoleons must be served the day they are made.

Variation: Classic Napoleons
photograph, p. 56
Follow the recipe above with the following changes: Omit strawberry jam; substitute 2 pounds (910 g) Pastry Cream flavored with ½ ounce (1½ cl) Kirschwasser for the whipped cream; spread it equally on both layers. For decoration spread Fondant directly on the top layer of puff paste. With melted dark chocolate or brown piping gel, pipe 8 to 10 narrow straight lines lengthwise; immediately draw a knife through the chocolate every ½ inch (12 mm) to create a fishbone pattern.

SMALL PEAR DELICACIES

photograph, p. 56

> Classic Puff Paste (see p. 36)
> Pastry Cream (see p. 242)
> pears
> cinnamon sugar
> Caramel Sauce II (see p. 236)

Roll out puff paste slightly thicker than ⅛ inch (3 mm) and as square as possible. Refrigerate the dough until firm. Using a sharp knife, cut out rectangles 5 × 3 inches (12.5 × 7.5 cm). While the dough is still firm (you may need to refrigerate some of the rectangles again), cut a smaller rectangle ¼ inch (6 mm) from the edge on the larger but not all the way through. Prick the inside. Using a no. 2 (4-mm) plain tip, pipe a layer of Pastry Cream on the inside rectangle. The cream, in addition to adding flavor, will prevent the inside from puffing up as high as the cutout frame.

Peel, core, and halve small ripe pears; place them in acidulated water to prevent browning. If needed, cut the pears to fit inside the frame; cut the halves crosswise into thin slices. Arrange 4 or 5 slices at each end of the rectangle to meet in the middle, forming a butterfly. Sprinkle a small amount of cinnamon sugar over the top. Bake at 375° F (190° C) oven until done, about 35 minutes.

Meanwhile, make the Caramel Sauce and keep it warm over hot water. Place tarts on warm dessert plates, and cover each with 2 ounces (6 cl) sauce. Serve immediately.

PÂTE À CHOUX

> 1 quart (9 dl, 6 cl) water
> 8 ounces (2 dl, 4 cl) coconut oil
> 1½ teaspoons (4.5 g) salt
> 8 ounces (225 g) cake flour
> 11 ounces (310 g) bread flour
> 1 small teaspoon (2 g) ammonium carbonate
> 1 quart (9 dl, 6 cl) fresh eggs, approximately

Heat water, oil, and salt to boiling. Sift the first five dry ingredients together and stir into the boiling water as quickly as the water can absorb it. Stir constantly until the mixture is smooth and comes away from the side of the pan, about 1 minute. Let dough cool slightly and transfer to a mixer bowl.

Add the ammonium carbonate. Using the paddle, mix in the eggs, two at a time. Add as many eggs as the paste can hold without getting runny. For best results, pipe the dough immediately.

If the Pâte à Choux is not to be frozen, bake it immediately. If frozen, bake it directly from the freezer. Bake at 425° F (220° C) until fully puffed and starting to show some color, about 10 minutes; reduce heat to 375° F (190° C). Bake about 10 to 12 minutes depending on size. As long as they do not overbrown you cannot overbake Pâte à Choux, so make sure they have been baked long enough to hold their shape and do not fall.

CHOCOLATE ECLAIRS

about 45 eclairs   *photograph, p. 56*

> ½ recipe Pâte à Choux (preceding recipe)
> Chocolate Glaze (see p. 247)
> strawberry jam
> Chocolate Cream (recipe follows)
> chocolate

Make the Pâte à Choux, and pipe out 3½-inch (9-cm) bars for buffet servings or 4½-inch (12-cm) bars for regular servings, using a no. 8 (16-mm) star tip. Do not put more than 30 small or 20 large bars on a pan because there must be enough space to bake them thoroughly. If you plan to freeze the eclairs, pipe them as close together as possible to conserve freezer space. (If the unbaked eclairs are covered, they can freeze for weeks without losing quality. Bake as needed directly from the freezer.)

Bake eclairs at 425° F (220° C) until puffed and starting to color, about 10 minutes; reduce heat to 375° F (190° C). Bake until dry enough so that they will not fall when you take them out, about 12 minutes. When eclairs have cooled, cut off the top third of each one and brush the top evenly with Chocolate Glaze. Pipe a small ribbon of strawberry jam in the bottom of the eclair; using a no. 5 (10-mm) plain tip, pipe Chocolate Cream in a coil shape on top of the jam (the coil shape makes it look as if there is more cream than there is). The cream should be at least ½ inch (12 mm) higher than the base of the eclair. Place the top on the cream at an angle so the cream shows nicely. Serve the eclairs as fresh as possible and do not use them after they are a day old. Pâte à Choux gets soggy and rubbery when it is too old.

Chocolate Cream for Eclairs

      3 pints (1 l, 4 dl, 4 cl) heavy cream
      7 ounces (200 g) dark chocolate, melted
      2 ounces (6 cl) Simple Syrup (see Index)
      2 ounces (6 cl) water

Whip the cream to the consistency of a thick sauce; be careful: if you overwhip the cream, it will break up when the chocolate mixture is added. Mix together the melted chocolate, Simple Syrup, and water. Heat the mixture to 130° F (55° C). Place a small amount of the whipped cream in a bowl and gradually add the chocolate mixture, mixing rapidly. Mix in the rest of the cream. If the chocolate cream seems too runny, whip it to a firmer consistency.

SWANS

approximately 55 swans
photograph, p. 56

      Pâte à Choux (see p. 47)
      strawberry jam
      whipped cream
      melted dark chocolate
      strawberry wedges
      powdered sugar

Make Pâte à Choux. Using a no. 7 (14-mm) star tip, pipe the dough into cone shapes, 3 inches (7.5 cm) long and 1¾ inches (4.5 cm) wide, on sheet pans lined with baking paper. It is important that the wide end also be quite high for a nice-looking swan. Save enough paste to make 10 to 12 more necks than you have bodies. To pipe out the necks, using a no. 0 (2-mm) plain tip, move the tip quickly about ¼ inch (6 mm) to make the strip thinner than the tip, stop for a second so you get a lump for the head, and continue in a smooth question mark. Bake the necks at 375° F (190° C) about 12 minutes.

    For best results, make the necks and bodies the day before, freeze them, and bake them straight from the freezer at 425° F (220° C) until puffed and slightly browned, about 10 minutes; reduce heat to 375° F (190° C). Bake until pastries can hold their shapes when out of the oven, about 12 minutes.

    When the cones have cooled, cut off the top third; then cut the top part lengthwise into halves, creating the two wings. Place the 2 halves on either side of the body. (This can be done with a knife, but a scissors is best.) After all the swan bodies are cut, pipe a thin ribbon of strawberry jam on the bottom of each shell. Using a no. 7 (14-mm) star tip, pipe in whipped cream in the same shape as you piped the paste. Arrange the wings in the whipped cream pointing upward and meeting at the top. Dip the bottom of each neck in chocolate so that the whipped cream will not soften it and make it fall; push the neck into the whipped cream so that the neck leans back slightly between the wings. For some color, put a small wedge of strawberry at the back end. Finally, sift a little powdered sugar over the top. As with all *pâte à choux* pastries, swans should be served the same day they are assembled.

SWEDISH PROFITEROLES

27 servings   color photograph, p. C-2

> 8 ounces (225 g) Short Dough (see p. 19)
> 3 ounces (85 g) granulated sugar
> ½ recipe Pâte à Choux (see p. 47)
> 2 pounds (910 g) Bavarian Cream (see p. 261)
>   powdered sugar
>   Chocolate Sauce (see p. 248)
>   whipped cream
>   shaved dark chocolate
>   strawberries and kiwis, thinly sliced

Make Short Dough, adding the granulated sugar. Roll dough out thin; cut 1¼-inch (30-mm) circles from the dough with a cookie cutter. Set aside.

Make Pâte à Choux. Using a no. 4 (8-mm) plain tip, pipe out mounds, 1¼ inches (30 mm) in diameter and 1 inch (25 mm) high. The profiterole should be about the size of a golf ball when baked. Put no more than 24 to 30 on a sheet pan. Put dough circles on top of the mounds immediately to prevent a skin from forming, and press lightly with your finger to be sure they stick. Profiteroles can be frozen at this point.

Bake profiteroles at 400° F (205° C) until puffed, about 10 minutes; reduce heat to 375° F (190° C). Bake until they will hold their shapes, approximately 10 minutes. When profiteroles are completely cooled, make small holes in the bottoms for the tip on a pastry bag, and fill them with Bavarian Cream. Dust the tops lightly with powdered sugar.

To serve: Spoon 1½ ounces (4.5 cl) Chocolate Sauce on a serving plate and arrange 3 profiteroles on top. Decorate with whipped cream and shaved chocolate on top and in the middle of the profiteroles. At 3 places at the side of the plate, place thin slices of kiwi and strawberry just touching the sauce.

APPLE STRUDEL, AUSTRIAN STYLE

24 to 26 servings   photograph, p. 56

photograph, p. 56

- 2½ pounds (1 kg, 135 g) peeled, cored, and sliced apples
- 4 ounces (115 g) granulated sugar
- 1 pound (455 g) bread flour
- 1 egg (50 g)
- 2 ounces (55 g) butter, softened
- pinch salt
- 9 ounces (2 dl, 7 cl) cold water
- 6 ounces (170 g) small croutons
- butter
- 8 ounces (225 g) raisins
- 8 ounces (225 g) nuts, coarsely crushed
- cinnamon sugar
- 7 ounces (200 g) butter
- powdered sugar
- Sauce Anglaise (see p. 258)
- whipped cream (optional)

Combine sliced apples and granulated sugar. Set aside.

To make the dough: Place flour in a bowl or on the table. Make a well in the middle and add the egg, 2 ounces butter, salt, and enough of the cold water to make a soft dough. Knead until dough is smooth and elastic. Divide the dough into 2 pieces, and roll each out on a cloth dusted with flour into a small rectangle. Let dough rest for 5 minutes; then stretch it out with your hands, and let it rest again for 5 minutes.

Sauté croutons in butter until golden brown and crisp; any leftover butter can be used to brush on the strudel during baking.

Finish stretching dough into rectangles, about 28 × 14 inches (70 × 35 cm). Sprinkle the apples and any juice that has developed on the pastry rectangles. Sprinkle on the raisins, nuts, cinnamon sugar to taste, croutons, and the 7 ounces (200 g) butter cut into small chunks. Distribute all ingredients evenly. Using the cloth to help, roll each strudel from the long side toward yourself at the same time as you push down. You want a tight roll that will not flatten out too much when it is baked.

Place each strudel, seam side down, in a horseshoe shape on a sheet pan. Bake at 375° F (190° C) about 35 minutes. Brush the strudel with the juices that spill out from time to time. If there are no juices after 15 to 20 minutes in the oven, melt some butter and brush it on.

When strudel has cooled somewhat, slice, sift powdered sugar over the tops, and serve hot or cold with Sauce Anglaise or whipped cream.

APPLE STRUDEL, GERMAN STYLE

15 servings   *color photograph, p. C-2*

          Short Dough (see p. 19)
          Classic or Quick Puff Paste (see pp. 36, 38)
  2 **pounds (910 g) apples, peeled, cored**
          Poaching Syrup (see p. 233)
  6 **ounces (170 g) shelled walnuts**
  8 **ounces (225 g) raisins**
  1 **ounce (30 g) cinnamon sugar**
  3 **ounces (85 g) Mazarin Filling (see p. 262)**
  4 **ounces (115 g) spongecake**
          Apricot Jam (see p. 238)
          Spongecake I or II (see pp. 92, 93)
          egg wash
          Sauce Anglaise (see p. 258)
          Apricot Glaze (see p. 239)
          Fondant (see p. 249)

Roll out a strip of Short Dough the length of a sheet pan, ⅛ inch (3 mm) thick and 4 inches (10 cm) wide; refrigerate.

Roll out puff paste, ⅛ (3 mm) thick, 8 inches (20 cm) wide, and as long as the Short Dough. Refrigerate.

Poach the apples lightly (they should still be firm), and cut them into ½-inch (12-mm) slices. Frozen or canned apples are an excellent substitute, but they must not be too soft. Chop the walnuts to the size of the raisins. Combine apples, nuts, raisins, cinnamon sugar, and mazarin filling thoroughly. Add the 4 ounces (115 g) spongecake, broken into small pieces.

Spread a thin layer of jam on the Short Dough the full length of the dough, leaving ½ inch (12 mm) of the dough exposed on each edge. Place a thin strip of Spongecake on top of the jam. With your hands, add and shape the apple mixture, evenly and slightly rounded, on the length of the strip, leaving ¼ inch (6 mm) Short Dough exposed on each edge.

Fold the puff paste lengthwise over a 1-inch (25-mm) dowel. Position the dowel so that there is a space of 2 inches (5 cm) between the fold and the dowel. With the back of a chef's knife and using the dowel as a guide, lightly mark (being careful not to cut) a line parallel to the fold and approximately 1½ inches (37 mm) away from it. Cut through the fold up to the line at ¼ inch (6 mm) intervals, making a series of 3-inch (7.5-cm) slits along the center of the dough when unfolded. Brush the exposed Short Dough on the strudel with egg wash. Now move the dowel enough toward the cut part so that you can pick up the puff paste with the aid of the dowel and place it on top of the strudel, positioning it so that the slits are in the middle. Fasten the puff paste to the Short Dough with your thumbs and cut the excess off both sides. Brush with egg wash. Bake at 375° F (190° C) until golden brown, about 45 minutes. You might have to place a second pan underneath to prevent the bottom from getting too dark.

Make Sauce Anglaise. When the strudel has cooled, glaze with Apricot Glaze, and brush on Fondant that has been thinned to look transparent.

To serve: Spoon 1½ ounces (4.5 cl) Sauce Anglaise on each serving plate, cut the strudel into 1½-inch (37-mm) slices, and arrange each slice on the sauce. The strudel can be served hot or cold.

Kiwi Tart

Raspberry-Lemon Tart

Walnut-Caramel Tart

Lemon-Almond Tartlets

*Cointreau Tart with Apple,
Pear, or Rhubarb*

Apple Mazarins

Tosca

Citrons

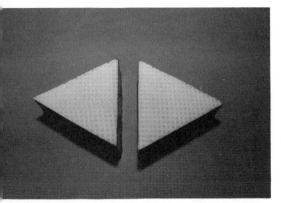

Green Triangles

Trier Squares

Almond Tart

Pecan Tarts

Apple Turnovers

Gâteau Saint-Honoré

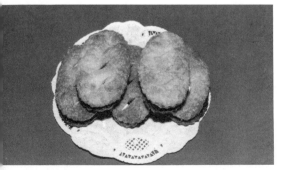

Pariser Waffles

Puff-paste Cuts with Fresh Fruit

Puff-paste Diamonds

Cream Horns

Swedish Napoleons

Classic Napoleons

Small Pear Delicacies

Chocolate Eclairs

Pâte à Choux Swans

Apple Strudel, Austrian Style

3

Breads

The baking of bread dates back to the Stone Age, when man first learned to grind seeds, probably barley and millet, in hand-operated mills made from stone. From the first porridges, it was not a great step to the making of bread. This early bread, heavy and unleavened, was cooked on heated stones (it was not called the Stone Age for nothing). Over the centuries the process of milling the grain was improved. The early Egyptians, with the aid of wind-powered fans and later of sieves, developed a way to remove parts of the chaff and bran. But it was not before the Romans and the Greeks that the cultivation and milling of grains started to develop; they produced different kinds of flour in various stages of refinement.

Baking bread has always had an important place in the European home. Different regions of various countries have their special types of bread that differ not only in flavor but in shape as well. Although today most bread baking is done industrially, it is still a favorite hobby of many. In fact bread baking is probably what the beginner will try first.

Basically, there are three types of bread: loaf bread in many shapes, breakfast items, such as croissants and Danish, and soft cakes, such as muffins and doughnuts. Some of these are leavened with baking powder or soda, but the majority are leavened with yeast.

Baking with yeast demands that the ingredients be in proper proportion. Yeast needs sugar to grow, but too much sugar can slow the process to the point where it stops altogether. Sugar also colors and flavors the bread. Salt is used in a yeast dough to add color and flavor and to retard the yeast just a little. When I see a loaf of baked bread that is pale instead of healthy golden brown, I know that the loaf was either baked at too low a heat or the salt was left out. Yeast fermentation is damaged in temperatures above

115° F (46° C), and the yeast is killed at 140° F (60° C). At the other end of the scale, yeast fermentation is slowed but not damaged at temperatures below 65° F (18° C) and is nonexistent at 40° F (4° C) or lower. In certain types of yeast dough, such as for Danish pastry, braided white bread, and croissants, it is essential that the yeast be kept cold to prevent fermentation while the dough is being made.

The easiest bread to make is plain white bread that has all white, glutenous flour and only the amount of sugar that is healthy for the yeast. It can therefore be made with cold milk, which slows the fermentation long enough to give one time to braid it into different kinds of loafs. In a bread with a high proportion of sugar, a sweet flour, such as rye, or flours with little or no gluten structure, such as whole wheat, it is very important to keep the dough from getting too cold. The ideal temperature for the yeast to develop is from 78° to 82° F (26° to 28° C); the dough should be kept as close to this temperature as possible by starting with a warm 105° F to 115° F (40° C to 46° C) liquid, but if the liquid is too hot, the yeast will be damaged or killed. Use a thermometer until you know your judgment is accurate. Take care in keeping the dough covered and away from drafts at all times.

There are two methods of fermenting the yeast. For the sponge method, a very soft dough is made of a small amount of flour, water, sugar (sugar is not necessary if milk is used because milk is naturally sweet), and most of the time, all of the yeast; then it rises covered in a warm place until doubled in volume. The sponge method allows the yeast to ferment in peace without any damaging enemies. The sponge is then mixed with all the remaining ingredients to make the dough.

For the straight-dough method, all the ingredients are mixed together at the beginning and, in most cases, kneaded to form a gluten structure. It is then given one or two periods to rise before being punched down and made into loaves or rolls.

In breads with a high sugar content, such as Swedish Orange Rye or Italian Triestine Bread, the sponge method is essential for a satisfactory result. Danish pastry and croissants depend on a thin layer structure to "help" the yeast. The fat particles steam when the Danish or croissant is baked, and that, together with the trapped air and of course the yeast, gives it the light flaky consistency. Or at least it should.

Most bread doughs should rise to double in volume as a rule of thumb, but this includes the rising that will occur in the oven before the bread reaches 140° F (60° C) when the yeast is killed. Therefore, prior to baking, the bread should rise to just around the half of its double-in-volume potential to allow for the final rise in the oven. A loaf that has risen too much is very crumbly, dries out faster because of the extra air, and loses part of its flavor because the flavor does not increase with the dough's volume. On the other hand, if the bread is not allowed to rise long enough, the gluten will not have formed all the elasticity it needs to expand, and, as a result, the loaf will crack, usually on the side and will be compact and heavy. Not enough rising time for Danish pastry or croissants will make part of the butter run out on the pan and result in a drier and heavier pastry.

Last, but certainly not least, it is very important that the proof box (the box where the yeast is fermenting in a dough in industrial baking) or other rising area is not too hot. Ideally it should be about 82° F (28°C) with 90% humidity. If you keep to all of these rules and guidelines, I can assure you that you will be very satisfied with the results of the following recipes.

BRAIDED WHITE BREAD

six 18-ounce (510-g) loaves   *photograph, p. 88*

> 4 ounces (115 g) fresh compressed yeast
> 1 quart (9 dl, 6 cl) cold milk
> 1½ ounces (40 g) salt
> 2 pounds (910 g) bread flour
> 2 pounds (910 g) cake flour
> 4 ounces (115 g) sugar
> 8 ounces (225 g) unsalted soft butter
> egg wash
> poppy or sesame seeds (optional)

Dissolve yeast in milk. Add salt, both flours, and sugar. Mix until dough forms a ball; mix in butter. Knead until a fine gluten structure develops, 8 to 10 minutes. Test by pulling off a small piece of dough and lightly stretching it; if it forms an almost translucent membrane, the dough has been kneaded enough. If the dough is overkneaded, the gluten structure will be permanently damaged, resulting in a loose and hard-to-work dough that will not rise properly, if at all, because the damaged gluten cannot trap enough air. Cover dough and let rise until doubled.

Punch down dough and divide into pieces for braiding. The total weight of the loaf should be 18 ounces (510 g); the weight of the pieces depends on how many braids are used; for example, 3 braids are 6 ounces (170 g) each and 6 braids are 3 ounces (85 g) each. Keep covered to prevent a skin from forming. Pound and roll each piece into a string, thicker in the center and thinner on the ends, 14 inches (35 cm) long. Do not roll all strings at once, but braid each loaf immediately after rolling out the strings for it. Take care not to braid too tightly.

Brush the loaves with egg wash and let rise again until half-doubled. For extra shine, the loaves can be brushed with egg wash before baking. Sprinkle with poppy or sesame seeds or leave the braids plain. Bake at 400° F (205° C) about 25 minutes. Cool on racks.

How to Make Braids

All braids except the 1-string braid have the following in common:

The individual pieces should be pounded free of any air bubbles (pockets) and rolled into a tapered shape, thicker in the middle and gradually thinner toward the ends.

For the 16- to 18-ounce (455- to 510-g) loaf, pieces should be rolled to about 12 inches (30 cm) in length. As you braid the strings, stretch the dough at the same time so that the braid ends up 12 inches (30 cm) long. As you place the braids, 4 to a pan, on sheet pans, stretch them to approximately 14 inches (35 cm). This procedure will give you nice uniform loaves.

As you follow the numbers in the different braids, count from left to right. When you move string no. 1 in a 6-string braid over 2, 3, 4, 5, and 6, no. 1 will be no. 6 and no. 2 will be no. 1. Doing it is not as complicated as reading about it.

1-string braid

This is usually made with a leftover piece of dough. Roll the dough out about ¾ inch (20 mm) thick. Place horizontally in front of you. Pick up the left end and form an inward loop (toward yourself): using two thirds of the string's length for the loop, bring the left end up and under the center of the remaining straight string, with the end protruding slightly. Make a half-turn in the loop to the left to form a figure eight. Pull the remaining straight string under and through the larger lower loop of the figure eight. Now turn the remaining loop to the right and repeat, each time alternating left to right, until the full length of the string is used.

2-string braid

Weigh the dough into 9-ounce (255-g) pieces. Roll each piece out 20 inches (50 cm) long, and place them in a wide X shape in front of you. Pick up the two ends of the bottom string, and move the two ends straight across the other string so they change sides, but they should not cross over each other. Repeat the procedure with the other string and so on, until the braid is finished.

3-string braid

Weigh the dough into 6-ounce (170-g) pieces and roll out. Braid 3 over 2, 1 over 2. Repeat.

4-string braid

Weigh the dough into 4½-ounce (130-g) pieces and roll out. Braid 2 over 3; 4 over 3, 2; 1 over 2, 3. Repeat.

5-string braid

Weigh the dough into 3½-ounce (100-g) pieces and roll out. Braid 2 over 3; 5 over 4, 3, 2; 1 over 2, 3. Repeat.

6-string braid

Weigh the dough into 3-ounce (85-g) pieces and roll out. Braid 1 over 2, 3, 4, 5, 6; 5 over 4, 3, 2, 1; 2 over 3, 4, 5, 6; 5 over 4, 3; 5 over 4, 3, 2, 1; 2 over 3, 4. Repeat last four.

7-string braid

Weigh the dough into 2½-ounce (70-g) pieces and roll out. Braid 7 over 6, 5, 4; 1 over 2, 3, 4. Repeat.

8-string braid

Weigh the dough into 2-ounce (55-g) pieces and roll out. Braid 2 under 3 and over 8; 1 over 2, 3, 4; 7 under 6 and over 1; 8 over 7, 6, 5. Repeat.

CHRISTMAS STAR

photograph, p. 88

> **Braided White Bread dough (recipe precedes)**
> **egg wash**
> **poppy and sunflower seeds, optional**

This bread is a striking centerpiece for any holiday table. The recipe is for a star that is 15 inches (37 cm) in diameter. If you want a smaller star, reduce the weight and length of the pieces. Even though you only have to know how to do a four-string braid to make this loaf, you should not attempt it before you are fairly successful in rolling out and forming the strings; if you take too long, the first string will have risen when you are still shaping the last one.

Make the bread dough, and weigh out sixteen 3-ounce (85-g) pieces (12 pieces for the points and 4 pieces for the center of the star). Keep pieces covered to prevent a skin from forming. Pound and roll each piece 18 inches (45 cm) long and taper the ends. Arrange them in an upside-down U so that you are getting two strings out of each piece. Place them on top of each other, so the left string of the second upside-down U is one third inside the first one, and so on (the same way you put two Vs together to form an upside-down W). Leave a 5-inch (12.5-cm) round space in the center. When you come to the twelfth string here, pick up the right string of the U and place it under and one third in on the first one. Then form 6 groups with 4 strings in each one, out of the 24 strings, and four-braid them. If the opening in the middle is becoming too large, move the separate pointed braids together as you braid. Cut remaining 4 pieces into 3 pieces each, making twelve 1-ounce (30-g) pieces. Roll each one out to approximately 8 inches (20 cm) but do not taper these. Form 4 groups of 3 each, and do the four-string braid again. Leave both ends of the braid open. Pick the braid up with both hands and push the two ends under so that you form a round loaf. You can also use this method on a normal-size loaf (increase the weight of each piece to 4 ounces (155 g) for a 1-pound (455-g) loaf). It will take a little extra time but looks very unusual and very few will know that it is only a four-string braid. Place the round loaf in the open middle of the star. Brush with egg wash. Let the dough rise again until half-doubled.

For a good shine, brush a second time with egg wash before baking. Sprinkle with poppy and/or sunflower seeds if you wish. Bake at 375° F (190° C) until golden brown, about 40 minutes.

BAGUETTES
five 13-ounce (370-g) thin loaves
photograph, p. 88

> 1¼ ounces (35 g) fresh compressed yeast
> 3 cups (7 dl, 2 cl) warm water, 110° F (43° C)
> ½ ounce (15 g) salt
> 2 pounds, 7 ounces (1 kg, 110 g) bread flour
>   cornmeal

Dissolve the yeast in warm water; stir in salt and bread flour. Knead until dough is smooth and elastic. Let rise covered until doubled.

Weigh into 13-ounce (370-g) pieces. Roll and pound each piece into a 23-inch-long (58-cm) *baguette* to fit the length of a sheet pan. Brush loaves with water and sprinkle with cornmeal. With a razor blade or very sharp knife, cut deep slits, 4 to 5 inches (10 to 12 cm) long, at a sharp angle on the tops of the loaves. Let rise until half-doubled.

Bake at 400° F (205° C). During the first 10 minutes of baking, place a cake pan with ice cubes in the oven, and keep adding ice cubes, 2 at a time, to create steam. After 10 minutes, remove the water, and bake the loaves until golden brown and crusty, about 25 minutes. Cool on a rack and use the same day.

BUTTER-WHEAT BREAD
seven 1-pound, 2-ounce (510-g) loaves   *photograph, p. 88*

        3 ounces (85 g) fresh compressed yeast
        1 quart (9 dl, 6 cl) cold water
    2½ pounds (1 kg, 135 g) bread flour
        1 pound (455 g) whole-wheat flour
        2 ounces (55 g) salt
        2 pounds (910 g) Puff-paste or Croissant scraps (see pp. 36, 38, 73) (If you are using Croissant scraps, reduce the yeast to 2 ounces (55 g)
           whole-wheat flour
           egg wash

This is a great way to use up puff-paste or croissant scraps that otherwise might go to waste. Scraps of Danish dough make a very good coffee ring.

Dissolve the yeast in the cold water. Add the flours, and mix 5 minutes on medium speed. Add salt and dough scraps; mix until dough is smooth, about 3 minutes. Add more whole-wheat flour if necessary for a medium-firm dough. Place the dough on a sheet pan, and let rise covered in a warm place until the dough starts to fall, about 1½ hours. Divide into 18-ounce (510-g) pieces, but do not knead them. Keep the pieces covered as you weigh them to prevent a skin from forming. Knead each piece between your palm and the table until the loaf is tight and round and the dough has enough tension to spring back when pressed. If kneaded too much, the skin will break, giving the loaf a ragged look.

Immediately after kneading, flatten each loaf lightly with your hand, brush with egg wash, and invert it on whole-wheat flour.

Place loaves on sheet pans, no more than 4 to a pan. Using a sharp paring knife, cut a flower *baguette* pattern ⅛ inch (3 mm) deep by first making one straight cut down the middle and then 3 fanned cuts from the left joining at the bottoms and the same pattern on the right. Let loaves rise until half-doubled.

Bake at 400° F (205° C) until loaves have a healthy brown color and test done (they should feel light when lifted up and sound hollow when tapped), about 48 minutes. Place them on racks to cool.

RUSSIAN ROLLED-WHEAT BREAD

ten 19-ounce (540-g) loaves   photograph, p. 88

            1 **pint, 2 ounces (5.4 dl) hot water**
            7 **ounces (200 g) light corn syrup**
            1 **pound, 2 ounces (510 g) rolled wheat**
            7 **ounces (2 dl, 1 cl) boiling water**
        3½ **ounces (100 g) rye flour**
        3½ **ounces (100 g) whole-wheat flour**
          ⅓ **ounce (10 g) salt**
            2 **pints, 3 ounces (1 l, 5 cl) warm water, 105° to 115° F (40° to
                  46° C)**
        3½ **ounces (10.5 cl) milk**
            6 **ounces (170 g) fresh compressed yeast**
        2⅓ **ounces (65 g) salt**
        3½ **ounces (100 g) butter**
          ½ **pound (225 g) whole-wheat flour**
        4½ **pounds (2 kg, 45 g) bread flour**
               egg wash
               rolled wheat

Heat 1 pint, 2 ounces (5.4 dl) hot water and the corn syrup to boiling; pour over the rolled wheat. Do not stir. Let stand overnight.

Pour the boiling water over the rye flour, 3½ ounces (100 g) whole-wheat flour, and ⅓ ounce (10 g) salt. Mix and add to the rolled-wheat mixture. Let stand for 1 hour.

Combine the warm water and milk in a mixer bowl, and dissolve the yeast in it. Add the rolled-wheat mixture, 2⅓ ounces (65 g) salt, the butter, and the remaining flours. Mix until smooth. Turn out on a floured table, and let rest, covered, for 30 minutes.

Divide the dough into 19-ounce (540-g) pieces. Shape each piece into a smooth round loaf. Flatten lightly with your hand. Brush with egg wash and sprinkle with rolled wheat. Using a 3-inch (7.5-cm) plain cookie cutter, cut a circle ⅛ inch (3 mm) deep in the center of each loaf, and slash the sides to the same depth with a sharp knife. Let rise until half-doubled. Bake at 400° F (205° C) about 35 minutes.

SWEDISH ORANGE RYE BREAD

eight 17-ounce (485-g) loaves   *photograph, p. 88*

> 2 cups (4 dl, 8 cl) molasses
> 5 cups (1 l, 2 dl) hot water, 130° F (54° C)
> 3 ounces (85 g) yeast
> 4 ounces (115 g) medium rye flour
> 2 pounds (910 g) bread flour
> 1 pound (455 g) rye flour
> 1 pound, 10 ounces (740 g) bread flour
> 10 ounces (285 g) candied orange peel, chopped to the size of raisins
> 1½ ounces (40 g) salt
> 1½ ounces (40 g) butter
>   vegetable oil

It is very important that the temperature of this dough does not fall below 75° F (25° C) because of the high amount of sugar in the recipe. Stir molasses into the hot water; add yeast, 4 ounces (115 g) rye flour, and 2 pounds (910 g) bread flour. Mix to a smooth sponge. Let rise covered in a warm place until the sponge just starts to fall, about 1 hour.

Add remaining ingredients except oil, but do not add more bread flour than is necessary to form the dough into a loaf. Do not overmix; the dough should be sticky and will not come away from the side of the bowl. Let dough rest covered 10 minutes; then divide into eight 17-ounce (485-g) pieces. Roll each piece into a tight circle and form into an oval loaf. The dough should spring right back when lightly pressed down. Place loaves in greased bread pans. Let rise again until doubled.

Bake at 375° F (190° C) about 45 minutes. You may have to protect the loaves from overbrowning by placing a second pan underneath or covering the tops with parchment paper. Brush loaves with vegetable oil as soon as they come out of oven. Unmold loaves and cool on racks.

SWEDISH PEASANT BREAD

eight 18-ounce (510-g) loaves   *photograph, p. 88*

  1 quart (9 dl, 6 cl) water
  1 ounce (30 g) salt
 12 ounces (340 g) whole-wheat flour
 12 ounces (340 g) rye flour
3½ cups (8 dl, 4 cl) warm water, 105° to 115° F (40° to 46° C)
  1 ounce (3 cl) white vinegar
 10 ounces (3 dl) light corn syrup
  3 ounces (85 g) fresh compressed yeast
  1 ounce (30 g) malt sugar or syrup
  8 ounces (225 g) butter
  ½ ounce (15 g) ground cumin
  ½ ounce (15 g) ground fennel
  4 pounds (1 kg, 820 g) bread flour
    egg wash

Heat 1 quart (9 dl, 6 cl) water to boiling; add salt, whole-wheat flour, and rye flour. Mix until smooth and let stand covered 1 hour.

Stir vinegar and corn syrup into the remaining warm water; dissolve the yeast in the liquid. Stir in the flour mixture, malt, butter, and spices. Add enough of the bread flour so that the dough is not sticky. Test the dough with some flour on your hand. Knead until smooth, 4 to 6 minutes. Turn dough out on a floured table, and let it rest covered 10 minutes.

Divide dough into 18-ounce (510-g) pieces. Roll each piece into a firm round loaf. The bread should spring back immediately when you lightly press it. With the side of your hand in the middle of each loaf, roll the loaf into 2 round halves, almost severing it. Place loaves on sheet pans. Brush with egg wash. Using a sharp knife, slash a few lines across the top of each loaf. Let loaves rise until doubled. Bake at 375° F (190° C) about 35 minutes. You can also invert the loaves in whole-wheat flour after you have brushed them with egg wash but before you slash the lines across the top.

RAISIN BREAD

seven 18-ounce (510-g) loaves   *photograph, p. 88*

> 1 quart (9 dl, 6 cl) milk
> 2 ounces (55 g) fresh compressed yeast
> ⅔ ounces (20 g) salt
> 3½ ounces (100 g) sugar
> 1 ounce (30 g) honey
> 3 pounds, 2 ounces (1 kg, 420 g) bread flour
> 2 ounces (55 g) butter
> 2 pounds (910 g) raisins
> egg wash
> cinnamon sugar

Due to the large amount of sugar in this bread, you must protect the dough from cooling below 75° F (25° C). Warm milk to 105° to 115° F (40° to 46° C) and dissolve the yeast in it. Stir in salt, sugar, and honey. Stir in enough of the bread flour to make a soft, smooth dough. Stir in the butter, but do not knead the dough at this point because it will be harder to knead in the raisins later. Place the dough on the table, and let it rest covered until almost doubled in bulk, about 45 minutes.

Knead in the raisins by hand (at the same time you are developing the needed gluten structure). Let dough rest covered 10 minutes. Divide dough into fourteen 9-ounce (255-g) pieces. Keep them covered. Starting with the first pieces you measured, shape each piece into a 10-inch (25-cm) string. Twist 2 strings loosely together, and place them in rectangular bread pans, 8 × 4 × 2½ inches (20 × 10 × 6 cm). Brush with egg wash and sprinkle with cinnamon sugar. Let loaves rise until half doubled. Bake at 375° F (190° C) about 40 minutes.

ROSEMARY BREAD

five 16½-ounce (470-g) loaves   *photograph, p. 89*

> 2 ounces (55 g) fresh compressed yeast
> 3 cups (7 dl, 2 cl) warm water, 105° to 115° F (40° to 46° C)
> 2 ounces (55 g) sugar
> 1 cup (2 dl, 4 cl) olive oil
> 1½ ounces (40 g) salt
> 1 ounce (30 g) rosemary, finely chopped
> 3 pounds, 12 ounces (1 kg, 705 g) high-gluten flour
> egg wash

Dissolve yeast in warm water; stir in sugar, oil, salt, rosemary, and enough of the flour to make a fairly stiff dough. (Regular bread flour can be substituted for the high-gluten flour, but the bread will not have the same springy texture.) Mix 6 to 8 minutes to develop the gluten structure. The dough will get a little looser as it gets smoother. Let rise covered 30 minutes. Punch down and let dough rise another 30 minutes. Punch down again and divide into 16½-ounce (470-g) pieces. Shape pieces into tight oval loaves. They should be tight enough to spring back when lightly pressed but not so tight that the skin on the dough breaks. Place loaves on sheet pans, brush with egg wash, and let rise until half-doubled.

Using a serrated knife, cut halfway down at a 45-degree angle in the middle of each loaf.

Bake at 475° F (240° C) 8 to 10 minutes; remove from the sheet pans to the oven racks. Reduce heat to 375° F (190° C); bake until loaves sound hollow when tapped, about 18 minutes. Place them on racks to cool.

Variation: Crisp Bread
Measure 8-ounce (225-g) pieces and form into round loaves. Let stand a few minutes to relax the loaves. Roll each out to a 10-inch (25-cm) circle. Cut a hole 3 inches (7.5 cm) in diameter in the center. Place the cutouts next to the doughnut-shaped circles. Start rolling the first loaf formed; if the dough is still rubbery, let it rest some more by rolling it out only halfway at first. When rolled out, rub loaves with olive oil and sprinkle lightly with kosher salt. Let them rise only halfway; bake at 375° F (190° C) about 30 minutes.

GARLIC BREAD
six 18-ounce (510-g) loaves   photograph, p. 89

2	ounces (55 g) minced garlic
	olive oil
2	ounces (55 g) fresh compressed yeast
1	quart (9 dl, 6 cl) lukewarm water, 105° to 115° F (40° to 46° C)
2	ounces (6 cl) egg whites
2	ounces (55 g) butter
1½	ounces (40 g) sugar
2	ounces (55 g) salt
½	ounce (15 g) dried oregano
½	ounce (15 g) dried basil
4	pounds, 6½ ounces (2 kg) bread flour
	salt

Sauté the garlic in olive oil until soft to remove some of the sting. If the garlic is very strong, reduce the amount. Dissolve yeast in warm water. Stir in remaining ingredients except unmeasured salt and ½ pound (225 g) (about a handful) of the flour. Knead the dough, adding the remaining flour, until the dough is fairly stiff and smooth. Let rise covered 1 hour.

Punch down and divide into six 18-ounce (510-g) pieces. Shape each piece into a round loaf; then, starting with the loaf first formed, shape them into tight oval loaves. They should spring back if lightly pressed. Place loaves seam sides down on sheet pans. Brush with water and sprinkle generously with salt. Make diagonal slashes across each loaf, about ¼ inch (6 mm) deep. Let rise until doubled. Bake at 375° F (190° C) about 30 minutes. Cool on racks.

ONION WALNUT BREAD
eight 17-ounce (485-g) loaves   *photograph, p. 89*

> 8 ounces (225 g) peeled white onions, minced
>   butter or olive oil
> 2 ounces (55 g) fresh compressed yeast
> 1¼ quarts (1 l, 2 cl) warm milk, 105° to 115° F (40° to 46° C)
> 2 ounces (55 g) sugar
> 2½ ounces (70 g) salt
> 1 cup (2 dl, 4 cl) olive oil
> 5 pounds (2 kg, 275 g) bread flour
> 8 ounces (225 g) chopped walnuts
>   egg wash
>   whole-wheat flour

Sauté the onions in butter or olive oil until golden. Use a stainless-steel or other noncorrosive bowl to mix the dough because the oil from the walnuts in contact with bare metal colors the dough grey. Dissolve yeast in warm milk; stir in sugar, salt, and 1 cup (2 dl, 4 cl) olive oil; mix in half the flour. Mix in walnuts and onions. Mix in enough of the remaining flour to make a quite firm dough; knead until smooth. Let rise covered until doubled.

Divide dough into 17-ounce (485-g) pieces, and knead the pieces into firm round loaves. Brush loaves with egg wash; invert on whole-wheat flour, completely covering the tops of the loaves with flour. Immediately mark the tops with 3 plain cookie cutters, firmly and deeply enough to leave a distinct depression without cutting into the loaf. Start with a 4½-inch (11-cm) cutter at the outside and space the other two smaller ones about ½ inch (12 mm) apart. Let loaves rise until doubled. Bake at 400° F (205° C) about 37 minutes.

Variation

Although in principle all bread doughs can be made into rolls, this dough makes up into rolls particularly well. Divide each 17-ounce (485-g) piece into 8 smaller pieces; shape and finish as instructed for the loaves, but use smaller cutters to mark them. Bake at 400° F (205° C) 20 minutes.

BANANA BREAD

6 small loaves   photograph, p. 89

> 1 pound (455 g) butter
> 1 pound, 12 ounces (795 g) granulated sugar
> 4 eggs
> 1 ounce (3 cl) water
>   few drops vanilla extract
> 2 pounds (910 g) puréed bananas, somewhat overripe
> 1 pound, 12 ounces (795 g) flour
> 2 teaspoons (7 g) salt
> ½ ounce (15 g) baking soda
> 12 ounces (340 g) coarsely chopped nuts
>   powdered sugar

Melt the butter and add the granulated sugar. Beat together for a few minutes. Stir in eggs, water, vanilla, and bananas. Mix the dry ingredients except powdered sugar; stir into the butter mixture.

Butter and flour *gugelhupf* forms or other desired molds. Spoon batter into forms, filling each three-quarters full. Bake at 350° F (175° C) until a toothpick inserted in the middle comes out dry, about 55 minutes. You may need to use a second pan underneath to ensure that the loaves do not get too dark while baking.

Unmold the loaves as soon as possible; they will get wet if left to cool in the pans. When cool, dust lightly with powdered sugar.

TRIESTINE

seven 15-ounce (430-g) loaves
photograph, p. 89

Sponge

    9 ounces (2 dl, 7 cl) warm milk, 105° to 115° F (40° to 46° C)
    ⅓ ounce (10 g) fresh compressed yeast
    ½ ounce (15 g) lard
    12 ounces (340 g) bread flour

Dough

    9 ounces (2 dl, 7 cl) warm milk, 105° to 115° F (40° to 46° C)
    2½ ounces (70 g) fresh compressed yeast
    1 ounce (30 g) malt sugar or syrup
    6 ounces (170 g) sugar
    ¾ ounce (20 g) salt
    4 eggs (200 g)
      grated zest of ½ lemon
    2 drops orange-flower water
    5 ounces (140 g) butter
    2 pounds (910 g) bread flour
    8 ounces (225 g) candied orange peel, finely chopped
    9 ounces (255 g) glazed or candied cherries, finely chopped
    8 ounces (225 g) blanched almonds, thinly sliced

Topping

    2½ ounces (70 g) almonds, finely ground
    1 ounce (30 g) granulated sugar
    1 to 1½ ounces (28 to 40 g) egg whites
    3 ounces (85 g) blanched almonds, thinly sliced
      powdered sugar

Make a sponge with 9 ounces (2 cl, 7 cl) warm milk, ⅓ ounce (10 g) yeast, ½ ounce (15 g) lard, and 12 ounces (340 g) bread flour. Let rise covered until doubled.

Stir in the ingredients for the dough in the order listed, but hold back a little flour in case you do not need it all. The dough should be fairly firm. Let rest covered 10 minutes. Divide dough into 15-ounce (430-g) pieces, and knead into round loaves. The loaf is kneaded enough when the dough springs back when lightly pressed. Flatten loaves slightly with your hands to make a surface for the topping.

To make the topping, combine ground almonds and granulated sugar; without overmixing, add enough egg white to make it spreadable but not runny. Spread the topping on the tops and halfway down the sides of the loaves. Top with sliced almonds, pressing them with your hand so they stick. Let loaves rise until doubled.

Before placing the bread in the oven, sift powdered sugar over the tops to cover the almonds. Bake at 375° F (190° C) until golden brown, about 35 minutes. You may need to protect these loaves from overbrowning by placing a second pan underneath or covering the top with paper parchment.

CROISSANTS

approximately sixty 2-ounce (55-g) croissants
photograph, p. 89

> 2½ pounds (1 kg, 340 g) sweet butter
> juice of ¼ lemon
> 3½ pounds (1 kg, 590 g) bread flour
> 3 ounces (85 g) fresh compressed yeast
> 1 quart (9 cl, 6 dl) cold milk
> 3 ounces (85 g) sugar
> 1 ounce (30 g) malt sugar or syrup
> 1½ ounces (40 g) salt
> egg wash or milk

This dough is easier to work with if prepared in the morning for finishing in the afternoon or prepared in the afternoon for finishing the next morning. In both cases, store it covered in the refrigerator.

First check and prepare the 2½-pound (1-kg, 340-g) butter if needed. Work in the lemon juice and 4 ounces (115 g) of flour. If it is too soft, place in the refrigerator to harden, and then work it smooth with your hands just as you would if it was too firm. Shape it into a 12-inch (30-cm) square on a piece of paper and set aside. If the room is warm, place it in the refrigerator.

Dissolve the yeast in the 1 quart (9 cl, 6 dl) milk; add sugar, malt, and salt. Mix for a few seconds using the dough hook, and start adding the flour. Mix in the flour to make a not-too-soft workable dough.

Place the dough on a table dusted with flour; roll it out to a 14-inch (35-cm) square. Place the butter square on the dough at an angle so that there are 4 triangles on the sides. Pat the butter lightly to make sure it is smooth; then fold the dough triangles toward the middle to seal in the butter. Give the dough 3 single turns (see Index). After the last turn, roll the dough out ½ inch (12 mm) thick. Refrigerate covered at least 2 hours.

To form Croissants, roll dough into a rectangle, 40 × 27 inches (100 × 67.5 cm). It should be slightly thinner than ¼ inch (6 mm) and as even as possible. Let dough rest 3 to 4 minutes so that it will not shrink when you cut it, and cut it lengthwise into three 9-inch (22.5-cm) strips. On the bottom edge of the strip closest to you, make a mark every 4½ inches (11.2-cm), working from left to right. Do the same on the top edge of the middle strip. Place a ruler from the first 4½-inch (11.2-cm) mark (this mark should be at the lower left corner) on the bottom strip up to the second mark on the middle strip (4½ inches (11.2-cm) from the left edge); cut the dough using a knife or pastry wheel, following the ruler through the top strip. Then cut from the second 4½-inch (11.2-cm) mark on the bottom strip to the third mark on the middle strip and across the top strip. Repeat for the length of the dough; then, beginning at the opposite end, follow the same pattern and cut from right to left. Pick away the scrap dough and save for the next batch of Butter-wheat Bread (see Index). Form the Croissants by rolling the tall triangles up tightly but without stretching the dough too much. Shape the triangles into crescent shapes; the point of the triangle should be inside the crescent shape and underneath the roll. Place no more than 16 to 18 Croissants on a full-size sheet pan to ensure that they bake evenly and not get overdone at the ends before they are fully baked in the middle.

Let the Croissants rise until half-doubled in a humid, 85° F (32° C) proof box. If the proof box is hotter, the butter will run out, which will also happen while they are being baked if you do not let them rise enough. Brush the Croissants with egg wash or milk, which is typical in France. Bake at 425° F (220° C) until golden and done, about 25 minutes.

DANISH PASTRY

    1 quart (9 dl, 6 cl) cold water
    1 pint (4 dl, 8 cl) whole eggs
    4 pounds (1 kg, 800 g) margarine
    4 ounces (115 g) fresh compressed yeast
    8 ounces (225 g) sugar
 1½ ounces (40 g) salt
 4½ pounds (2 kg) bread flour
    4 ounces (115 g) margarine, softened
    1 tablespoon (3 g) ground cardamom

All ingredients except the softened margarine must be cold. Mix water and whole eggs and freeze until cold; freeze bread flour at least 1 hour before making dough. Or place all these ingredients in the refrigerator the day before. On really hot days, you may want to decrease the amount of yeast slightly so the dough does not rise too fast.

Shape the margarine into a 12-inch (30-cm) square; refrigerate it so that it is firm and cold but not hard when the dough is ready. A good margarine gives a better layer structure and is more elastic than butter, which is why it is used in this dough, where the light and flaky texture is more important than the butter flavor.

Dissolve yeast in mixed water and eggs; stir in salt and sugar. Start mixing in flour; add softened butter when about two-thirds of the flour has been added and dough has the consistency of soft butter. Add enough of the remaining flour to make a sticky dough. Place dough on floured table and shape into a 14-inch (35-cm) square. Place the butter block on the dough at an angle so that there are 4 dough triangles showing. Fold these toward the middle to seal in the margarine. Roll the dough into a rectangle, 30 × 20 inches (75 × 50 cm), using plenty of flour to prevent it from sticking to the table. Roll it out as carefully and evenly as possible. Give the dough a single turn (see Index). Roll out and give it a double turn (see Index). Cover and refrigerate for 30 minutes. Roll out and make one more single turn. Carefully place the dough on a sheet pan. Refrigerate covered 30 minutes.

Roll the dough out about ½ inch (12 mm) thick, cover with plastic wrap, and place it in the refrigerator or freezer, depending on how hot it is in the room you are working and when you are going to make up the Danish. In either case, the dough should chill at least 30 minutes before being finished.

Make up the Danish and let the pieces rise until half-doubled. Be observant of their rise; if they rise too long, they will lose their flakiness and get spongy; if they do not rise long enough, the fat will run out. If Danish are to be frozen, it is best to freeze them before they are baked—either made up in individual pieces or in sheets, but they must thaw slowly before being placed in the proof box to rise.

Do not brush with egg wash before baking unless you are covering the Danish with an almond or streusel topping; brush instead with Simple Syrup as soon as the pastry is removed from the oven. When pastries have cooled, spread on Fondant lightly, using a small spatula.

Danish Filling I

1 pound (455 g) butter
2 pounds (910 g) almond paste
1 pound (455 g) granulated sugar
1 pound, 2 ounces (515 g) finely ground nuts or cake crumbs
Pastry Cream (see p. 242)

Beat butter into the almond paste and sugar, a little at a time to avoid lumps. Stir in the nuts or cake crumbs and Pastry Cream as needed. Make the filling quite firm for bear claws but loose enough to spread easily for wreaths and such items.

Danish Filling II

10 ounces (285 g) butter or margarine
2 pounds, 3 ounces (995 g) almond paste
7 ounces (200 g) Pastry Cream (see p. 242)

Beat butter gradually into the almond paste to avoid lumps; stir in just enough of the Pastry Cream to make it easy to spread or pipe, depending on use.

Cream-Cheese Filling

2 pounds, 9 ounces (1 kg, 170 g) filling

1 pound, 6 ounces (630 g) cream cheese
3½ ounces (100 g) sugar
3½ ounces (100 g) butter, softened
3 eggs
1½ ounces (40 g) bread flour
½ teaspoon (3 g) vanilla extract
4 ounces (115 g) raisins
4 ounces (1 dl, 2 cl) milk

Place cream cheese and sugar in a mixer bowl; mix in butter gradually at medium speed; mix until smooth. Mix in eggs and flour; then mix in vanilla extract, raisins, and enough milk so that it can be piped.

BEAR CLAWS

color photograph, p. C-2

Danish Pastry (recipe precedes)
Danish Filling I (recipe precedes)
egg wash
sliced almonds
Simple Syrup (see Index)
Fondant (see Index)

Roll dough into a rectangle, ⅛ inch (3 mm) thick and a width that allows you to cut 4½-inch-wide (11.2-cm) strips without wasting dough, for example, 9 inches (22.5 cm), 13½ inches (33.7 cm), and so on. Cut the strips. Using a no. 4 (8-mm) plain tip in a pastry bag, pipe Danish Filling I on the upper part of the strip the entire length. Brush the lower edge with egg wash and fold the strip down two times to enclose the filling. The strip is now one-third its original size but fatter. Lightly flatten and shape the strip with your palm. Using a so-called bear-claw cutter, which looks like a miniature water wheel with a handle, roll along the lower edge of the strip to make the typical claw pattern. The next best tool is a multiple pastry wheel with the wheels pushed together. If you have neither, a chef's knife will do; it just takes a little longer. Make ¾-inch (20-mm) cuts along the length of the strip. If you are making more than one strip, push them together with a dowel or ruler and brush with egg wash. Sprinkle generously with sliced almonds and cut into the desired size. Pick them up and gently shake loose any almonds that are not sticking. Place on paper-lined sheet pans; bend each strip into a half-circle so that the cuts open up. Let rise until half-doubled. Bake at 425° F (220° C) about 16 minutes. Brush with Simple Syrup immediately; ice with Fondant when they have cooled.

ENVELOPES

Danish Pastry (see p. 74)
Danish Filling I or II (see p. 76)
egg wash
Pastry Cream or Apricot Jam (see pp. 242, 238)
sliced almonds
Simple Syrup (see p. 233)
Fondant (see p. 249)

Roll dough ¼ inch (6 mm) thick and to a size that can be divided by the size pastry you are making. For example, for a 2-ounce (55-g) Danish, you need to cut the pastry into 3½-inch (8.7-cm) squares; the dough would be rolled to a 14-inch (35-cm) square for which you would need 2 pounds (910 g) dough. Let dough rest for a few minutes before you cut it so that the squares do not end up as rectangles due to shrinkage. Mark and cut the dough into 3½-inch (8.7-cm) squares using a ruler as a guide, or cut with that handy multiple pastry wheel adjusted to 3½ inches (8.7 cm). Brush egg wash lightly on the cuts. Pipe a dot of Danish Filling I or II the size of a cherry in the middle of each square. Fold the 4 points of each small square to meet the middle. Push the middle down firmly with your thumb to prevent the dough from unfolding.

Place on paper-lined sheet pans. Pipe Pastry Cream or jam on top in the space created by your thumb. Sprinkle sliced almonds lightly on top; they will stick to the topping. Let rise until half-doubled. Bake at 425° F (220° C) until golden brown, about 14 minutes. Brush with Simple Syrup immediately; ice with Fondant when cooled.

DANISH TURNOVERS

Danish Pastry (see p. 74)
egg wash
Cream-cheese Filling (see p. 76)
sliced almonds
Simple Syrup (see p. 233)
Fondant (see p. 249)

Roll out and cut dough as directed for Envelopes. Brush egg wash on the lower triangle of the square and pipe cheese filling in the middle. Pick up a top corner and fold it diagonally almost to the opposite bottom corner; press it into the egg wash with your thumb. Do not press or seal the sides. You now have a triangle. Repeat with the remaining dough. Place on paper-lined sheet pans. Let rise until half-doubled. Pipe a dot of cheese filling on each top. Sprinkle lightly with sliced almonds. Bake at 425° F (220° C) about 16 minutes. Finish as directed for Envelopes.

Of course, Danish Turnovers and Envelopes can be made with other fillings, such as Apple Filling (see Index) or plum jam.

BUTTERHORNS

Danish Pastry (see p. 74)
egg wash
cinnamon sugar
Streusel (see p. 263)
Fondant (see p. 249)

Roll dough into a rectangle, 10 inches (25 cm) wide and ¼ inch (6 mm) thick. Trim sides if they are not even, and brush dough with egg wash. Sprinkle generously with cinnamon sugar and fold the two long sides to meet in the middle. Brush again with egg wash; fold in half in the same direction (double turn). Roll the strip gently with a rolling pin to make it even. Dust flour in front of the strip; cut into ¾-inch-wide (20-mm) strips. Turn each strip over with the knife so that the cut side is up. When all the dough is cut and turned, brush the top with egg wash and sprinkle a ½-inch-thick (12-mm) layer of Streusel on top. Place them carefully on paper-lined sheet pans. Press the Streusel lightly on the top with the palm of your hand. Let rise until half-doubled. Bake at 425° F (220° C) until golden brown, about 16 minutes. Ice with Fondant when cooled.

RAISIN SNAILS

Danish Pastry (see p. 74)
egg wash
raisins soaked in water
cinnamon sugar
Simple Syrup (see p. 233)
Fondant (see p. 249)

Roll dough into a 14-inch-wide (35-cm) strip, ⅛ inch (3 mm) thick. Brush dough with egg wash. Sprinkle generously with the soft raisins and then quite heavily with cinnamon sugar. Roll over it with a rolling pin to press the raisins into the dough. Starting at the top, roll up the dough evenly, stretching it if necessary. Place it at the edge of the table with the seam underneath; with a sharp knife, cut it into 2-ounce (55-g) pieces. If the raisins were not soft, you will not be able to cut through them and, instead, will push them to the bottom with the knife, creating a less attractive snail. Put the ends under the snails as you place them on paper-lined sheet pans so that they will not unfold when baking. Let rise until half-doubled. Bake at 400° F (205° C) until golden brown, about 20 minutes. Brush with

Simple Syrup as soon as they come out of the oven, and ice with Fondant when they are cool.

DANISH TWISTS

Danish Pastry (see p. 74)
Pastry Cream (see p. 242)
Apricot Jam (see p. 238)
cherry filling
Simple Syrup (see p. 233)
Fondant (see p. 249)

This is a very simple, quickly made Danish pastry. It does require a carefully rolled and well-chilled dough in order to achieve the characteristic crispness around the topping. The crispness is also lost if the dough is rolled too thin and the strips are cut too wide or if the Danish is left to rise too long before baking.

Roll out a good piece of dough (avoid end pieces) to a ¼-inch (6-mm) thickness. If you accidentally roll the dough too thin, it is better to make Envelopes or Turnovers from the piece and start again. Making sure the dough is still firm, cut ¼-inch-wide (6-mm) strips with a sharp knife or a pastry wheel, using a dowel as a guide. Twist the strips tight and form into Singles, Figure Eights, or Cherry Twists (see below). Let rise until half-doubled. Bake at 425° F (220° C) until golden brown, about 14 minutes. Brush with Simple Syrup as soon as you remove from the oven. Ice with Fondant when cool.

Singles
color photograph, p. C-2
Twist the strips and form into the shape of a paper clip. Fold and secure the end piece underneath. Place on paper-lined sheet pans. Pipe a line of Pastry Cream down the long central strip of each Danish.

Figure Eights
color photograph, p. C-2
Twist the strips and form into figure-eight shapes. Overlap both end pieces enough to protrude into the centers of holes of the eight. Invert onto paper-lined sheet pans. Pipe a line of Apricot Jam onto the eight shape.

Cherry Twists
Twist the strips and shape into a loose spiral. Secure the end piece underneath as you place them on paper-lined sheet pans. Pipe cherry filling onto the center of each twist.

SUGAR BUNS

Danish Pastry (see p. 74)
egg wash
Pastry Cream (see p. 242)
melted butter
sugar

Roll out and cut dough as for Envelopes. Brush the edges lightly with egg wash; pipe a mound of Pastry Cream about the size of an unshelled walnut onto the middle (too much will be hard to fold in but not enough will be absorbed by the dough when baked, leaving a dry inside). Pick up the corners and fold as directed for Envelopes but stretch the dough to fit around the cream. Pinch the seams together so the cream will not leak out. Place them seam sides down on paper-lined sheet pans or in paper baking cups. Let rise until half-doubled. Bake at 400° F (205° C) until golden brown, about 20 minutes. Because of the Pastry Cream inside, they will puff up as high as a large profiterole, so it is important that they are baked long enough to hold their shape when removed from the oven. Let cool completely. Brush the tops and sides with melted butter. Fill a bowl with enough sugar and make a well deep enough in the sugar to fit a bun so that they can be coated without being flattened. Dip each bun into the sugar well so that the sugar sticks to the butter, and serve.

MAYOR'S WREATH
one 10-inch (25-cm) wreath   photograph, p. 89

Danish Pastry (see p. 74)
Danish Filling II (see p. 76)
egg wash
sliced almonds
Simple Syrup (see p. 233)
Fondant (see p. 249)

Weigh 1 pound (455 g) dough. Roll out to a strip 8 inches (20 cm) wide, 18 inches (45 cm) long, and ⅛ inch (3 mm) thick. Cut this strip lengthwise into 3 equal strips. Using a no. 3 (6-mm) plain tip in a pastry bag, pipe Danish Filling II along the length and approximately ½ inch (12 mm) from the top of each strip. The filling should not be too soft because the strips will be braided later. Brush egg wash on the bottom of each strip and roll each strip into a string from the top to the bottom. Carefully roll each string even and to 20 inches (50 cm) in length. Place them next to each other with the seam sides down and braid as a 3-braid loaf, starting in the middle and working to the ends.

Carefully place the braid, seam sides down, on a paper-lined sheet pan. Shape into a wreath 10 inches (25 cm) in diameter. Stretch the braid slightly if necessary so that it is 24 inches (60 cm) long. Fold the ends together so the seam shows as little as possible. Brush with egg wash and sprinkle lightly with sliced almonds. Let rise until half-doubled. Bake at 375° F (190° C) about 30 minutes. Brush with Simple Syrup immediately. When cooled, ice with Fondant.

DANISH CINNAMON WREATH
one 10-inch (25-cm) wreath

> Danish Pastry (see p. 74)
> Danish Filling I or II (see p. 76)
> cinnamon sugar
> egg wash
> sliced almonds
> Simple Syrup (see p. 233)
> Fondant (see p. 249)

Roll 1 pound (455 g) dough into a strip about 22 inches (55 cm) long, 7 inches (17.5 cm) wide, and ⅛ inch (3 mm) thick. Spread filling ⅛ inch (3 mm) thick on top. (It is a common misconception that spreading on a little extra filling will make the wreath especially tasty but this is not so! The filling will overpower the dough, and it will be like eating filling flavored with some dough. In addition, part of the filling will run out and burn on the sheet pan.) Sprinkle cinnamon sugar to taste on top and roll the strip into a tight string, starting from the top. Roll it evenly and to about 24 inches (60 cm) in length. Place on a paper-lined sheet pan, and shape into a wreath 10 inches (25 cm) in diameter, making sure the seam is on the bottom. Seal the ends by pushing one inside the other.

Holding a scissors at a 45° angle from the wreath, make ¼-inch-wide (6-mm) cuts almost to the center of the wreath. With your free hand, turn these cuts to the side, alternating between left and right. Brush with egg wash and sprinkle lightly with sliced almonds. Let rise until half-doubled. Bake at 400° F (205° C) about 28 minutes. Brush with Simple Syrup immediately; when cooled, ice the wreath with Fondant.

SISTER'S PULL-APART COFFEE CAKE
10-inch (25-cm) cake

Danish Pastry (see p. 74)
Danish Filling I or II (see p. 76)
Pastry Cream (see p. 242)
sliced almonds
Simple Syrup (see p. 233)
Fondant (see p. 249)

Weigh 1¼ pounds (570 g) dough. Roll out as directed for in Danish Cinnamon Wreath (preceding recipe). Cut a 7-inch (17.5-cm) piece from one end of the strip and set aside. Spread filling on top of the remaining piece of dough ⅛ inch (3 mm) thick. Roll the strip up tight, starting from the top. Roll it even and cut it into 16 equal pieces. Roll the reserved piece of dough to a 10-inch (25-cm) circle. Place it on the bottom of a 10-inch (25-cm) cake pan. Using a no. 3 (6-mm) tip in a pastry bag, pipe a spiral of Pastry Cream on top of the dough. Arrange the 16 pieces evenly, cut sides up, on the cream. Press them lightly with the palm of your hand. Pipe a dot of Pastry Cream, about the size of a hazelnut, on top of each piece. Sprinkle with sliced almonds. Let rise until half-doubled. Bake at 375° F (190° C) about 35 minutes. Brush with Simple Syrup as soon as it is removed from the oven. When the cake has cooled down some, but not completely or the bottom will be wet, unmold and ice with Fondant.

SWEDISH BREAKFAST SNAILS (GOSEN)
twelve dozen 2-ounce (55-g) snails   photograph, p. 89

Dough
6 ounces (170 g) fresh compressed yeast
1 quart (9 dl, 6 cl) cold milk
12 eggs
10 ounces (285 g) sugar
1½ ounces (40 g) salt
5 pounds, 10 ounces (2 kg, 555 g) bread flour
2 pounds, 10 ounces (1 kg, 195 g) butter, softened
egg wash

Dissolve yeast in milk, and stir in the eggs, sugar, and salt. Mix enough of the flour to make a sponge with the consistency of soft butter; then mix in the remaining flour and the butter. This method ensures that you will not get lumps from the butter by adding it to a cold dough. Mix until smooth. Spread the dough evenly on a sheet pan, and refrigerate (or, if necessary, freeze) until dough is firm.

Filling

　　2 pounds, 10 ounces (1 k, 195 g) butter
　14 ounces (400 g) roasted hazelnuts, finely ground
　1½ pounds (680 g) brown sugar
　1½ pounds (680 g) granulated sugar
　1½ ounces (40 g) ground cinnamon
　　 Pastry Cream (see p. 242), optional

Mix all ingredients except the Pastry Cream until smooth and spreadable. If the filling is not freshly made (it is certainly a good idea to make a large batch to save time), it may be necessary to add Pastry Cream to make the mixture spreadable (the nuts absorb moisture).

Topping

　　1 pound, 2 ounces (510 g) butter
　3½ ounces (1 dl) heavy cream
　14 ounces (400 g) sugar
　3½ (100 g) light corn syrup
　　8 ounces (225 g) sliced almonds, slightly crushed

Place butter and cream in a saucepan over heat. When the butter starts to melt, add sugar and corn syrup. Boil to 215° F (102° C), remove from heat, and add the almonds, slightly crushed. Boil at medium heat about 5 minutes. The hotter the sugar mixture gets (as it is being reduced), the smaller and slower the bubbles will become. Let the topping cool until it is firm enough to be spread with a spatula. If the topping hardens completely or is premade and must be reheated, the butter will separate; stir in 1 ounce (3 cl) heavy cream to bring it back together.

Cut the dough into 2 pieces, and roll each piece out about 14 inches (35 cm) wide, 6 feet (2 m, 45 cm) long, and ⅛ inch (3 mm) thick. Spread the filling evenly over the dough. If you are not making the snails in paper cups, leave a ½-inch (12-mm) strip at the bottom to brush with egg wash so snails do not unfold as they are rising. Roll the strip tightly, starting at the top edge.

Cut each roll into 2-ounce (55-g) pieces. An easy way to do this is to cut the string into 4 sections and cut each section into 18 pieces. Place them level in muffin-size paper cups. These can be placed in muffin tins to keep the snails from spreading too flat. Let the snails rise, but do not let these rise too long or a lot of the topping will be lost when they expand in the oven. Spread the topping on with a spatula. Bake at 375° F (190° C) until golden brown, about 40 minutes.

BRAN MUFFINS
about 30 muffins

>   5 ounces (140 g) brown sugar
>   6½ ounces (185 g) butter
>   5½ ounces (1 dl, 6.5 cl) molasses
>   5 ounces (140 g) honey
>   5 eggs
>   few drops vanilla extract
>   1 pound, 4 ounces (570 g) bread flour
>   ½ ounce (15 g) salt
>   ¾ ounce (20 g) baking soda
>   ½ ounce (15 g) baking powder
>   1 quart (9 dl, 6 cl) buttermilk
>   1 cup (2 dl, 4 cl) light cream
>   sugar
>   bran

Cream brown sugar and butter. Mix molasses, honey, eggs, and vanilla and mix into the butter mixture. Add dry ingredients alternately with buttermilk mixed with light cream, mixing after each addition. Always start and finish with the dry ingredients. Butter and flour muffin tins. To prevent the muffins from getting discolored by the flour, use a flour-to-butter ratio of 1 to 4. Also butter the tops of the muffin tins to prevent the batter from sticking as it rises during baking.

Using a no. 8 (16-mm) plain tip in a pastry bag, pipe the batter in a dome shape in each cup slightly above the rim. Sprinkle them with a mixture of equal amounts of sugar and bran. Bake at 375° F (190° C) until dark brown and done, about 18 minutes. They should have a healthy crust.

BLUEBERRY GINGER MUFFINS
about 30 muffins   *photograph, p. 90*

    14 ounces (400 g) brown sugar
    14 ounces (400 g) butter
     7 ounces (2 dl, 1 cl) molasses
     2 ounces (6 cl) honey
     5 eggs
       few drops vanilla extract
    ⅓ ounce (10 g) salt
     1 teaspoon (8 g) baking powder
     1 teaspoon (4 g) baking soda
     1 teaspoon (2 g) ground ginger
     1 pound, 14 ounces (855 g) bread flour
     1 cup (2 dl, 4 cl) buttermilk
     1 pound, 2 ounces (510 g) fresh or frozen blueberries

Cream brown sugar and butter together. Mix in molasses, honey, eggs, and vanilla. Mix the dry ingredients, and mix into the sugar mixture alternately with the buttermilk. Stir in the blueberries carefully so that the berries do not color the batter blue. If frozen berries are used, they should not be thawed before adding. Coat muffin tins with a mixture of 1 part flour to 4 parts butter. Also coat the tops of the tins so that the batter does not stick as it rises.

Using a large plain tube in a pastry bag, pipe the mixture in a dome shape slightly above the rim of each cup. If you are using frozen berries, the batter will be too firm because of the cold berries; use a medium-size ice-cream scoop to fill the cups. Bake at 375° F (190° C) until done and the crust is brown, about 35 minutes.

PUMPKIN MUFFINS

about 30 muffins   *photograph, p. 90*

1	pound (455 g) butter
13	ounces (370 g) brown sugar
4	eggs
8	ounces (225 g) molasses
1	teaspoon (4 g) salt
1	teaspoon (2 g) ground ginger
1	teaspoon (2 g) ground cinnamon
1	teaspoon (2 g) ground allspice
½	teaspoon (1 g) grated nutmeg
1½	teaspoons (3 g) baking powder
1½	teaspoons (4 g) baking soda
2	pounds (910 g) bread flour
9	ounces (225 g) dark raisins
1	teaspoon (6 g) vanilla extract
1	cup (2 dl, 4 cl) buttermilk
15	ounces (430 g) pumpkin purée

Cream butter and brown sugar. Mix in eggs and molasses. Sift dry ingredients together, and mix in the raisins so that they are coated with flour, which will prevent them from sinking to the bottom. Mix vanilla, buttermilk and pumpkin. Mix pumpkin mixture alternately with the dry ingredients into the butter mixture. Start and finish with the dry ingredients. Coat muffin tins inside and on top with a mixture of 4 parts butter and 1 part flour.

Pipe the batter into each cup slightly above the rim, or spoon into the cups with an ice-cream scoop. Bake at 375° F (190° C) until done and crust is brown, about 35 minutes.

Braided White Bread

Christmas Star

Baguettes

Butter-Wheat Bread

Russian Rolled-wheat Bread

Swedish Orange Rye Bread

Swedish Peasant Bread

Raisin Bread

Rosemary Bread

Garlic Bread

Onion Walnut Bread

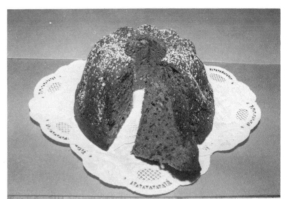

Banana Bread

Triestine

Croissants

Mayor's Wreath

Swedish Breakfast Snails

Blueberry Ginger Muffins

Pumpkin Muffins

4

Cakes

SPONGECAKE I

three 10-inch (25-cm) layers, or 2 16 × 24-inch (40- × 60-cm) sheet cakes

    12 eggs
     6 egg yolks
    13 ounces (370 g) sugar
    ½ teaspoon (3 g) vanilla extract
     7 ounces (200 g) bread flour
     3 ounces (85 g) cornstarch

Whip eggs, egg yolks, and sugar to maximum volume. Beat at medium speed 4 to 5 minutes to let the batter stabilize. The batter should now have stiff peaks. Add vanilla. Sift flour and cornstarch together and fold in carefully by hand. Divide the batter evenly among 3 greased and floured 10-inch (25-cm) cake pans. Bake immediately at 375° F (190° C) until the cake springs back when pressed lightly in the middle, about 20 minutes. Remove cakes carefully from the pans before they cool completely.

If you are making sheet cakes, divide the batter between 2 sheets of parchment paper, 24 × 16 inches (60 × 40 cm), and spread batter out evenly. Pull the sheet papers onto pans. Bake immediately at 425° F (220° C) about 10 minutes. Slide the sheets onto cool pans as soon as they come out of the oven.

SPONGECAKE II
two 10-inch (25-cm) layers

    12 eggs
     2 egg whites
    10 ounces (285 g) sugar
        few drops lemon juice
        pinch salt
     6 ounces (170 g) cake flour
     6 ounces (170 g) bread flour
     5 ounces (140 g) melted butter

Place whole eggs, egg whites, sugar, lemon juice, and salt in a mixing bowl; heat to about 130° F (55° C) over hot water, whipping lightly. Then whip at high speed until cold and peaks are stiff. Sift the flours and fold in carefully by hand. Lastly, fold in the melted butter. Divide the mixture between 2 greased and floured 10-inch (25-cm) cake pans. Bake immediately at 375° F (190° C) about 20 minutes.

CHOCOLATE SPONGE I
three 10-inch (25-cm) layers, or 2 16- × 24-inch (40- × 60-cm) sheet cakes

    12 eggs
     6 egg yolks
    13 ounces (370 g) sugar
     1 teaspoon (3 g) vanilla extract
     6 ounces (170 g) bread flour
     2 ounces (55 g) cornstarch
     2 ounces (55 g) cocoa powder

Whip eggs, egg yolks, and sugar until stiff. Beat at medium speed 4 to 5 minutes to let the batter stabilize. Add vanilla. Sift flour, cornstarch, and cocoa powder together, and fold in carefully by hand. Divide mixture among 3 greased and floured 10-inch (25-cm) cake pans. Bake immediately at 375° F (190° C) until cake springs back when pressed lightly in the middle, about 20 minutes. Remove cakes carefully from the pans before they cool completely.

If you are making sheet cakes, divide the mixture between 2 sheet papers, 24 × 16 inches (60 × 40 cm), and spread batter out evenly. Pull the sheet papers onto pans. Bake cakes immediately at 425° F (220° C) about 10 minutes. Slide the sheets onto cool pans as soon as they come out of the oven.

CHOCOLATE SPONGE II
two 10-inch (25-cm) layers

  12 eggs
   2 egg whites
  10 ounces (285 g) sugar
      few drops lemon juice
      pinch salt
   4 ounces (115 g) cake flour
   6 ounces (170 g) bread flour
   2 ounces (55 g) cocoa powder
   5 ounces (140 g) melted butter

Place eggs, egg whites, sugar, lemon juice, and salt in a mixing bowl, and heat to about 130° F (55° C) over hot water, whipping lightly. Then whip the mixture at high speed until cold and peaks are stiff. Sift the flours and cocoa powder together, and fold in carefully by hand. Lastly, fold in the butter. Divide the mixture between 2 prepared 10-inch (25-cm) cake pans. Bake immediately at 375° F (190° C) about 20 minutes.

BISCUIT AU CHOCOLAT
four 10-inch (25-cm) cakes

  14 ounces (400 g) egg yolks
  13 ounces (370 g) sugar
   7 ounces (200 g) almond paste
3½ ounces (1 dl, 1 cl) water
      pinch salt
      few drops vanilla extract
  14 ounces (400 g) egg whites
  13 ounces (370 g) bread flour
4½ ounces (130 g) cocoa powder

Whip egg yolks and four ounces (115 g) of the sugar to the ribbon stage. Soften and smooth almond paste; work in water, a little at a time. Add salt and vanilla to the almond paste; then mix the almond paste into the yolk mixture. Whip egg whites with remaining sugar to stiff peaks. Fold the yolk mixture into the whites. Sift flour with cocoa and fold into the batter. Divide mixture among 4 buttered and floured, 10-inch (25-cm) cake pans. Bake at 400° F (205° C) until the sponge springs back when lightly pressed, 12 to 15 minutes.

BISCUIT VIENNOISE
two 10-inch (25-cm) cakes

> 5 eggs (250 g)
> 5½ ounces (155 g) sugar
> pinch salt
> few drops lemon juice
> 3½ ounces (100 g) bread flour
> 4 ounces (115 g) cornstarch
> 2 ounces (55 g) melted butter

Beat eggs, sugar, salt, and lemon juice over hot water until the batter reaches about 130° F (55° C). Remove from heat and continue whipping until the batter is cool to the touch and has a creamy consistency. Sift flour with cornstarch and fold in carefully by hand; then fold in butter. Divide mixture between 2 prepared 10-inch (25-cm) cake pans. Bake at 400° F (205° C) about 12 minutes.

CARAMEL CAKE
three 10-inch (25-cm) cakes

> ½ recipe Spongecake II (see p. 93)
> ½ recipe Chocolate Sponge II (see p. 94)
> three 10-inch (25-cm) short-dough bottoms (see p. 17)
> 1 pound, 12 ounces (800 g) sugar
> 14 ounces (4 dl, 2 cl) water
> 2 quarts (1 l, 9 dl, 6 cl) heavy cream
> ⅔ ounce (20 g) unflavored gelatin
> 4 ounces (1 dl, 2 cl) warm water, 130° F (54° C)
> Apricot Jam (see p. 238)
> crushed roasted almonds

Make spongecakes and short-dough bottoms.

Caramelize the sugar (see Caramel in Index) to a light golden color. Pour about one-third out onto a lightly oiled marble slab or oiled sheet pan. Add 14 ounces (4 dl, 2 cl) water to remaining caramel; as you do this, it will lump up. Place the saucepan back on the heat and cook out the lumps. Set aside to cool; or cool in an ice bath if it is needed immediately. In the meantime, whip the heavy cream to soft peaks; fold in the cooled caramel carefully by hand. (If the caramel is warm, the cream will break.) Measure 1 pound (455 g) of the cream mixture, and place it in the refrigerator to ice the cake later.

Dissolve the gelatin in 4 ounces (1 dl, 2 cl) water and heat to 150° F (65° C). Add dissolved gelatin to a small part of the remaining cream mixture; working quickly, combine that mixture with the rest of the cream.

Cut each spongecake into 3 equal layers. Using a 6-inch (15-cm) template, cut the center out of all the layers. Place the dark centers inside the light cakes and vice versa. Place the short-dough bottoms on a support, such as a cardboard, and spread on a thin layer of smooth Apricot Jam. Place a dark doughnut with light center on each of the short-dough bottoms. Divide the cream mixture among the 3 cakes and spread it evenly. Place remaining sponge layers on top. Spread tops and sides of the cakes with the chilled cream in a thick layer so that there is none left over. Cover the sides with crushed almonds.

Crush the hard caramelized sugar finely, but not to a powder. Place the 6-inch (15-cm) template you used to cut the sponges on top of each cake, and sprinkle the caramelized sugar around the edge.

SWEDISH CHOCOLATE CAKE

four 10-inch (25-cm) cakes   photograph, p. 137

2 recipes Chocolate Sponge II (see p. 94)
1 recipe Chocolate Buttercream (see p. 242)
    Chocolate Rectangles (see p. 245)
    Chocolate Squares (see p. 245)
¼ recipe Pastry Cream (see p. 242)
    strawberries

Make the batter for chocolate sponge cake, and divide it evenly among 4 buttered and floured 10-inch (25-cm) cake pans. Bake at 375° F (190° C) about 20 minutes.

Make Chocolate Buttercream (1 pound, 9 ounces (700 g) for each cake), Chocolate Rectangles, Chocolate Squares, and Pastry Cream.

Cut the skins off the baked cake layers. Slice each cake into 3 equal layers. Use the bottom layer as the base, but save the better of the remaining two for the top. Spread a ¼-inch (6-mm) layer of Pastry Cream on the bottom layer. Place the second cake layer on top and spread a ¼-inch (6-mm) thick layer of the Chocolate Buttercream on the second layer. Place the third layer on top. Spread the top and sides with Chocolate Buttercream just thick enough to cover the sponge. Be sure to save some for decoration. Refrigerate the cakes until the buttercream is firm, so that the cakes will slice cleanly.

Cut each cake into the desired number of pieces. Using a no. 4 (8-mm) plain tip, pipe one straight line of Chocolate Buttercream next to the cut on each piece. At the same time, pipe a small mound of buttercream at the edge of each slice. Place a Chocolate Rectangle alongside each line of buttercream, pointing slightly up toward the middle of the cake. Fasten a Chocolate Square on the side of each slice. Top each buttercream mound with half a strawberry. Buttercream always tastes better served at room temperature.

GÂTEAU MALAKOFF
four 10-inch (25-cm) cakes   photograph, p. 137

> Chocolate Genoise (recipe follows)
> 14 dozen Ladyfingers (see p. 158)
> four 10-inch (25-cm) short-dough bottoms (see p. 17)
> Maraschino Cream (recipe follows)
> strawberry jam
> Simple Syrup (see p. 233)
> rum
> Ganache (see p. 247)
> whipped cream

Make Chocolate Genoise and divide the batter among 4 buttered and floured 10-inch (25-cm) cake pans. Bake immediately at 400° F (205° C) until done, approximately 12 minutes. Make Ladyfingers, piping them out 1½ inches (37 mm) long, and bake. Roll out and bake the short-dough bottoms. Make the Maraschino Cream.

Place the short-dough bottoms on cardboard for support. Spread a thin layer of strawberry jam on their tops. Slice the cakes into 2 layers each; they should be very thin. Save the best-looking layer for the top and place the other on top of the short-dough bottom. If the Maraschino cream is not thick enough to hold its shape, cool it by stirring, not whipping. Spread half the cream evenly on top of the bottom cake layers.

Dip the Ladyfingers into a mixture of 3 parts Simple Syrup and 1 part rum until they are soaked; you will need about 18 for each cake. Place them flat side by side on the cream in a circle 1 inch (25 mm) from the edge of the cake, working quickly so the filling does not set. Divide remaining cream and spread evenly on top. Finally, place the second chocolate layer on top and press down gently to make sure top is even. Refrigerate the cakes at least 2 hours to set the cream.

Heat Ganache until quite liquid and very glossy. Spread Ganache just thick enough to cover the sponge on top of the cakes, working rapidly so it does not harden before you finish spreading. As soon as Ganache has started to harden, score it into ½-inch (12-mm) diamonds, using the back of a chef's knife. Spread the sides of the cakes with whipped cream.

Cut cakes into desired number of pieces. Stand 1 or 2 Ladyfingers, depending on the size of the piece, upright on the edge of each piece.

Chocolate Genoise
four 10-inch (25-cm) cakes

> 16 eggs (800 g)
> 14 ounces (400 g) sugar
> 7½ ounces (215 g) bread flour
> 1½ ounces (40 g) cornstarch
> 3 ounces (85 g) cocoa powder
> 3 ounces (85 g) dark chocolate
> 7 ounces (200 g) butter

Separate the eggs, being sure to keep the whites clean. Whip the yolks with half the sugar to the ribbon stage. Sift the flour, cornstarch, and cocoa powder together. Melt the chocolate and butter and mix them. Whip the whites with the remaining sugar to stiff peaks; fold into the yolks. Fold in the dry ingredients carefully. Fold in the melted (but not hot) butter mixture.

Maraschino Cream

       7 ounces (2 dl, 1 cl) white dry wine
    1 ⅙ ounces (35 g) gelatin
       5 egg yolks (100 g)
       6 ounces (170 g) sugar
       5 pints, 4 ounces (2 l, 5 dl, 2 cl) heavy cream
       4 ounces (1 dl, 2 cl) maraschino liqueur

Dissolve the gelatin in wine, and heat to 140° F (60° C). In the meantime, whip yolks and sugar on the side of a bowl, just until combined. Pour the wine mixture into the yolks in a steady stream with one hand, whisking it rapidly with the other. Place over hot water; heat the *sabayon* to 155° F (68° C), stirring constantly. It should be thick and foamy. Remove from heat; stir in the maraschino liqueur, and cool to slightly below body temperature. In the meantime, whip the heavy cream to soft peaks. Then fold the cool *sabayon* gradually into the whipped cream.

CHOCOLATE HAZELNUT CAKE

four 10-inch (25-cm) cakes   photograph, p. 137

          Vanilla Cake Base (recipe follows)
     ½ **recipe of Biscuit au Chocolat (see p. 94)**
      5 **pounds (2 kg, 265 g) Buttercream (see p. 239)**
      6 **ounces (170 g) hazelnut paste (see p. 8)**
      6 **ounces (170 g) dark chocolate, melted**
          crushed roasted hazelnuts
          roasted whole hazelnuts
          Chocolate Rounds (see p. 245)
          sugar for caramelizing hazelnuts

Make Vanilla Cake Base and Biscuit au Chocolat. Flavor 3 pounds (1 kg, 356 g) of the Buttercream with hazelnut paste; flavor remaining Buttercream with the dark chocolate.

Cut the chocolate cakes into halves and the vanilla cakes into 3 equal layers. Spread hazelnut buttercream ⅛ inch (3 mm) thick on the chocolate layers; place the first vanilla layers on top, saving the best looking for the top of the cake. Add the remaining layers the same way. Spread a thin layer of chocolate buttercream on the top and sides. Put crushed roasted hazelnuts on the sides. Refrigerate the cake until the buttercream is set.

Make Chocolate Rounds. Caramelize roasted whole hazelnuts (see Index). When they have cooled, place one in the middle of each Chocolate Round.

(You can also dip the nuts in boiling Florentina, which is less time-consuming and easier on your fingers than caramelizing them, but the nuts will not be as crunchy.)

Cut or mark the cake into the desired number of pieces. Using a no. 1 (3-mm) plain tip, pipe 2 straight lines of chocolate buttercream down the middle of each piece, starting about one-third from the center of the cake. Pipe a third line slightly longer in between and on top of the first two. Finally, place a Chocolate Round at a slight angle on top of the three lines at the end of each slice.

Vanilla Cake Base
four 10-inch (25-cm) cakes

      1 pound (455 g) bread flour
      3 ounces (85 g) cornstarch
     24 egg yolks (480 g)
     12 ounces (340 g) sugar
     16 egg whites (480 g)
        pinch salt
   1½ teaspoons (9 g) vanilla extract
      6 ounces (170 g) melted butter

Sift the flour and cornstarch together. Whip egg yolks with half the sugar to the ribbon stage. Whip egg whites with remaining sugar to stiff peaks, and fold into the yolk mixture carefully. Fold the flour/cornstarch mixture into the egg mixture with the salt and vanilla. Fold in the melted butter. Divide among 4 buttered and floured 10-inch (25-cm) cake pans. Bake immediately at 400° F (205° C) about 12 minutes.

GÂTEAU MOKA CARROUSEL
four 10-inch (25-cm) cakes   photograph, p. 137

        Japonaise Batter (see p. 147)
        Chocolate Sponge I (see p. 93)
      1 pound (455 g) Ganache (see p. 247)
        Mocha Whipped Cream (recipe follows)
   1½ pounds (680 g) whipped cream
        crushed roasted almonds
      2 ounces (55 g) finely ground coffee

Draw four 10-inch (25-cm) circles on parchment papers. Heat oven to 275° to 300° F (135° to 150° C). Make the Japonaise Batter. Using a no. 3 (6-mm) plain tip, pipe a 1-inch-wide (25-mm) frame inside the 4 marked circles. Divide the remaining batter among the circles, and spread it evenly with a spatula. Bake until golden brown, about 35 minutes.

Make the batter for Chocolate Sponge I. Prepare one 10-inch (25-cm) cake pan and fill two-thirds full with batter. Bake at 375° F (190° C) until done, about 18 minutes. Spread remaining batter evenly on sheet pans, 24 × 16 inches (60 × 40 cm). Bake at 425° F (220° C) just until done, about 10 minutes. Be careful not to overbake the thin sheets.

Spread a thin layer of soft Ganache, 4 ounces (115 g) per cake, on the cooled Japonaise bottoms. Adjust cake rings to 10 inches (25 cm) in diameter and place on the Ganache. Cut strips, 1 inch (25 mm) wide, lengthwise out of the thin chocolate sheets; stand the strips up in the Ganache, making 5 evenly spaced concentric circles, starting at the outside against the ring.

Make Mocha Whipped Cream; pipe it between the chocolate circles with a no. 6 (12-mm) plain tip. Even the top with a spatula.

Cut the 10-inch (25-cm) Chocolate Sponge into 4 thin layers, and place one on top of each cake. Refrigerate until cream is set, at least 2 hours.

Cut off any Japonaise that protrudes outside the sponge. Spread the entire surface of each cake with a thin layer of plain whipped cream. Cover the sides with crushed almonds. Cut or mark the cakes into serving pieces. Using a no. 3 (6-mm) plain tip and whipped cream, pipe a horn of plenty on each piece. Decorate each serving piece with a sprinkle of coffee.

Mocha Whipped Cream

    2 quarts, 3 cups (2 l, 6 dl, 4 cl) heavy cream
    1 ounce (30 g) sugar
      mocha paste or strong coffee to taste
    ⅘ ounces (24 g) unflavored gelatin
    6 ounces (1 dl, 8 cl) water

Whip cream and sugar to soft peaks and flavor with mocha paste. Soften the gelatin in the water and heat it to 150° F (65° C) to dissolve it. Rapidly beat the gelatin into a small part of the whipped cream; then beat the mixture into the remaining cream.

BLACK FOREST CAKE

six 10-inch (25-cm) cakes   *color photograph, p. C-2*

   2 recipes of Chocolate Sponge II (see p. 94)
   7 pounds (3 kg, 185 g) canned sour cherries
     Simple Syrup (see p. 233) or sugar
     red food color
 5½ ounces (155 g) cornstarch or potato starch
     sugar
     six 10-inch (25-cm) short-dough bottoms (see p. 17)
  12 ounces (340 g) soft Apricot Jam (see p. 238)
 1¾ quarts (1 l, 6 dl, 6 cl) whipping cream
   6 ounces (1 dl, 8 cl) Kirschwasser
   2 pounds, 4 ounces (1 kg, 25g) whipped cream
     Chocolate Squares, from dark chocolate (see p. 245)
     shaved dark chocolate
     powdered sugar

Make the chocolate spongecakes.

To make the cherry filling: Drain the liquid from the canned cherries, pressing the cherries firmly without crushing them. Continue draining while you make short-dough bottoms (liquid must be thoroughly drained to prevent the filling from being too runny). Measure the liquid; add Simple Syrup or sugar to taste, and enough water to make 2 quarts (1 liter, 9 dl, 2 cl). Add a few drops of food color so that the filling is a rich color when the starch is added. Add enough liquid to the starch (potato starch holds up better over time) so that it can be easily poured. Heat the remaining liquid to boiling; stir in the starch mixture; cook, stirring constantly, until thick. Stir in the cherries carefully so that they are not crushed. Set aside to cool. Sprinkle sugar lightly on top to keep a skin from forming. The filling will cool more quickly if spread out on a sheet pan.

Place a short-dough bottom on a round piece of cardboard and spread with a thin layer of jam. Cut the skin off the 4 spongecakes and slice each into 3 equal layers. Save 6 of the best-looking layers for the tops. Place 6 remaining layers on the short-dough bottoms. Divide the cherry filling among the 6 cakes and spread it out carefully.

Whip the whipping cream to stiff peaks and add the Kirschwasser. Spread the whipped cream evenly on top of the cherries. Place the second cake layer on top and make sure the cakes are even. Cover the cakes and freeze so that the cream and cherries can be cut cleanly.

To finish, cut any of the short dough that protrudes outside the sponge. Spread 4 ounces (115 g) whipped cream on the top and sides of each cake to cover. Mark and cut cakes into serving pieces; for best results, the cakes should be halfway thawed. Pipe a rosette of whipped cream on the edge of each piece, using a no. 4 (8-mm) plain tip for buffet servings, or a no. 8 (16-mm) for regular servings. Decorate each piece with Chocolate Squares on the side, shaved chocolate on the top, and lightly sifted powdered sugar over the shaved chocolate.

CHOCOLATE MOUSSE CAKE WITH BANANA
four 10-inch (25-cm) cakes

> Almond Sponge I (recipe follows)
> currant jelly
> four 10-inch (25-cm) short-dough bottoms (see p. 17)
> 10 medium-size ripe bananas
> Chocolate-Cognac Cream (recipe follows)
> whipped cream
> crushed roasted almonds
> Dark Chocolate Figures (see p. 246)

Make the almond spongecakes. When cool, cut them into 2 layers each. Spread a thin layer of jelly on short-dough bottoms. Cover with a layer of cake. Place an adjustable cake ring loosely around the cakes. Unless your cake rings are stainless steel, line the insides of the rings with parchment paper or plastic strips to prevent the metal from staining the cakes. Slice the bananas lengthwise in half, bend the halves carefully (they will break slightly but it will not show in the finished cake), and arrange 2 rings of bananas on each cake, the first close to the edge and the smaller second ring about 2 inches (5 cm) toward center. Make the Chocolate-Cognac cream, and spread it evenly and very smoothly on the tops. Refrigerate until the cream is set, 1 to 2 hours.

To finish: Remove the rings and paper or plastic. Spread a thin layer of plain whipped cream on the sides and cover with crushed almonds. Cut or mark into serving pieces. Pipe a mound of whipped cream on the edge of each piece, using a no. 7 (14-mm) plain tip. Decorate each mound with a piped chocolate figure.

This cake should not be made more than one day in advance and cannot be frozen because of the bananas.

Almond Sponge I

two 10-inch (25-cm) cakes

- 3½ ounces (100 g) egg yolks
- 3½ ounces (100 g) almond paste
- ⅔ ounce (20 g) water
  pinch salt
- 5 ounces (140 g) sugar
  few drops lemon juice
- 5⅓ ounces (150 g) egg whites
- 2½ ounces (75 g) flour
- 2⅓ ounces (65 g) cornstarch
- 3 ounces (85 g) melted butter

Work egg yolks, almond paste, water, salt, and 2 ounces of the sugar until smooth. Beat egg whites with remaining (90 g) sugar and the lemon juice until stiff, as directed for French Meringue (see Index). Mix in almond paste mixture. Sift flour and cornstarch together and fold in by hand. Fold in the melted butter. Divide between 2 greased and floured 10-inch (25-cm) cake pans. Bake at 400° F (205° C), about 12 minutes.

Chocolate-Cognac Cream

- 3 quarts, 2 ounces (2 l, 9 dl, 4 cl) whipping cream
- 14 ounces (400 g) dark chocolate, melted
- 8½ ounces (2 dl, 5 cl) Simple Syrup (see p. 233)
- 3 ounces (9 cl) Cognac
- 1 ounce (30 g) unflavored gelatin
- 6 ounces (1 dl, 8 cl) hot water (150° F, 65° C)

Whip the cream to the consistency of a thick sauce; if you overwhip the cream, it will break when the chocolate mixture is added. Mix melted chocolate and Simple Syrup; add Cognac. Dissolve gelatin in water heated to 150° F (65° C); stir into chocolate mixture. The temperature of this mixture should be about 130° F (55° C). Place a small amount of the cream in a bowl; add the chocolate mixture gradually; then mix it with the rest of the cream, working rapidly. If the mixture seems too runny, whip it until it has a firmer consistency.

SICILIAN MACAROON CAKE

four 10-inch (25-cm) cakes   *photograph, p. 137*

> Almond Meringue (recipe follows)
> Almond Sponge II (recipe follows)
> four 10-inch (25-cm) cocoa short-dough bottoms (see pp. 17, 19)
> melted dark chocolate
> currant jelly
> Macaroon-Maraschino Whipped Cream (recipe follows)
> 1 pound, 4 ounces (570 g) whipped cream
> crushed roasted almonds
> shaved dark chocolate
> Macaroon Coins (see p. 160)

Make the Almond Meringue, Almond Sponge II, and short-dough bottoms.

Brush cooled meringue bottoms on both sides with a thin layer of melted chocolate. Place short-dough bottoms on cardboard for support; spread with jelly and top with a meringue bottom. Put a ring adjusted to 10 inches (25 cm) on top of the meringue and line with parchment paper or plastic strips. Fill each ring with Macaroon-Maraschino Whipped Cream. Top with a layer of spongecake. Refrigerate at least 2 hours.

Trim the sides of the cake so that meringue and short-dough do not overhang filling. Spread each cake with a thin layer of whipped cream, 5 ounces (140 g) per cake, and put crushed almonds on the sides. Place a 6-inch (15-cm) round template on top of the cake, and cover the middle with shaved chocolate. Mark or cut serving pieces. Pipe a small whipped cream mound on the edge of each piece, and decorate each mound with a Macaroon Coin dipped halfway into chocolate.

Almond Meringue

four 10-inch (25-cm) bottoms

> 8 ounces (2 dl, 4 cl) egg whites
> 11 ounces (310 g) sugar
> 1 ounce (30 g) cornstarch
> 4 ounces (115 g) finely ground almonds

Whip egg whites with sugar to peaks. Mix cornstarch and almonds and fold into whites. Using a no. 3 (6-mm) plain tip, pipe out four 10-inch (25-cm) filled circles. Bake at 300° F (150° C) 60 minutes.

Almond Sponge II

    10 ounces (285 g) almond paste
    1½ ounces (4.5 cl) water
        pinch salt
    ⅓ ounce (10 g) ground cinnamon
    ⅓ ounce (10 g) grated lemon zest
    10 ounces (3 dl) egg whites
    4 ounces (115 g) sugar
    4 ounces (115 g) cornstarch

Work almond paste, water, salt, cinnamon, and lemon zest until smooth. Whip egg whites with sugar to peaks. Sift cornstarch and fold into egg whites. Fold egg whites into almond paste mixture. Divide mixture among 4 greased and floured 10-inch (25-cm) cake pans. Bake at 300° F (150° C) 10 minutes.

Macaroon-Maraschino Whipped Cream

    1 pound, 5 ounces (595 g) macaroon pieces
    6½ ounces (2 dl) maraschino liqueur
    3 pounds, 15 ounces (1 liter, 8 dl, 9 cl) heavy cream
    9 ounces (255 g) egg yolks
    5 ounces (140 g) sugar
    1⅔ ounces (50 g) unflavored gelatin
    1 cup (2 dl, 4 cl) cold water
    5½ ounces (1 dl, 6.5 cl) warm milk

This cream is a good opportunity to use up some old and dry macaroon cookies. If they have to be made fresh, use Macaroon Paste I (see Index), but bake the macaroons slightly on the dry side so they do not fall apart when mixed with the cream.

Cut the macaroons roughly into pieces the size of a quarter. Macerate macaroons in maraschino liqueur. Whip cream to soft peaks and set aside. Whip egg yolks with sugar to the ribbon stage. Dissolve gelatin in water and heat to 150° F (65° C). Add to the egg mixture. Add milk. Add the whipped cream rapidly by hand, in small enough portions to blend each addition thoroughly. Fold in macerated macaroons.

BÛCHE DE NOËL
two 11-inch (27.5-cm) logs   photograph, p. 137

> Chocolate Sponge II (see p. 94)
> sugar
> 1 pound, 12 ounces (795 g) Chocolate Buttercream (see p. 242)
> 4 ounces (115 g) dark chocolate, melted
> 12 ounces (340 g) Marzipan (see p. 255)
> Rum-ball Mixture (see p. 194)
> Marzipan, colored green (see p. 255)
> meringue mushrooms
> marzipan mistletoes

Make batter for chocolate sponge and spread it evenly on a paper-lined sheet pan, 24 × 16 inches (60 × 40 cm). Bake at 425° F (220° C) about 10 minutes. Cool. Refrigerate covered until needed, up to 5 days.

Remove the crust or skin on top of the sponge. If it was baked the day before, it will come off with little effort; otherwise, simply remove what comes off easily, being careful not to tear the sponge. Sprinkle sugar lightly on parchment paper. Turn the sheet cake upside down onto the sugar and peel the paper off the back. (If you are rolling up a number of cakes, use this paper for the next cake, placing it with the used (baked) side on the table. It saves paper and makes it easier to roll up the roulade because the paper will not slide.) Cut the 2 long edges of the cake even.

Spread a layer of Buttercream, about ¼ inch (6 mm) thick, on the sponge; reserve about 5 ounces (140 g) of the Buttercream to use later. Spread the cream very thinly on the bottom 1 inch (25 mm) of the cake so that it will not ooze out as you roll the cake. Roll up the cake, pulling the paper towards you as you proceed. Refrigerate covered, seam side down, until firm. Turn a sheet pan upside down, place parchment paper on the pan, and place the roll seam down at one end of the pan. Spread a thin layer of reserved Buttercream on the sponge, evening it out by pulling the paper around the roulade.

Roll out white Marzipan ¹⁄₁₆ inch (2 mm) thick, and cover the roulade smoothly with the Marzipan. Rapidly spread the remaining dark chocolate, heated to body temperature, on top of the roulade to cover the Marzipan; keep spreading back and forth until the chocolate starts showing signs of hardening.

Trim the ends of the cake to even, and cut into two 11-inch (27.5-cm) logs with a warm knife. Cover the ends with Buttercream to keep them from drying out.

Roll Rum-ball Mixture into round strings, 1½ inches (35 mm) in diameter; cover with Marzipan. Refrigerate until cold. Cut into 2-inch (5-cm) pieces, straight at one end and slanted at the other. You need two for each log. Dip these branches into dark chocolate and let cool. Dip the slanted ends into chocolate again and fasten them to the log, one on each side. Roll out a strip of green Marzipan and write *Merry Christmas* on it. Place in the middle of the log. Decorate as desired with meringue mushrooms and marzipan mistletoe.

Variation: Chocolate Roulade

Follow recipe above but cut roulade into 1-inch-wide (25-mm) pieces with a serrated knife. Place in paper cups, pressing the bottoms of the paper cups flat on both sides of the slice to create a base. Decorate with chocolate Buttercream piped in an *S* with a no. 1 (3-mm) plain tip; place a small candied violet in the middle.

WHISKEY-COFFEE CAKE

four 10-inch (25-cm) cakes   *photograph, p. 137*

> four 10-inch (25-cm) short-dough bottoms (see p. 17)
> Biscuit Viennoise (see p. 95)
> Biscuit au Chocolat (see p. 94)
> currant jelly
> Coffee Cream (recipe follows)
> Whiskey Cream (recipe follows)
> whipped cream
> shaved dark chocolate
> dark chocolate for piping
> marzipan or candy coffee beans

Make short-dough bottoms, Biscuit Viennoise and Biscuit au Chocolat. Split each cake into 2 layers. Place the short-dough bottoms on cardboard for support and spread a thin layer of jelly on each. Place a chocolate layer on each. Make the Coffee Cream and spread equally on the cakes. Place the second chocolate layer on top; refrigerate.

Make the Whiskey Cream and spread it in a dome shape on the cakes. Cover with the Biscuit Viennoise layers. Refrigerate covered until cream is set, at least 2 hours or overnight.

To finish, spread the entire surface of cake with a thin layer of whipped cream. Put shaved dark chocolate on the sides. Cut the cake into serving pieces. Using a no. 2 (4-mm) plain tip, pipe a hook on each piece with whipped cream. Pipe a thin line of dark chocolate on top following the line of the hook. Finish with a marzipan or candy coffee bean at the edge of each slice.

Coffee Cream

  7 ounces (2 dl, 1 cl) milk
  3 ounces (85 g) sugar
  3 ounces (85 g) egg yolks
 1⅓ ounces (40 g) instant coffee powder
  ⅓ ounce (10 g) unflavored gelatin
  2 ounces (6 cl) water
  1 quart, 10 ounces (1 l, 2 dl, 6 cl) heavy cream

Heat milk and sugar to scalding. Gradually fold into egg yolks; stir in coffee powder. Dissolve gelatin in water and add to the milk mixture. Set aside to cool. Whip cream to soft peaks. Fold cooled milk mixture into the whipped cream.

Whiskey Cream

  6 ounces (1 dl, 8 cl) Irish whiskey
  ⅔ ounce (20 g) unflavored gelatin
  1 quart, 10 ounces (1 l, 2 dl, 6 cl) heavy cream
  5 ounces (140 g) sugar

Dissolve the gelatin in the whiskey and heat to about 150° F (65° C). Whip the cream and sugar to a soft consistency. Stir the gelatin into a small part of the cream; then rapidly mix the two cream mixtures.

GÂTEAU LUGANO

four 10-inch (25-cm) cakes

 Cocoa Almond Sponge (recipe follows)
 Arrack-flavored Buttercream (recipe follows)
 crushed roasted almonds
 cocoa powder
 strawberries

Make Cocoa Almond Sponge. A heavy sponge such as this will always bake higher in the middle because the batter next to the hot metal of the pan will not have as much time to rise as the batter in the middle. (Usually such a cake is cut even at the same time the skin is cut from the cake. In this case, evening the cake is not necessary because only the center of the top layer will be used.) Cut the skin from each sponge and slice into 3 layers; then, using a 6-inch (15-cm) template or cookie cutter, cut each top layer into a 6-inch (15-cm) circle.

Make the buttercream. Use 1 pound, 7 ounces (655 g) of the buttercream for each cake. Spread buttercream ⅛ inch (3 mm) thick on the bottom layers and place the second layers on top. Spread enough buttercream on top to cover the sponge. Spread the sides with a thin layer of buttercream and cover with crushed roasted almonds.

Spread buttercream on the tops and sides of the 6-inch (15-cm) top layers. Refrigerate all layers until buttercream is firm. Turn a cake cooler upside down on top of a 6-inch (15-cm) layer. (The cake cooler should be lightweight so it does not sink into the buttercream.) Sift cocoa powder through a fine sieve over the layer; then remove the cake cooler carefully so that the pattern is not disturbed. Repeat with 3 remaining top layers. Make the 10-inch (25-cm) cakes with the same template used to cut the top layers to show where the top layer goes; then carefully place the small sponge layers on top. Refrigerate until the buttercream is set.

Mark or cut the cake into the desired number of pieces. Using a no. 6 (12-mm) plain tip, pipe a mound of buttercream the size of a Bing cherry at the edge of each piece. Cut small strawberries of equal size in half, and place one half, cut side up, on each mound. Serve at room temperature.

Cocoa Almond Sponge
four 10-inch (25-cm) cakes

> 1 pound, 4 ounces (560 g) egg yolks
> 1 pound, 5 ounces (600 g) almond paste
> 10 ounces (285 g) sugar
> pinch salt
> ½ teaspoon (3 g) vanilla extract
> 1 pound, 10 ounces (740 g) egg whites
> 14 ounces (400 g) sugar
> 15 ounces (430 g) flour
> 6 ounces (170 g) cocoa powder
> 11⅓ ounces (320 g) melted butter

Mix egg yolks, one at a time, into the almond paste, 10 ounces (320 g) sugar, the salt, and vanilla; mix until smooth. Do not add yolks too fast to prevent lumps. Whip egg whites with 14 ounces (400 g) sugar to stiff peaks;

fold into almond mixture. Sift flour with cocoa powder and fold in. Fold in melted butter. Divide batter among 4 greased and floured 10-inch (25-cm) cake pans. Bake immediately at 400° F (205° C) about 18 minutes.

Arrack-flavored Buttercream

     1 pound (455 g) egg whites
     2 pounds (910 g) sugar
       pinch salt
     2 pounds (910 g) butter, softened
    10 ounces (285 g) margarine, softened
    ½ teaspoon (3 g) vanilla extract
     2 ounces (6 cl) arrack or rum

Heat egg whites, sugar, and salt over hot water until sugar and salt are dissolved (130° F/55° C). Whip egg whites to stiff peaks. Add vanilla and arrack or rum; gradually mix in butter and margarine. Store covered at room temperature.

LEMON CHIFFON CAKE

six 10-inch (25-cm) cakes   photograph, p. 137

     8 lemons
     2 oranges
       Spongecake I (see p. 92)
     7 ounces (2 dl, 1 cl) water
     9 ounces (255 g) sugar
    16 egg yolks
     2 quarts (1 l, 9 dl, 2 cl) heavy cream
     1 cup (2 dl, 4 cl) water
     2 ounces (55 g) unflavored gelatin
       few drops yellow food color
       few drops tartaric acid
       whipped cream, for icing and piping
       Pectin Glaze (see p. 237) or shaved dark chocolate
       Chocolate Squares (see p. 245)
       lemon wedges

Grate the zest of 8 lemons. Juice the lemons and oranges, combine grated zest and juice, and set aside. Make three 10-inch (25-cm) spongecakes using the Spongecake I recipe. Remove skins from the tops of the cakes, and slice into 2 layers each. Place the layers on sheet pans, 3 to a pan, and place adjustable rings around them. Unless the rings are stainless steel, line them with parchment paper or plastic strips to prevent discoloration.

Heat 7 ounces (2 dl, 1 cl) water and the sugar to 230° F (107° C). Beat egg yolks until half-whipped. Pour syrup into egg yolks; whip until the mixture is cold and reaches the ribbon stage.

Whip the heavy cream to soft peaks. Dissolve gelatin in 1 cup (2 dl, 4 cl) water and heat to 150° F (65° C). Mix egg-yolk mixture, whipped cream, and citrus juice and zest. Mix in food color and tartaric acid. Place about one-fifth of the cream mixture in a small bowl, and rapidly add all the gelatin at once; then mix the gelatin mixture quickly into the remaining cream mixture. Spread the lemon cream equally on the 6 prepared cakes. Place 10-inch (25-cm) plain doilies on the lemon cream to prevent skins from forming. Let it set at least 2 hours.

Spread 10 ounces (285 g) plain whipped cream ¾ inch (20 mm) thick on top of each cake and a very thin layer on each side. Spread a layer of Pectin Glaze over the center of the cake not all the way to the edge, and let the glaze set; or shave some dark chocolate in the middle to offset the plain color of the whipped cream. Cut or mark the cakes into serving pieces. Place a Chocolate Square on the side of each piece. Pipe a whipped cream rosette on the edge of each piece and decorate with a small lemon wedge.

PRINCESS CAKE

one 10-inch (25-cm) cake   *photograph, p. 138*

> ½ recipe Spongecake II (see p. 93)
> 2 ounces (55 g) strawberry jam, softened
> 10 ounces (285 g) Bavarian Cream (see p. 261)
> 1 pound, 6 ounces (620 g) whipped cream
>   Marzipan, colored green (see p. 255)
>   powdered sugar

Make the spongecake, remove the skin, and cut level if necessary. Slice into 3 layers. Spread jam on the bottom layer, top with the second layer, and spread Bavarian Cream on top. Place the third layer on top; cover with whipped cream in a dome shape, about 1 inch (25 mm) thick in the middle, and a thin glaze at the edge. Spread a thin layer of whipped cream on the side. Refrigerate until set.

Roll out green Marzipan into a circle, 15 inches (37.5 cm) in diameter and a little thinner than ⅛ inch (3 mm). If the cake is to be used the next day (this is an excellent cake to make up ahead because the Marzipan keeps the cake fresh for days if refrigerated), spread a thin glaze of buttercream on the bottom side of the Marzipan to keep the Marzipan from getting wet. Cover the cake evenly with the Marzipan, making sure that the sides are not wrinkled. Cut into serving pieces, cutting twice from the outside in, the first time to cut through the Marzipan and the second time to cut through the cake. Dust lightly with powdered sugar. If a decoration is desired, make it before dusting the cake with powdered sugar.

GÂTEAU ISTANBUL
four 10-inch (25-cm) cakes   color photograph, p. C-2

> Cocoa Almond Sponge (see p. 110)
> 4 10-inch (25-cm) short-dough bottoms (see p. 17)
> Nougat Butter (recipe follows)
> Hazelnut Cream (recipe follows)
> whipped cream
> crushed roasted almonds
> cocoa powder
> crescent cookies made from Cocoa Short Dough (see p. 19)
> dark chocolate, optional

Make the 4 spongecakes; cut each sponge into 2 layers. Place the short-dough bottoms on cardboard, and spread the Nougat Butter evenly on all four. Place a sponge layer on top, saving the best-looking layers for the tops. Spread Hazelnut Cream on the 4 cakes evenly. Place the second sponge layer on top, pressing it down lightly. Cover cakes and freeze.

When cakes are completely frozen, cut off any short dough that protrudes outside the sponge. Spread the tops and sides with a thin layer of whipped cream and cover the sides with crushed roasted almonds. Place a 10-inch (25-cm) round template with a 6-inch (15-cm) hole cut out of the center in the middle of the cake, and sift on enough cocoa powder to cover the whipped cream.

When the cake is halfway thawed, cut into serving pieces. (Do not allow the cake to thaw too much, or you will push the nuts into the cake, rather than slicing through them.) Using a no. 7 (14-mm) plain tip, pipe a mound of whipped cream the size of a cherry at the edge of each slice. Decorate each mound with a crescent cookie.

To make the crescent cookies, roll out Cocoa Short Dough no thicker than ⅛ inch (3 mm). Using a plain cookie cutter the size of a quarter, cut out circles; then cut halfway into each circle to get a crescent. The cookies can be left plain or dipped into melted dark chocolate.

Nougat Butter

 3½ ounces (100 g) butter, softened
 3½ ounces (100 g) hazelnut paste

Work the soft butter gradually into the hazelnut paste so that it does not get lumps.

Hazelnut Cream

  1 pound (455 g) roasted whole hazelnuts
  2 quarts, 4 ounces (1 l, 9 dl, 4 cl) heavy cream
 12 ounces (340 g) hazelnut paste

Rub nuts between your hands to remove as much skin as will come off easily. To remove all of the skin on the nuts, they must be blanched in water with baking soda before they are roasted, but this is quite time-consuming. Whip the cream to a soft consistency; if it is too firm, it will break when the rest of the ingredients are added. Mix cream gradually into the hazelnut paste. Mix in the nuts. If the cream is too soft to hold its shape, keep mixing until it holds a peak.

FLORENTINE TORTE
one 10-inch (25-cm) cake

   very finely ground nuts
 10 ounces (285 g) mixed nuts
  7 ounces (200 g) granulated sugar
 7½ ounces (215 g) chocolate, shredded
 1½ ounces (40 g) candied citron or grated zest of 2 lemons or 1
   orange
  8 egg yolks (160 g)
   vanilla extract
  8 egg whites (225 g)
   powdered sugar
   Ganache (see p. 247)
   pecan quarters

Butter a 10-inch (25-cm) cake pan lined with a plain doily on the bottom, and sprinkle it with ground nuts. Grind the 10 ounces (285 g) mixed nuts with some sugar (to absorb the fat from the nuts and keep them from caking) to the consistency of whole-wheat flour. Combine nuts, 7 ounces (200 g) sugar, the chocolate, citron, egg yolks, and vanilla to taste.

Beat egg whites until stiff but not dry. Fold about one-fifth of the whites into the nut mixture to loosen it; then carefully fold in the remaining whites. Pour into prepared pan. Bake at 350° F (175° C) about 30 minutes. Cool cake in pan a few minutes; then carefully turn out of pan while still warm to prevent damage to the skin.

Sprinkle very lightly with powdered sugar. Cut into serving pieces. Using a no. 3 (6-mm) plain tip, pipe Ganache that has been softened to a slight shine in a cone at the edge of each slice with the point of the cone facing towards the middle of the cake. Decorate with a pecan piece.

This torte will improve in flavor if made 1 to 2 days in advance.

GÂTEAU AU DIPLOMATE
two 10-inch (25-cm) cakes   *photograph, p. 138*

> **Spongecake II (see p. 93)**
> **strawberry jam**
> 2 **pounds, 7 ounces (1 kg, 110 g) Pastry Cream (see p. 242)**
> **crushed sliced almonds (unroasted)**
> 1 **pound (455 g) Macaroon Paste II (see p. 159)**
> **fresh fruit**
> **Apricot or Pectin Glaze (see pp. 239, 237)**

Slice both light spongecakes into 3 layers. Cover the bottom with a thin layer of jam, and add the second layer of sponge. Spread the second layer with Pastry Cream ¼ inch (6 mm) thick, and top with the third layer. Spread the cakes with Pastry Cream, ⅛ inch (3 mm) thick on top and thinner on the sides. Cover the sides with crushed almonds.

Place cakes on doubled baking pans and mark serving pieces. Using the macaroon paste and a no. 2 (4-mm) plain tip, pipe a petaled flower on each cake, one petal on each slice. Bake at 425° F (220° C) until paste is golden brown and the almonds are toasted, about 10 minutes. Decorate flower petals with 2 or 3 sliced fruits and glaze with Apricot or Pectin Glaze, and cut between petals to serve.

Variation: Gâteau au Sénateur
Pipe softened and strained apricot and strawberry jams alternately in the petals before baking.

PRALINE CAKE WITH RUM
four 10-inch (25-cm) cakes   photograph, p. 138

> four 10-inch (25-cm) short-dough bottoms (see p. 17)
> Biscuit Viennoise (see p. 95)
> Chocolate Cream (recipe follows)
> currant jelly
> Praline-rum Cream (recipe follows)
> whipped cream
> shaved light chocolate
> Chocolate Rounds (see p. 245)

Make short-dough bottoms and Biscuit Viennoise. Slice both cakes into 2 layers each. Make Chocolate Cream.

Place cardboard beneath the short-dough bottoms for support; spread jelly on each and top with a cake layer. Spread Chocolate Cream on each cake into a dome. Place an adjustable cake ring around each cake layer; if the ring is not stainless steel, line it with a strip of parchment paper or plastic. Refrigerate the cakes until the dome is firm enough to hold praline cream on top.

Make Praline-rum cream. Divide and spread it smoothly on top of the chocolate mounds so the cake is now level. Refrigerate until set, about 2 hours.

Spread a thin layer of whipped cream on the sides. Place a 7-inch (17.5-cm) round template on the center of a cake, and decorate the side and the exposed top with shaved light chocolate. Repeat with remaining cakes. Mark or cut into serving pieces. Using a no. 6 (12-mm) plain tip, pipe a whipped cream mound on each piece in the middle of the shaved chocolate border. Stand a Chocolate Round, the size of a quarter, in each mound.

Chocolate Cream
> 2 pints, 10 ounces (1 l, 2 dl, 6 cl) heavy cream
> 7 ounces (200 g) dark chocolate, melted
> 5 ounces (1 dl, 5 cl) Simple Syrup (see p. 233)
> 3 ounces (9 cl) crème de cacao
> ½ ounce (15 g) unflavored gelatin
> 4 ounces (1 dl, 2 cl) water

Fruit Tartlets

Raspberry Turnovers

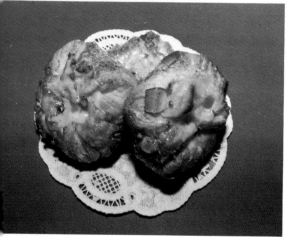

Choux Surprise

Swedish Hazelnut Tart

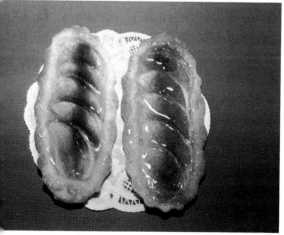

Fruit Waffles

Apple Cross-over Strips

Swedish Profiteroles

Apple Strudel, German Style

Danish Pastries: Singles, Bear Claws, and Figure Eights

Black Forest Cake

Gâteau Istanbul

German Poppy-seed Cake

Mocha Meringues

Vacherin à la Vanille

Meringue Landeck

Heide Sand Cookies

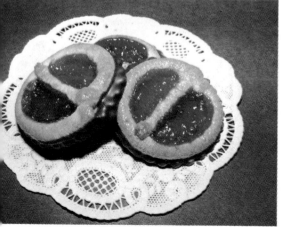

Almond Doubles

Marie Puffs

Petits Fours

Fruit Barrels

Crêpes Vienna

Charlotte with Pears and Caramel Sauce

Banana Poppy-seed Ice Cream

Ice-Cream Cake Jamaica

Whip heavy cream to soft peaks; set aside. Mix together chocolate, Simple Syrup, and crème de cacao. Dissolve gelatin in water and heat to 150° F (65° C). Add to the chocolate mixture. The mixture should now be about 130° F (55° C). Place a small amount of the whipped cream in a bowl. Gradually incorporate the chocolate mixture, mixing rapidly; work this into the remaining whipped cream.

Praline-rum Cream

> 1½ quarts, 1 ounce (1 l, 4 dl, 7 cl) heavy cream
> 3 ounces (85 g) sugar
> 7 ounces (200 g) crushed Hazelnut Praline (see p. 237)
> ⅚ ounce (25 g) unflavored gelatin
> 7 ounces (2 dl, 1 cl) water
> 4 ounces (1 dl, 2 cl) rum

Whip heavy cream and sugar to a soft consistency; mix in Hazelnut Praline. Dissolve the gelatin in water and heat to 150° F (65° C); stir in rum. Rapidly mix the gelatin into part of the whipped cream; mix into remaining cream.

RASPBERRY CAKE
four 10-inch (25-cm) cakes   photograph, p. 138

> Almond Butter Cake (recipe follows)
> raspberry jam
> four 10-inch (25-cm) short-dough bottoms (see p. 17)
> Raspberry Cream (recipe follows)
> raspberries
> Buttercream (see p. 239)
> crushed roasted almonds
> Marzipan (see p. 255)
> shaved dark chocolate
> fluted small Short-dough Cookies (see p. 18)
> melted dark chocolate

Make Almond Butter Cake. Slice each cake into 2 layers each. With cardboard beneath for support, spread jam on short-dough bottoms. Top with a layer of almond sponge. Place an adjustable cake ring lined with paper around each cake layer. Make Raspberry Cream. Spread half the Raspberry Cream on the 4 cakes. Arrange whole raspberries, round sides up, in 3 concentric rings in the cream. Spread the remaining cream evenly over the raspberries. Place remaining cake layers on top and press lightly to level. Refrigerate or freeze until cream is set.

Spread a very thin layer of Buttercream over the cakes, and cover the sides with crushed almonds. Roll out Marzipan about 1/16 inch (2 mm) thick; mark with a waffle-patterned roller, and cut into 4 circles the size of the cakes. Cut out circles, 2½ to 3 inches (6 to 7.5 cm) in diameter, from the centers of the larger circles so that they look like doughnuts. Cut the Marzipan from hole of the doughnut to about 2 inches (5 cm) from the outside edge to align with the cuts for serving pieces. Roll up the Marzipan pieces gently toward the outside of the cake, making a petal pattern. Place Marzipan on the tops of the cakes. Cover the center of the cake with shaved chocolate. Cut the cake into serving pieces. Decorate the end of each piece with a cookie dipped in chocolate and topped with a raspberry.

Variation:

This cake can be made with blackberries with the following changes in the Raspberry Cream: Omit raspberry purée, add 8 ounces (225 g) more whipped cream, and substitute maraschino liqueur for the Framboise.

Almond Butter Cake

four 10-inch (25-cm) cakes

> 8 ounces (225 g) egg yolks
> ⅓ ounce (10 g) grated lemon zest
> ⅓ ounce (10 g) salt
> 9 ounces (255 g) almond paste
> 13 ounces (370 g) egg whites
> 8 ounces (225 g) sugar
> 7 ounces (200 g) bread flour
> 7 ounces (200 g) cornstarch
> 5 ounces (140 g) butter, melted

Whip egg yolks; mix gradually into almond paste, lemon zest, and salt. Whip egg whites and sugar as directed for French Meringue. Fold into almond paste mixture. Fold in sifted flour and cornstarch. Fold in melted butter. Divide among 4 prepared 10-inch (25-cm) cake pans. Bake immediately at 400° F (205° C) until cakes spring back when lightly pressed, about 12 minutes.

Raspberry Cream

    5 egg yolks
    6 ounces (170 g) sugar
    7 ounces (2 dl, 1 cl) white wine
1⅙ ounces (35 g) unflavored gelatin
    4 ounces (1 dl, 2 cl) water
    4 ounces (1 dl, 2 cl) framboise
4½ pints (2 l, 1 dl, 6 cl) cream
    1 cup (2 dl, 4 cl) strained puréed raspberries

Whip egg yolks, sugar, and wine over hot water until thick and heated to about 130° F (55° C). Dissolve gelatin in the water; mix gelatin and liqueur into egg yolk mixture until gelatin is completely incorporated and heat to 150° F (65° C); stir in raspberry purée. Whip heavy cream to soft peaks; fold in raspberry mixture, mixing it first into part of the cream.

STRAWBERRY-KIRSCH CAKE

four 10-inch (25-cm) cakes   *photograph, p. 138*

Spongecake II (see p. 93)
strawberry jam
four 10-inch (25-cm) short-dough bottoms (see p. 17)
100 small fresh strawberries, roughly equal in size
Kirsch Whipped Cream (recipe follows)
Buttercream
crushed roasted almonds
Marzipan (see p. 255)
dark chocolate

Cut each spongecake into 4 thin layers. Spread a thin layer of jam on the short-dough bottoms and top with a sponge layer. Place an adjustable cake ring, lined with parchment paper, around each cake. Arrange strawberries, points up, over the surface of each layer. Cut the strawberries that are placed next to the ring in half, and place the cut sides to the outside. Spread the Kirsch Whipped Cream on the 4 cakes. Place second cake layers on cream; refrigerate until set, at least 2 hours.

    Spread a thin layer of Buttercream on top of each cake. Cut a strip of parchment paper wide enough to cover the strawberries and ½ inch of the cake; wrap the paper around the strawberry layer and ¼ inch (6 mm) of the cake above and below the berries. Ice the exposed cake with a thin layer of Buttercream; cover with crushed almonds. Remove paper carefully.

Roll out marzipan ⅛ inch (3 mm) thick, cut it into circles to fit the tops of the cakes, and place on the tops. Cut or mark into serving pieces. Pipe an "L" on each piece with dark chocolate.

This cake cannot be frozen because of the strawberries.

Kirsch Whipped Cream

5	ounces (140 g)	egg yolks
8	ounces (225 g)	sugar
4½	pints (2 l, 1 dl, 6 cl)	heavy cream
1⅙	ounces (35 g)	unflavored gelatin
6	ounces (1 dl, 8 cl)	water
10	ounces (3 dl)	dry white wine
4	ounces (1 dl, 2 cl)	Kirschwasser

Whip yolks and sugar to the ribbon stage. Whip cream to soft peaks; mix with yolks. Dissolve gelatin in water; stir in wine and Kirschwasser and heat to 150° F (65° C). Rapidly mix into a small part of the cream; stir into remaining cream.

SACHER TORTE

three 10-inch (25-cm) cakes   photograph, p. 138

	Sacher Sponge (recipe follows)
3	recipes hot Apricot Glaze (see p. 239)
	Marzipan (see p. 255)
15	ounces (430 g) Chocolate Glaze (see p. 247)
	melted light chocolate
	dark chocolate for piping

Make Sacher Sponge, and divide among 3 greased and floured 10-inch (25-cm) cake pans. Bake at 375° F (190° C), about 21 minutes. When cakes are cold, cut off the skins and then even the cakes if necessary. Slice each one into 2 layers.

Spread hot Apricot Glaze, forcing it into the sponge and adding another ⅛ inch (3 mm), on the bottom half; immediately, before a skin forms, place the top layers on the glaze and press down firmly. Spread glaze as thinly as possible on the tops and sides of the cakes.

Roll out Marzipan ¹⁄₁₆ inch (2 mm) thick and place on tops of the cakes. Turn cakes over and refrigerate. Make Chocolate Glaze. Place the cakes, marzipan sides up, on screens with sheet pans underneath. Spread the tops and sides as thinly as possible with Chocolate Glaze (5 ounces (140 g) per cake). Before the glaze sets, move the cakes to cardboards, and let the glaze dry until it does not run.

Meanwhile, make the decoration: Spread melted light chocolate (100° F/38° C) in a thin layer on baking paper. With a plain cookie cutter, cut out ¾-inch (20-mm) circles. Pipe an "S" in the middle of each circle with dark chocolate. With a little chocolate fasten a chocolate circle at the edge of each cake slice. If you prefer, you can pipe the "S" directly on the cake, using light or dark chocolate.

Sacher Sponge

       21 eggs
        1 pound, 3 ounces (540 g) sugar
       10 ounces (285 g) flour
        2 ounces (55 g) cornstarch
        4 ounces (115 g) cocoa powder
     4½ ounces (130 g) nuts, finely crushed
     4½ ounces (130 g) chocolate
   10½ ounces (300 g) butter

Separate the eggs. Whip the yolks and half the sugar to the ribbon stage. Sift the flour, cornstarch, and cocoa powder together, and mix in the crushed nuts. Melt the chocolate and butter and mix the two. Whip the whites with the remaining sugar to stiff peaks; fold into the yolks. Fold in the dry ingredients carefully. Fold in the melted, but not hot, chocolate mixture.

REINE DE SABA
four 10-inch (25-cm) cakes   *photograph, p. 138*

   Reine de Saba Sponge (recipe follows)
   Short Dough (see p. 19)
   melted dark chocolate
   4 pounds, 1 ounce (1 kg, 850 g) Ganache (see p. 247)
   1 pound, 13 ounces (825 g) Buttercream (see p. 239)
   crushed roasted hazelnuts
   Marzipan (see p. 255)
   red piping gel

Make Reine de Saba Sponge. While sponge is baking and cooling, roll out Short Dough ⅛ inch (3 mm) thick, and cut out fluted cookies 1¼ to 1½ inches (30 to 35 mm) in diameter. Cut 3 holes in each cookie with a no. 2 (4-mm) plain tip. Bake cookies at 375° F (190° C) until golden brown, about 10 minutes. When cooled, line them up and streak with very thin lines of dark chocolate.

Cut the skins from the cooled sponges and at the same time even the tops. Slice each cake into 2 layers. Mix 3 pounds, 7 ounces (1 kg, 565 g) of the Ganache with 1 pound, 13 ounces (825 g) Buttercream (1 pound, 6 ounces (625 g) mixture per cake). Spread the mixture ¼ inch (6 mm) thick on the bottom layers. Place the top layers upsidedown on top of the Ganache. Reserve 3 ounces (85 g) of the Ganache mixture for decorating; spread the remaining mixture just thick enough to cover the sponge. Cover the sides with crushed hazelnuts. Roll out Marzipan ¹⁄₁₆ inch (2 mm) thick, and cut into circles to fit the tops of the cakes. Place each Marzipan circle on a cardboard and slide it carefully on top of the cake. Turn the cakes upside down to flatten the tops.

Warm remaining Ganache until quite loose and shiny but still controllable. Turn cakes right side up and spread a thin layer of Ganache on the Marzipan (2½ ounces (70 g) per cake). With the back of a chef's knife make a ¾-inch (20-mm) diamond pattern in the Ganache. Refrigerate cakes.

Cut cakes into serving pieces. Using a no. 6 (12-mm) plain tip, pipe a mound of the reserved mixture at the edge of each piece, place a short-dough cookie at an angle on the cream, and pipe a dot of red piping gel in one hole for some color.

Reine de Saba Sponge

four 10-inch (25-cm) cakes

> 2 pounds (910 g) dark chocolate
> 1 cup (2 dl, 4 cl) rum
> 2 pounds (910 g) butter, softened
> 2 pounds, 10 ounces (1 kg, 195 g) sugar
> 24 eggs, separated
> 1 pound, 5 ounces (595 g) cake flour
> 14 ounces (400 g) ground roasted hazelnuts

Melt the chocolate, stir in rum, and set aside. Cream butter and 2 pounds (910 g) of the sugar until light and fluffy. Beat in egg yolks, a few at a time. Stir chocolate and rum into a small part of the butter mixture; then rapidly mix the two together. Whip egg whites and remaining sugar to stiff peaks. Sift the flour, and mix with the nuts. Fold the whites alternately with the dry ingredients into the butter mixture. Divide among four 10-inch (25-cm) greased and floured cake pans. Bake at 350° F (175° C) about 40 minutes.

GUGELHUPF (Direct Method)

six 6-inch (15-cm) cakes   *photograph, p. 138*

        9 ounces (255 g) raisins
           grated zest of 2 lemons
     1½ ounces (4.5 cl) Cointreau
    10½ ounces (300 g) butter
       13 ounces (370 g) sugar
        6 eggs
        1 pound, 5 ounces (595 g) cake flour
        1 ounce (30 g) baking powder
        7 ounces (200 g) finely ground almonds
        2 cups (4 dl, 8 cl) lukewarm milk
           crushed sliced almonds
           powdered sugar

Macerate raisins and lemon zest in Cointreau. Cream butter and sugar. Add in eggs, one at a time, as quickly as they will be absorbed. Sift flour and baking powder together, and mix in ground almonds. Fold dry ingredients alternately with milk into the egg mixture. If you overmix, incorporating too much air, the *gugelhupf* will be dry and crumbly. Stir in raisins, zest, and Cointreau.

Coat six 6-inch (15-cm) *gugelhupf* forms with a mixture of 4 parts melted butter to 1 part flour; then coat with crushed almonds. Fill forms three-quarters full with batter. Bake at 350° F (175° C) until done, about 50 minutes. Before serving, sift powdered sugar lightly over the cakes.

CHOCOLATE GUGELHUPF
2 large or 4 small cakes

8 ounces, (225 g) butter, softened
1 pound, 2 ounces (510 g) sugar
6 eggs
11 ounces (310 g) boiled potatoes, smoothly mashed
15 ounces (430 g) cake flour
1½ ounces (45 g) cocoa powder
5 teaspoons (10 g) baking powder
pinch salt
8 ounces (225 g) blanched almonds, finely ground
9 ounces (2 dl, 7 cl) heavy cream
1½ teaspoons (9 g) vanilla extract

Beat the butter and sugar until creamy. Beat in the eggs, a few at a time; then beat in potatoes. Sift flour, cocoa powder, baking powder, and salt together; mix in almonds. Fold the dry ingredients alternately with the cream and vanilla into the butter mixture.

Coat the desired forms with a mixture of 4 parts melted butter to 1 part flour. (This mixture can be used over and over; warm it up and stir.) Spoon the batter into the forms to fill them two-thirds. Bake at 350° F (175° C) until a toothpick inserted in the middle comes out dry, about 1 hour. Unmold immediately. When cakes have cooled, wrap in plastic wrap to keep them from drying out.

CHOCOLATE CRISP CAKE
five 1-pound, 7-ounce (655-g) cakes   photograph, p. 139

1 pound (455 g) sugar
1 pound, 2 ounces (510 g) butter
10 eggs
1 teaspoon (6 g) vanilla extract
1 pound, 12 ounces (795 g) bread flour
½ ounce (15 g) baking powder
9 ounces (255 g) chopped dark chocolate
10½ ounces (300 g) crushed roasted hazelnuts
grated zest of 1 orange
11 ounces (3 dl, 3 cl) milk, room temperature
Apricot Glaze, optional (see p. 239)
dark chocolate, optional

Beat sugar and butter until fluffy; beat in the eggs, two at a time. Mix in vanilla. Sift the flour and baking powder together; stir in chopped chocolate, the hazelnuts, and orange zest, and fold into the butter mixture alternately with milk. Butter and flour 5 rectangular fluted forms; divide the mixture among them (1 pound, 7 ounces (655 g) batter for each pan). Bake at 350° F (175° C) about 60 minutes. Let cool completely.

Serve plain or brush tops with a thin layer of Apricot Glaze and ice with dark chocolate.

This cake tastes better if served 1 to 2 days later.

RAISIN CAKE
six 6½-inch (13½-cm) cakes
photograph, p. 139

> 2 pounds, 2 ounces (970 g) butter, softened
> 2 pounds (910 g) sugar
> 1 teaspoon (6 g) vanilla extract
> 13 eggs
> 1 pound, 2 ounces (510 g) bread flour
> 14 ounces (400 g) potato flour or cornstarch
> 2 tablespoons (14 g) baking powder
> 9 ounces (255 g) raisins
>   fine dry bread crumbs

Beat butter, sugar, and vanilla until creamy but do not overmix. Mix in the eggs, a few at a time. Sift the flours and the baking powder together. Add the raisins, coating them with flour. Fold dry ingredients into the butter mixture.

Butter *gugelhupf* forms or other pans and coat them thoroughly with fine dry bread crumbs. Spoon in enough batter to fill pans two-thirds. Bake at 375° F (190° C) until cake springs back when lightly pressed, about 35 minutes.

This batter can also be baked in muffin cups; bake in a slightly hotter oven and not quite as long. Wrap and store this cake 1 day before serving.

SAND CAKE

four 1-pound, 6-ounce (625 g) cakes
photograph, p. 139

>   1 pound, 12 ounces (795 g) butter
>   1 pound, 12 ounces (795 g) sugar
>   12 eggs
>   4 ounces (1 dl, 2 cl) brandy
>   1 teaspoon (6 g) vanilla extract
>   14 ounces (400 g) cake flour
>   14 ounces (400 g) potato starch or cornstarch
>   4 teaspoons (8 g) baking powder
>   2 ounces (55 g) blanched almonds, finely ground
>   fine dry bread crumbs

Melt butter and let it cool. Stir the butter for a few minutes and stir in the sugar. Continue stirring 5 to 10 minutes; then stir in the eggs, a few at a time, the brandy, and vanilla. Sift the flour, starch, and baking powder together, mix in the almonds, and stir into the butter mixture.

Butter large *gugelhupf* forms and dust with fine dry bread crumbs. Pour batter into the forms to fill two-thirds. Bake at 350° F (175° C) until cake springs back when lightly pressed, about 60 minutes. Unmold cakes immediately.

When cakes have cooled, wrap in plastic and store in the refrigerator or freezer.

APPLE CAKE

three 1-pound, 6-ounce (625-g) cakes
photograph, p. 139

>   14 ounces (400 g) soft butter
>   1 pound, 2 ounces (510 g) sugar
>   8 eggs, room temperature
>   3 cups (7 dl, 2 cl) half and half, slightly warm
>   ½ teaspoon (3 g) vanilla extract
>   1 pound, 11 ounces (765 g) cake flour
>   1½ ounces (45 g) baking powder
>   fine dry bread crumbs
>   7 small apples
>   cinnamon sugar

Beat butter until light and fluffy. Whip the sugar and eggs to the ribbon stage, and mix into the butter. Gradually beat in the warm half-and-half and vanilla. If the batter looks broken, do not panic because the flour will pull it together. Sift flour and baking powder; fold into the batter.

Butter 3 large *gugelhupf* forms thoroughly and dust with fine dry bread crumbs. Pour the batter into the forms.

Peel, core, and slice apples into ½-inch (12-mm) wedges. Coat them with cinnamon sugar, and press into the middle of the batter about ¼ inch (6 mm) apart. The apples can also be cut into crouton-size pieces, coated with cinnamon sugar, and mixed into the batter before it is poured into the forms.

Bake cakes at 350° F (175° C) until baked through, about 55 minutes. Unmold immediately and let cool completely. Wrap in plastic and store in the refrigerator.

TIGER CAKE

four 17-ounce (485-g) cakes
photograph, p. 139

> 8 eggs
> 1 pound, 2 ounces (510 g) sugar
> 6 ounces (1 dl, 8 cl) milk
> 1 pound, 6 ounces (625 g) butter, melted
> 14 ounces (400 g) cake flour
> 1 tablespoon (7 g) baking powder
> 1 ounce (30 g) cocoa powder
>   grated zest of 2 lemons
> ½ teaspoon (3 g) vanilla extract
>   fine dry bread crumbs

Separate the eggs. Cream the yolks with half the sugar until fluffy. Beat in milk and melted, but not hot, butter. Sift flour and baking powder together and fold into butter mixture. Whip the egg whites with remaining sugar to stiff peaks; fold into the butter mixture carefully by hand.

Add the cocoa powder to one-third of the batter by placing cocoa powder in a bowl and gradually adding one-third of the batter. This method prevents the cocoa from causing lumps. Mix lemon zest and vanilla into the remaining two-thirds of the batter.

Butter and flour four 17-ounce *gugelhupf* forms; coat them with bread crumbs. (It is very important to coat the cake forms carefully, especially if you are using fluted forms or forms with any pattern; always melt the butter and always apply it with a brush. Bread crumbs are used because they are neutral in taste and turn a beautiful golden brown color when baked; only very fine crumbs should be used because coarse ones will not look as good.) Starting and finishing with the white batter, spoon alternating layers of white and chocolate batters into the forms, filling each two-thirds full. Bake immediately at 360° F (180° C) until cake springs back when lightly pressed, about 55 minutes. Unmold forms immediately.

When cakes are completely cool, wrap them in plastic wrap and store in the refrigerator.

HAWAIIAN PINEAPPLE CAKE

four 10-inch (25-cm) cakes   photograph, p. 139

> Egg Sand Cake (recipe follows)
> 10 ounces (285 g) Apricot Jam (see p. 238)
> four 10-inch (25-cm) short-dough bottoms (see p. 17)
> Pineapple Whipped Cream (recipe follows)
> whipped cream
> crushed roasted almonds
> diced pineapple
> Pectin or Apricot Glaze (see pp. 237, 239)
> pineapple wedges
> shaved dark chocolate

Make Egg Sand cake, and slice into 2 layers each. Place cardboard beneath short-dough bottoms for support. Spread a thin layer of jam on each short-dough bottom and place a cake layer on top. Place adjustable cake rings lined with paper around the cakes.

Make Pineapple Whipped Cream. Allow to thicken slightly to prevent the pineapple from sinking to the bottom of the mixture. Spread it evenly on the four cakes. Place the second cake layers on top and press lightly to level. Refrigerate cakes until cream sets, about 2 hours.

Spread a ⅛-inch (3-mm) layer of whipped cream on the top and sides of each cake; place crushed almonds a third to a half of the way up the side.

Mark but do not cut the serving pieces. Mark a 3½-inch (8.5-cm) circle and a 7-inch (17.5-cm) circle on top of each cake. Using a no. 4 (8-mm) plain tip, pipe 2 circles of whipped cream on the marked circles. Fill the space between circles with finely diced (not crushed) pineapple. Using a paper tube, cover pineapple with Pectin or Apricot Glaze. Let glaze set completely before cutting.

Pipe a mound of whipped cream on the edge of each piece and decorate each mound with a small wedge of pineapple. Sprinkle a little shaved chocolate around the edge for contrast.

Egg Sand Cake
four 10-inch (25-cm) cakes

```
 8  ounces (225 g) egg yolks
 9  ounces (255 g) egg whites
 7  ounces (200 g) sugar
    pinch salt
    few drops lemon juice
 4  ounces (115 g) cake flour
 4  ounces (115 g) bread flour
3½  ounces (100 g) melted butter
```

Mix yolks, whites, sugar, salt, and lemon juice. Whip over hot water until the mixture is warm to the touch, 130° F (55° C). Remove from heat; continue whipping until cold and peaks are stiff. Sift flours and fold into the egg mixture. Fold in the butter. Divide among 4 prepared 10-inch (25-cm) cake pans. Bake immediately at 375° F (190° C) about 20 minutes.

Pineapple Whipped Cream

```
8½  ounces (240 g) egg yolks
11  ounces (310 g) sugar
 3  pints, 1 ounce (1 l, 4 dl, 7 cl) heavy cream
1⅙  ounces (35 g) unflavored gelatin
 5  ounces (1 dl, 5 cl) water
 6  ounces (1 dl, 8 cl) pineapple juice
 4  ounces (115 g) pineapple purée
 1  pound, 12 ounces (795 g) pineapple chunks
```

(If fresh pineapple is used, it must be blanched first because it contains the enzyme bromelain, which destroys the gelling ability of the gelatin. Bromelain is not present in canned or cooked pineapple.)

Whip eggs yolks and sugar to the ribbon stage. Whip heavy cream to soft peaks. Dissolve gelatin in water and add pineapple juice; heat to 150° F (65° C). Combine whipped cream and egg mixture. Place a small amount of this mixture into a separate bowl and rapidly add the gelatin. Work this into the remaining cream mixture. Stir in purée and chunks.

CARROT CAKE
four 10-inch (25-cm) cakes
color photograph, see front book jacket

> **Carrot Sponge (recipe follows)**
> **Cream-cheese Filling (recipe follows)**
> **crushed roasted hazelnuts**
> **Marzipan (see p. 255)**
> **red and yellow food colors**
> **slivered blanched pistachios, skinned**
> **powdered sugar**
> **melted dark chocolate**

Make Carrot Sponges and Cream-cheese filling. Trim the tops of the cakes level and split each one into 2 layers. Spread a 3/16-inch (5-mm) layer of filling on the bottom layers. Top with the top layers and coat the cakes with a thin layer of the filling. Put crushed hazelnuts on the sides. Roll out Marzipan 1/16 inch (2 mm) thick. Cut out circles to fit the tops of the cakes and place them on the cakes. Turn the cakes upside down onto pieces of cardboard and refrigerate.

To make Marzipan carrots for decoration: Color Marzipan orange using red and yellow food colors. Roll out to 1/4-inch (6-mm) strings and cut into 1-inch (25-mm) pieces. Cover the pieces you are not working with so that they stay moist. Work each piece in your hand, shaping into carrots 1 1/4 inches (30 mm) long. Mark them lightly with the blade of a paring knife to make them look slightly ringed, and make a small round opening at the top of each carrot. Place a small sliver of pistachio in the openings.

Turn the cakes right side up, and cut into the serving pieces. Sift powdered sugar very lightly on the tops. Pipe a dot of chocolate the size of a dime in the middle of the outside edge of each serving. Place a carrot on top before the chocolate hardens.

Carrot Sponge
four 10-inch (25-cm) cakes

16 eggs (800 g)
3 cups (7 dl, 2 cl) oil
3 pounds, 8 ounces (1 kg, 590 g) sugar
2 teaspoons (7 g) salt
2 pounds, 4 ounces (1 kg, 25 g) bread flour
1 ounce (30 g) ground cinnamon
1 tablespoon (12 g) baking soda
1 teaspoon (2 g) baking powder
4 pounds (1 k, 820 g) peeled carrots, grated finely
10 ounces (285 g) chopped walnuts

Whip the eggs to the ribbon stage; beat in oil gradually. Adjust mixer speed to low, and mix in the sugar and salt. Sift together the remaining dry ingredients and add to the egg mixture. Fold in the carrots and walnuts. Do not overmix. Divide the batter among 4 greased and floured 10-inch (25-cm) cake pans. Bake at 375° F (190° C) about 55 minutes.

Cream-cheese Filling

7½ ounces (215 g) butter, softened
1 pound, 14 ounces (855 g) cream cheese
1 pound, 2 ounces (520 g) powdered sugar
vanilla extract

Mix butter into cream cheese slowly. Cream until smooth but do not overmix. Stir in sifted powdered sugar and vanilla to taste.

SOFT GINGERBREAD CAKE
six 15-ounce (430 g) cakes   photograph, p. 139

1 pound, 9 ounces (710 g) brown sugar
8 eggs (400 g)
1 pound, 9 ounces (710 g) bread flour
1⅓ ounces (40 g) baking powder
1 ounce (30 g) ground cinnamon
1 tablespoon (7 g) ground ginger
1 tablespoon (7 g) ground cloves
1 tablespoon (4 g) ground cardamon
pinch salt
1 pound, 2 ounces (510 g) butter
14 ounces (4 dl, 2 cl) light cream, lukewarm
powdered sugar

Beat brown sugar and eggs thoroughly. Sift all dry ingredients and mix into sugar mixture. Melt the butter and stir into the cream; then carefully stir into the batter. Coat 6 fluted rectangular forms with a mixture of 4 parts melted butter and 1 part flour. Divide the batter among them, using 15 ounces (430 g) of batter for each cake. Bake at 350° F (175° C) about 45 minutes. Unmold cakes while still warm.

When cakes have cooled, place a template 1 inch (25 mm) down the length of the cake; dust each cake lightly with powdered sugar and remove the template.

This cake, as is true of many coffee cakes, gets moister if kept refrigerated for a day or two.

GERMAN POPPY-SEED CAKE
four 10-inch (25-cm) cakes   color photograph, p. C-2

> 1½ pounds (680 g) butter
> 3 pounds (1 kg, 365 g) sugar
> 12 ounces (340 g) bread flour
> 12 ounces (340 g) cake flour
> 3 tablespoons (21 g) baking powder
> 1 pound, 2 ounces (510 g) poppy seeds
> 2 pints (9 dl, 6 cl) milk, room temperature
> 1 pint (4 dl, 8 cl) egg whites
>   whipped cream
>   strawberries, thinly sliced
>   crushed roasted almonds
>   dark chocolate

Cream butter and half the sugar until light and fluffy. Sift flours and baking powder together; mix in poppy seeds. Fold dry ingredients alternately with milk into the butter mixture, starting and finishing with the dry ingredients. The milk should not be above room temperature or it will soften the batter, causing the poppy seeds to sink to the bottom of the sponge. Whip egg whites and remaining sugar to soft peaks; fold carefully into the poppy-seed mixture. Divide batter among 4 buttered and floured 10-inch (25-cm) cake pans. Bake at 350° F (175° C) until cake springs back when lightly pressed, about 45 minutes.

Cut tops of sponge cakes even and slice in half. Spread ⅛ inch (3 mm) whipped cream on the bottom layer and arrange thinly sliced strawberries on top of the cream. Spread another ⅛ inch (3 mm) whipped cream on the strawberries and place the top layers on the cream. Ice the cakes with whipped cream just thick enough to cover the sponge. Put crushed almonds on the sides.

Mark or cut into serving pieces, and decorate with whipped-cream rosettes, strawberry wedges, and dark chocolate shavings.

CHEESECAKE

6 regular or 8 buffet-size cheesecakes
photograph, p. 139

> 1 pound, 3 ounces (540 g) graham cracker crumbs
> 8 ounces (225 g) melted butter
> 10 pounds, 5 ounces (4 kg, 690 g) cream cheese
> 20 eggs
> 3 pounds, 1 ounce (1 kg, 395 g) sugar
> 9 pounds (4 kg, 95 g) sour cream
> 1 pound, 5 ounces (595 g) sugar
> Flavorings (procedures to follow)

Mix graham-cracker crumbs with just enough of the melted butter to hold the crumbs together. Divide the crumbs among springform pans and pat them evenly on the bottoms.

The cream cheese should soften overnight at room temperature. In a large mixer fitted with a paddle, mix the cheese on low speed just until smooth. Mix the eggs and 3 pounds, 1 ounce (1 kg, 395 g) sugar together lightly by hand, and mix gradually into the cream cheese, scraping the sides frequently. Do not overmix. Divide the mixture among the prepared pans, and spread it evenly. Bake at 375° F (190° C) just until done, about 30 minutes. The cakes become firmer as they cool. An overbaked cake will be dry. Let cool at least 20 minutes.

Mix the sour cream and 1 pound, 3 ounces (540 g) sugar and divide it equally among the cakes. Pipe on flavoring in a spiral pattern. Pull the back of a knife through the spirals, from inside to outside. Bake at 375° F (190° C) to set the sour cream, about 5 minutes.

Lingonberry Topping
Lingonberries are a quite expensive Scandinavian delicacy that look a lot like small cranberries but taste different. They are available as jam in most delicatessens. Pipe lingonberry jam with a no. 4 (8-mm) plain tip.

Ganache
Pipe Ganache (see Index) using a no. 3 (6-mm) plain tip after the sour cream is baked.

Cappuccino
Remove about 1 cup (2 dl, 4 cl) of the sour cream before it is spread on

the cheesecakes, mix it with very strong coffee or mocha paste (see Index), and pipe out in a spiral pattern.

Lemon Curd
Add a little sour cream to Lemon Curd (see Index) for body, and pipe with a no. 3 (6-mm) plain tip.

APRICOT CREAM CAKE
four 10-inch (25-cm) cakes   photograph, p. 140

> four 10-inch (25-cm) short-dough bottoms (see p. 17)
> Almond Butter Cake (see p. 118)
> 8 ounces (225 g) soft Apricot Jam (see p. 238)
> Apricot Whipped Cream (recipe follows)
> 1 pound (445 g) whipped cream
> crushed roasted almonds
> cocoa powder
> Vanilla Buttons (recipe follows)

Make short-dough bottoms and Almond Butter Cake. Let them cool. Cut cakes into 2 layers each. Spread jam on short-dough bottoms and top each with an almond layer. Place an adjustable cake ring lined with parchment paper around each cake. Fill with Apricot Whipped Cream; place the second almond layer on top and refrigerate overnight to set the cream.

Spread cakes with whipped cream, ⅛ inch (3 mm) thick on top and thinner on the sides. Save some cream for decorating the cakes. Cover the sides with crushed almonds. Place a 6-inch (15-cm) template on top of each cake, and sift on cocoa powder to cover the center. Mark or cut the cakes into serving pieces. Using a plain tip, pipe a whipped cream mound at the edge of each piece. Decorate each mound with a Vanilla Button to look like an apricot half.

Apricot Whipped Cream
> 7 ounces (200 g) egg yolks
> 11 ounces (310 g) sugar
> 3 pints, 1 ounce (1 l, 4 dl, 7 cl) heavy cream
> 1⅓ ounces (40 g) unflavored gelatin
> 1 cup (2 dl, 4 cl) hot water
> 10 ounces (3 dl) Cointreau
> 4 ounces (1 dl, 2 cl) apricot juice
> 4 ounces (115 g) apricot purée
> 2 pounds, 3 ounces (1 k) apricot chunks

Whip egg yolks with sugar to ribbon stage. Whip the cream to soft peaks; fold into egg yolk mixture. Dissolve gelatin in water, and add Cointreau and apricot juice; heat to 150° F (65° C). Gradually add this mixture to a small part of the cream mixture, beating rapidly. Add to remaining cream mixture. Stir in apricot purée and chunks. Allow to thicken slightly before using to prevent apricot chunks from sinking to the bottom.

Vanilla Buttons

    3½ ounces (100 g) whole eggs
      3 ounces (85 g) sugar
      3 ounces (85 g) bread flour
      3 drops vanilla extract
        Apricot Glaze (see p. 239)

Whip eggs and sugar over hot water to 125° F (52° C). Remove from heat; continue whipping until cooled. Fold in bread flour and vanilla. Using a small plain tip, pipe out small buttons the size of a quarters on sheet pans. Let dry 1 hour; then bake at 400° F (205° C) about 10 minutes. When cooled, glaze only the buttons that will be used immediately by dipping them into Apricot Glaze.

HAZELNUT SURPRISE
30 servings

    ½ recipe Spongecake II (see p. 93)
      Hazelnut Nougat Cream (recipe follows)
  4½ ounces (130 g) Apricot Jam (see p. 238)
    ½ recipe Pâte à Choux (see p. 47)
    8 ounces (225 g) whipped cream
      powdered sugar

Make the batter for Spongecake II and spread it evenly on a half-sheet pan, 16 × 12 inches (40 × 30 cm). Bake at 400° F (205° C) about 10 minutes. Make Hazelnut Nougat Cream. Spread a thin layer of soft jam on the spongecake. Spread hazelnut cream evenly over the jam. Refrigerate until set, at least 1 hour.

In the meantime, draw a 1-inch (25-mm) diamond pattern the same size as the spongecake on parchment paper. Turn the paper over. Make batter for Pâte à Choux, but leave out 2 eggs for a slightly stiffer batter. With a no. 3 (6-mm) star tip, pipe out the *choux* paste following the lines. Bake at

400° F (205° C) until golden brown and dry enough to hold its shape, about 12 minutes.

Spread a ¼-inch (6-mm) layer of whipped cream on top of the hazelnut cream. Place the Pâte à Choux screen on top. Cut into rectangles 3 × 2 inches (7.5 × 5 cm) with a sharp knife, holding the knife at a 90° angle. Dust the top lightly with powdered sugar and serve.

Hazelnut Nougat Cream

    3 pints (1 l, 4 dl, 4 cl) heavy cream
    7 ounces (200 g) hazelnut paste (see p. 8)
10 ounces (285 g) Pastry Cream (see p. 242)
    ½ ounce (15 g) gelatin
    4 ounces (1 dl, 2 cl) water

Whip the cream to stiff peaks and set aside. Combine hazelnut paste with the Pastry Cream. Dissolve the gelatin in water, and heat to about 150° F (65° C). Add rapidly to the pastry cream mixture. Finely incorporate the whipped cream.

Swedish Chocolate Cake

Gâteau Malakoff

Chocolate Hazelnut Cake

Gâteau Moka Carrousel

Sicilian Macaroon Cake

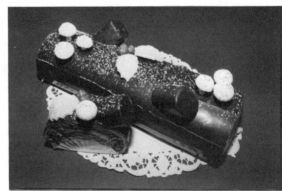

Bûche de Noël

Whiskey-Coffee Cake

Lemon Chiffon Cake

Princess Cake

Gâteau au Diplomate

Praline Cake with Rum

Raspberry Cake

Strawberry-Kirsch Cake

Sacher Torte

Reine de Saba

Gugelhupf (Direct Method)

Chocolate Crisp Cake

Raisin Cake

Sand Cake

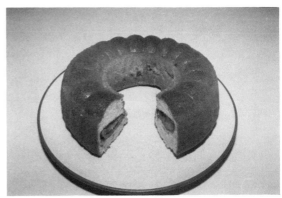

Apple Cake

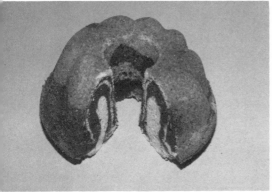

Tiger Cake

Hawaiian Pineapple Cake

Soft Gingerbread Cake

Cheesecake

Apricot Cream Cake

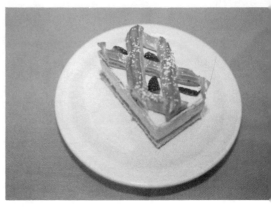

Hazelnut Surprise

5

Meringues

By *meringue,* I mean egg whites whipped fast with sugar, which also incorporates air, to make soft or stiff peaks. Egg whites whipped without sugar until stiff are not a meringue but simply whipped egg whites. Meringue whipped to a soft peak will not hold its shape but slowly settles or falls instead. Meringue whipped to a stiff peak will simply not move. Be careful: There is a fine line between stiff peaks and overwhipped, or dry, peaks. Meringue that is dry is hard to pipe out into any precise shape and impossible to mix into a batter without getting small lumps of meringue throughout the batter.

If you take the following precautions when making meringue, you should have no problems with the recipes in this chapter.

Do not use egg whites for meringue that are not clean and free of any egg yolk or fat particles.

Be sure that the whites are not so old that they have started to deteriorate and get cloudy.

Cold egg whites are preferable but not essential for making a good meringue.

Make sure that the sugar and tools are clean.

A copper bowl and balloon whip are useful, though not essential, tools for making meringue.

In this chapter there are two basic types of meringue. The cold method, also called French Meringue, is easier and more commonly used. The warm method, Italian Meringue, is a bit more complicated. The French Meringue is best for baking *au naturel,* mixing with nuts, and for the bottoms of cakes and desserts. It will, if made and baked correctly, be very soft, light, and fragile. French Meringue should not be held for more than ten minutes before baking to prevent the egg whites from separating from the sugar. Italian Meringue is a better choice if the meringue has to stand for some

142

time or is served almost raw, as in baked alaska or lemon meringue pie; it will keep for several hours, even overnight, if properly made and refrigerated. It is also used for buttercreams and combined with other nonbaked desserts. It is denser, because of the partially cooked egg whites, and so holds up longer in raw form. Italian Meringue will be harder and not as tender as the French type if baked. Always store baked meringue in a warm, dry place. Plain meringue will keep for weeks if stored this way, but not if nuts have been added, which will get rancid.

FRENCH MERINGUE

    1 **pound (455 g) egg whites (1 pint, 4 dl, 8 cl)**
    3 **drops lemon juice or tartaric acid**
1½ to 2 **pounds (680 to 910 g) granulated sugar**

Whip the whites and lemon juice or tartaric acid to a foam; then add the sugar very slowly (3 to 4 minutes), whipping at high speed. Whip until peaks are stiff but not dry.

If you use a copper bowl to whip the meringue, you can omit the lemon juice or acid. The meringue will be smoother and stiffer if you use the full amount of sugar, but, if you lack experience, use the smaller amount. The less weight added to the egg whites, the easier it is to beat them to stiff peaks.

ITALIAN MERINGUE

1½ **pounds (680 g) sugar**
  8 **ounces (225 g) light corn syrup**
  1 **cup (2 dl, 4 cl) water**
  1 **pound (455 g) egg whites (1 pint, 4 dl, 8 cl)**

Boil sugar, corn syrup, and water to 230° F (110° C). Start whipping egg whites when the sugar has reached 220° F (105° C). (If you do not have a sugar thermometer you will come close enough if you boil the syrup for 10 minutes; start whipping the egg whites when the sugar has boiled for 7 minutes.) Pour syrup in a thin steady stream into the whites, whipping at high speed. Whip until cooled.

MOCHA MERINGUES

about 90 pastries   color photograph, p. C-3

> French Meringue (recipe precedes)
> 3 pounds (1 kg, 365 g) Buttercream (see p. 239)
> mocha paste or strong coffee
> crushed roasted almonds
> Chocolate Cigars (see p. 246)
> powdered sugar

Make French Meringue. Using a no. 8 (16-mm) plain tip, pipe out meringues into 1¾-inch (45-mm) domes on parchment paper. Make sure the tops are flat. Bake at 250° F (120° C) until slightly puffed, about 5 minutes. Lower the heat immediately to 200° F (90° C); open the oven door for a few minutes. Let meringues dry at this temperature until done, 3 to 4 hours. These meringues can be made up weeks in advance if they are kept covered in a warm place.

Flavor Buttercream with mocha paste or with strong coffee (10 times normal strength) to taste. Line up meringues on a sheet pan. Using a no. 5 (10-mm) plain tip, pipe a mound of Buttercream on half the meringues. Place the remaining meringues on top and press lightly to center and level the top. Spread a thin layer of Buttercream on the sides and roll them in crushed almonds.

Using a no. 2 (4-mm) plain tip, pipe a pattern of parallel lines with the remaining Buttercream to cover the top of the meringue. Roll out Chocolate Cigars to fit on the meringues; place 2 crosswise on top of the Buttercream. Line up 6 to 8 meringues, cover the centers with a ¾-inch-wide (20-mm) strip of cardboard, and sift powdered sugar on top. If you do not have time to make Chocolate Cigars, substitute small Chocolate Rectangles (see Index).

MERINGUES GLACÉS CHANTILLY

about 50   photograph, p. 156

> Vanilla Ice Cream (see p. 220)
> French Meringue (recipe precedes)
> melted dark chocolate
> whipped cream
> strawberries

Make Vanilla Ice Cream, preferably the day before serving the meringues. Make French Meringue also the day before serving if possible. Using a no. 6 (12-mm) star tip, pipe the meringue out into cone shapes, about 4 inches (10 cm) high, on parchment paper. Bake at 250° F (120° C) oven until slightly puffed, 4 or 5 minutes; lower the heat to about 200° F (90° C), and continue drying meringues 3 to 4 hours. When meringues are dry and cooled, dip each pointed end diagonally into melted chocolate to cover half the meringue. You need 2 meringues for each serving.

Put a scoop of ice cream into each chilled champagne glass, and put 2 meringue shells on opposite sides of the ice cream with the points meeting in the middle. Using a no. 6 (12-mm) star tip, pipe whipped cream in the same shape as the meringues on the other two sides. Place the 2 thin strawberry wedges on the whipped cream. Serve immediately.

MERINGUE BASKETS WITH RASPBERRIES

45 to 50 baskets   *photograph, p. 156*

> ½ recipe French Meringue (see p. 143)
> melted dark chocolate
> Short Dough (see p. 19)
> whipped cream flavored with strawberry jam or crushed fresh
>   raspberries
> whole strawberries or raspberries
> Simple Syrup (see p. 233)

Cut paper into cones of the desired size. Grease the outside surface of each cone twice and place upside down on baking sheets.

Make French Meringue, which must be very firm. Using a no. 4 (8-mm) plain tip, pipe meringue around the cones, following the shape of the paper cone almost to the top. Bake at 250° F (120° C) until slightly puffed, about 5 minutes. Lower the heat and let dry at about 200° F (90° C) for 4 hours. Carefully remove the cones, loosening them with a small knife. Cut the cones flat on the narrow end, so that they will stand up straight. Dip each wide rim into melted dark chocolate; coat the inside thoroughly with chocolate, making sure there is a solid layer in the bottoms of the baskets.

Cut out and bake fluted short-dough cookies, about 1½ inches (35 mm) in diameter and ⅛ inch (3 mm) thick. Dip each cookie into chocolate, and, before the chocolate sets, fasten the basket to the cookie base.

No more than 2 hours before they are served, fill the baskets with the flavored softly whipped cream. Cover the top with fresh berries. Pipe out basket handles of chocolate thickened with Simple Syrup and place in the cream.

MERINGUE LANDECK

15 servings, one 24-inch (60-cm) strip   color photograph, p. C-3

> French Meringue (see p. 143)
> Ladyfingers (see p. 158)
> granulated sugar
> ½ recipe Spongecake I (see p. 92)
> 1¾ pints (8 dl, 4 cl) softly whipped cream
> mocha paste or strong coffee
> ¼ ounce (8 g) unflavored gelatin
> 1 ounce (3 cl) water
> 3 ounces (85 g) Apricot Jam (see p. 238)
> melted dark chocolate
> powdered sugar
> Marzipan Rose (see p. 253)

Make French Meringue. Using a no. 8 (16-mm) plain tip, pipe out lines of meringue on parchment paper the full length of a 16- × 24-inch (40- × 60-cm) sheet pan. Bake at 250° F (120° C) until slightly puffed, 2 or 3 minutes. Turn off the oven and open the oven door to cool it quickly to about 200° F (90° C). Close the door except for a small opening, and let the meringues dry 3 to 4 hours.

Make the batter for Ladyfingers, and pipe out 4 lines on parchment paper to the same size as the meringue. Sprinkle with granulated sugar; holding the paper, shake off excess sugar. Bake immediately at 425° F (220° C) until golden brown, about 12 minutes. You may need to use a second pan underneath the first.

Make the batter for Spongecake I, and spread it out on a sheet pan. Bake the spongecake. When cake is cool, cut out one strip, 4 inches (10 cm) wide and the length of the pan.

Flavor whipped cream to taste with mocha paste or strong coffee (10 times normal strength). Reserve about 4 ounces (115 g) for decorating.

Dissolve gelatin in water; heat to 150° F (65° C). Mix with a small amount of the whipped cream; then incorporate the remaining whipped cream. Spread Apricot Jam on the spongecake, and line with 1 strip meringue, 1 strip Ladyfinger, and 1 strip meringue. Spread a ¼-inch (6-mm) layer of flavored whipped cream on top. Place 2 strips ladyfinger and 1 strip of meringue with the meringue in the middle on the whipped cream. Spread the remaining flavored whipped cream on the top and sides of the strip. Finally, top with a layer of 2 strips meringue, coated with dark chocolate for contrast, and 1 strip ladyfinger. Refrigerate until cream is set.

Slice strip into 1½-inch (37-mm) pieces. Dust pieces lightly with powdered sugar. Pipe a small mound of the reserved whipped cream on each serving, and place a Marzipan Rose on the cream.

Chocolate Flavor
Follow above recipe but omit gelatin and mocha flavoring. Add 1 ounce (30 g) cocoa powder, 1 ounce (3 cl) water, and 1 ounce (3 cl) Simple Syrup (p. 233) to a small amount of the whipped cream. Mix well and incorporate into the remaining cream.

JAPONAISE BATTER

> 10 ounces (285 g) blanched almonds
> 14 ounces (400 g) granulated sugar
> ½ ounce (15 g) cornstarch
> 9 ounces (2 dl, 7 cl) egg whites

Prepare sheet pans, pastry bag, template, if you are using one, and heat oven to 275° to 300° F (135° to 150° C). Grind the almonds very finely with half the sugar and all the cornstarch. Whip the egg whites and remaining sugar to stiff peaks. Fold dry ingredients carefully into egg whites by hand; and pipe or spread out immediately.

JAPONAISE
about 35   *photograph, p. 156*

> Japonaise Batter (recipe precedes)
> Buttercream (see p. 239)
> hazelnut paste (see p. 8)
> melted dark chocolate or Fondant (see p. 249)

With a heavy pen, draw 2¼-inch (6-cm) circles, 1 inch (25 mm) apart, on parchment paper. Fasten the pattern to the table with a dab of batter in each corner. Place another parchment paper over the pattern. Make Japonaise Batter. Using a no. 4 (8-mm) plain tip, pipe batter into circles following the pattern under the parchment paper. Drag the filled paper onto a sheet pan and repeat. (Another way to make the circles is to count the number of turns you make as you pipe.) Bake immediately at 275° to 300° F (135° to 150° C) until meringues are completely dry, about 30 minutes. Make sure the oven is not too hot to keep the Japonaise from rising too much, making the shells very hard to work with.

When shells have cooled, set aside about 1 dozen of the worst-looking shells. Trim any remaining shells that are too big or unshapely so that all the shells are about the same size. Flavor Buttercream with hazelnut paste. Using a no. 4 (8-mm) plain tip, pipe Buttercream ¼ inch (6 mm) thick on half the remaining shells. Place the top shell on the Buttercream, pressing slightly to make sure the 2 shells are even. Refrigerate until cold.

Meanwhile, crush the dozen shells you set aside and any shavings from the others into very fine crumbs. When the shells are firm, spread a thin layer of Buttercream on the side and top of each shell. If the shells are the same size, you can spread Buttercream on the sides of 2 at the same time by holding them on top of each other; then separate them and spread Buttercream on the tops individually. Roll the shells in meringue crumbs; shake off any excess. Pipe a small dot of dark chocolate or light pink Fondant on each top.

GÂTEAU ARABE
four 10-inch (25-cm) cakes   *photograph, p. 156*

> Meringue Noisette (recipe follows)
> 1½ recipes Biscuit au Chocolat (see p. 94)
> 4½ pounds (2 kg, 45 g) Buttercream (see p. 239)
> strong coffee or mocha paste
> currant jelly
> roasted almonds, lightly crushed
> Chocolate Rounds (see p. 245)
> Simple Syrup (see p. 233)
> melted light chocolate

Make the Meringue Noisette and let them dry. Make the batter for Biscuit au Chocolat; divide it among four 10-inch (25-cm) pans, and bake the layers. Flavor the Buttercream to taste with strong coffee (10 times normal strength) or with mocha paste.

Cut the skin off the chocolate layers and slice into 2 layers. Spread a thin layer of jelly on the bottom layer, and cover with a meringue bottom. Spread a 1/8-inch (3-mm) layer of flavored Buttercream on each meringue bottom, and cover with the second meringue bottom. Top with another layer of Buttercream, and place the second chocolate layer on top. Spread the tops and sides with a thin layer of Buttercream. Place a 6-inch (15-cm) round template in the middle of each cake and cover the tops and sides with almonds. Refrigerate.

Make a Chocolate Round for each cake serving. Add a few drops of Simple Syrup to the chocolate to thicken it, and pipe the letter "A" on each round.

Mark or cut the cakes into serving pieces of the desired size. Using a no. 2 (4-mm) plain tip, pipe 2 straight lines of Buttercream in the middle of each slice. Place a Chocolate Round on top at the edge of each slice.

Meringue Noisette
eight 10-inch (25-cm) layers

> 14 ounces (400 g) egg whites
> 14 ounces (400 g) granulated sugar
> 14 ounces (400 g) powdered sugar, sifted
> 3 ounces (85 g) cornstarch, sifted
> 5⅔ ounces (160 g) roasted hazelnuts, skins removed, finely ground

Draw eight 10-inch (25-cm) circles on 3 sheets of parchment paper that fit full 16- × 24-inch (40- × 60-cm) sheet pans. Turn the paper over, so that the lead or ink does not touch the meringues, and place on sheet pans. Whip egg whites and granulated sugar to stiff peaks. Mix powdered sugar, cornstarch, and ground hazelnuts, and carefully fold by hand into the meringue. Using a no. 3 (6-mm) plain tip, pipe meringue in a 1-inch (25-mm) frame on each circle. Divide the remaining meringue evenly among the 8 frames and spread evenly with a spatula. Bake meringues at 200° to 225° F (90° to 105° C) until dry, 40 minutes.

VACHERIN À LA VANILLE

20 servings   *color photograph, p. C-3*

> ½ recipe French Meringue (see p. 143)
> melted dark chocolate
> Vanilla Ice Cream (see p. 220), softened
> whipped cream
> strawberries or other fresh fruit
> candied violets

Make French Meringue, and pipe out 3-inch (7½-cm) filled circles using a no. 4 (8-mm) plain tip. (See method for Japonaise shells.) Pipe 2 circles on top of each other at the edge of the meringue circle so that they look like 3 rings on top of each other from the outside. Bake at 250° F (120° C) until slightly puffed, about 4 to 5 minutes. Turn off the heat and open the door long enough to reduce the heat to 200° F (90° C). Bake at 200° F (90° C) until completely dry, preferably overnight but at least 4 hours.

Brush chocolate on the rims. At serving time, fill the meringue case almost to the top with soft ice cream. Pipe a lattice of whipped cream on top, and decorate with strawberries, chocolate, and candied violets. Serve immediately.

CHOCOLATE MERINGUE CREAM CAKE

four 10-inch (25-cm) cakes

> Chocolate Sponge II (see p. 94)
> Meringue Noisette II (recipe follows)
> melted dark chocolate
> Chocolate Whipped Cream (recipe follows)
> whipped cream
> shaved dark chocolate
> cocoa powder
> Chocolate Squares (see p. 245)
> maraschino cherry halves

Bake Chocolate Sponge II and Meringue Noisette II. Cut each spongecake into four ½-inch-thick (13-mm) layers. Place each layer on a cardboard circle and set aside. Brush the meringue bottoms with a thin layer of chocolate on both sides.

Make the Chocolate Whipped Cream and spread half on the spongecakes. Place a meringue bottom firmly on the cream and spread with remaining cream. Place the second meringue bottom on the cream and press down firmly and evenly. Freeze covered 3 to 4 hours or, preferably, overnight.

To finish, cut the meringue clean on the sides and spread a ⅛-inch (3-mm) layer of whipped cream on the tops and sides. When the cake is half thawed, cut into serving pieces. Using a no. 5 or 8 (10- or 16-mm) star tip, depending on the size of the piece, pipe a rosette of whipped cream at the edge of each slice. Shave dark chocolate over the center of the cake, inside the rosette, and sift cocoa powder lightly over the whole cake. Finally, place a Chocolate Square on the side of each piece, and decorate each rosette with a cherry half.

Meringue Noisette II
eight 10-inch (25-cm) layers

> 18 ounces (5 dl, 4 cl) egg whites
> 1 pound, 10 ounces (740 g) sugar
> 2½ ounces (70 g) cornstarch
> 8 ounces (225 g) hazelnuts, skins removed, finely ground
> 1 teaspoon (6 g) vanilla extract

Whip egg whites to a foam; gradually beat in sugar, taking 3 to 4 minutes to do so. Mix cornstarch and hazelnuts; carefully fold nut mixture and vanilla in the meringue by hand. Draw eight 10-inch (25-cm) circles on 4 full sheet papers, turn them upside down, and using a no. 3 (6-mm) plain tip, pipe a 1-inch (25-mm) meringue frame on each of eight 10-inch (25-cm) circles drawn by hand on parchment paper. Divide remaining meringue evenly among the 8 circles and spread it out evenly. Bake at 250° to 275° F (120° to 135° C) until dry, about 1 hour.

Chocolate Whipped Cream

> 3½ pints (1 l, 6 dl, 8 cl) heavy cream
> 1 pound (455 g) dark chocolate, melted
> 6 ounces (1 dl, 8 cl) water
> 2 ounces (6 cl) Kirschwasser

Whip the cream to the consistency of a thick sauce; do not overwhip as this may cause the cream to break up when the chocolate mixture is added. Mix melted chocolate with water and Kirschwasser, and heat to 150° F (65° C). Place a small amount of the cream in a bowl. Add the chocolate mixture gradually while mixing rapidly. Combine with the rest of the cream. If the mixture does not have stiff peaks, work it a little longer until it does.

MARJOLAINE
35 servings   *photograph, p. 156*

   ⅓ **recipe Spongecake I (see p. 92)**
      Nut Meringue (recipe follows)
      Praline Buttercream (recipe follows)
      Light Chocolate Cream (recipe follows)
   2 **pounds, 2 ounces (1 l, 2 cl) whipping cream**
   ⅙ **ounce (5 g) unflavored gelatin**
   1 **ounce (3 cl) water**
   1 **drop vanilla extract**
   1 **pound, 6 ounces (625 g) Ganache (see p. 247)**
      cocoa powder

This fabulous dessert is worth all the trouble it takes to make. It is the best-known recipe of the famous late French chef, Fernand Point, owner of the 3-star La Pyramide. Exactly why he picked this name I do not know, but it could have something to do with a special lady who liked chocolate. Marjolaine is a girl's name in France. The original recipe, of course, has been changed (possibly improved) over the years to suit each chef's taste. Here is my version—enjoy!

Make spongecake and spread the batter evenly on a a half-sheet pan. Bake immediately at 400° F (205° C) about 10 minutes. Make Nut Meringue, Praline Buttercream, and Light Chocolate Cream.

Whip the whipping cream to soft peaks. Dissolve gelatin in water, and heat to 150° F (65° C). Mix into a small amount of the cream before mixing it in with the rest.

Cut the 2 meringue sheets in half to make 4 meringue layers, 16 × 12 inches (40 × 30 cm) each. Do not separate the meringue from the paper at this time.

Spread 14 ounces (400 g) Ganache on top of the spongecake. Pick up the first meringue layer by the paper, invert it on the Ganache, and peel off the paper. Spread on Light Chocolate Cream. Add the second meringue layer and spread with Praline Buttercream. Add the third meringue layer and spread with whipped cream. Add the last meringue layer. Place a sheet pan on top and press lightly to level the top. Warm the remaining Ganache until runny, and spread it thinly on top. Before the Ganache sets completely, mark a diamond pattern on it with the back of a knife. Dust lightly with cocoa powder. Refrigerate cake until thoroughly cold and gelatin is set, about 2 hours.

Using a sharp knife dipped in hot water, cut about ¼ inch (6 mm) off 2 sides; mark into 2¼-inch (5.7-cm) square pieces; then, starting from clean, cut sides, cut the pieces, holding the knife at a 90° angle. This cake will keep for several days in the refrigerator if the sides are covered to keep them from drying out.

Nut Meringue

        12 ounces (340 g) roasted almonds
         8 ounces (225 g) hazelnuts
         1 ounce (30 g) flour
           pinch salt
         1 pound (455 g) egg whites
        11 ounces (310 g) sugar

Grind nuts until fine; mix with flour and salt. Whip whites and sugar as directed for French Meringue. Fold in dry ingredients by hand. Divide evenly between 2 paper-lined sheet pans, 24 × 16 inches (60 × 40 cm). Bake immediately at 375° F (190° C) about 10 minutes.

Praline Buttercream

        20 ounces (570 g) Buttercream (see p. 239)
        1½ ounces (40 g) hazelnut paste (see p. 8)
         2 tablespoons (8 g) espresso coffee
         1 ounce (3 cl) hot water
         1 ounce (30 g) ground roasted hazelnuts.

Mix Buttercream, hazelnut paste, espresso coffee dissolved in hot water, and the hazelnuts until the Buttercream has a smooth consistency.

Light Chocolate Cream

         3 cups (7 dl, 2 cl) heavy cream
         5 ounces (140 g) dark chocolate, melted
        2½ ounces (7.5 cl) water

Whip cream to the consistency of a thick sauce. Be careful not to overwhip, or the cream will break up later when the chocolate is added. Mix the melted chocolate and water; heat to 130° F (55° C). Place a small amount of the cream in a bowl. Add the chocolate mixture, working rapidly; mix in with the remaining cream. If the cream seems too runny to hold its shape when spread, whip until it has a firmer consistency.

RASPBERRY MOUSSE WITH MERINGUES
about 20 servings

> 6 ounces (1 dl, 8 cl) egg whites
> 8 ounces (225 g) sugar
> 3 ounces (85 g) ground roasted hazelnuts
> Raspberry Mousse (recipe follows)
> whipped cream
> fresh raspberries

Whip egg whites and sugar as directed for French Meringue. Fold in hazelnuts by hand. Using a pastry bag fitted with a no. 3 (6-mm) plain tip, pipe meringue in 3-inch (7.5-cm) circles on parchment paper placed over a pattern paper, keeping the circles within the markings. The circles should fit into individual soufflé ramekins. Bake at 250° F (120° C) until the meringue starts to increase in volume, several minutes. Open the door only a little to lower the temperature to approximately 200° F (90° C). Let dry at 200° F (90° C) about 2 hours.

Make Raspberry Mousse.

These desserts should be completed just before they are served. Unmold the mousse by quickly warming the ramekins in hot water, using a fork to pick the mousse out of the form. Place one meringue shell on a chilled plate, put the mousse on top, and top with a second meringue shell. Using a no. 4 (8-mm) star tip, pipe small dots of whipped cream in a border on the top shell. Hold a no. 3 (6-mm) plain tip over the larger one, and pipe a second border on the plate around the bottom shell. Place fresh raspberries on top in the middle. Serve immediately.

Raspberry Mousse

> 1 pound (455 g) fresh raspberries
> 10 ounces (285 g) egg whites
> pinch salt
> few drops tartaric acid
> 18 ounces (510 g) sugar
> 2½ cups (6 dl) whipping cream
> 3 ounces (9 cl) framboise

Purée and strain raspberries. Whip egg whites, salt, and tartaric acid for about 1 minute, to a thick foam; gradually fold in sugar. Whip to stiff peaks. Whip cream to soft peaks and mix in framboise. Fold cream into meringue and fold in the raspberry purée. Pipe into 3-inch (7.5-cm) ramekins to about ¼ inch (6 mm) from the top. Freeze until hard, at least two hours.

Meringues Glacés Chantilly

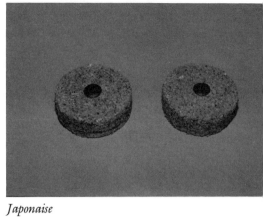

Japonaise

Meringue Baskets with Raspberries

Gâteau Arabe

Marjolaine

Cookies and Small Cakes

LADYFINGERS

about 250 cookies

> 6 ounces (170 g) sugar
> 6 ounces (170 g) cornstarch
> 13 egg whites
> 12 egg yolks
> 5 ounces (140 g) bread flour
> granulated sugar

Before starting the recipe, have ready a pastry bag with a no. 3 (6-mm) plain tip, sugar to sprinkle on top, 3 sheet pans lined with parchment paper, and an oven heated to 425° F (220° C). Draw 4 pairs of heavy lines spaced 2 inches (5 cm) apart the length of the parchment paper. Turn the papers over on the sheet pans.

Mix sugar and cornstarch; add half to the egg whites. Whip at full speed until foamy; gradually beat in the remaining sugar mixture. Whip yolks by hand until creamy. When the peaks on the meringue are stiff but not dry, blend a small amount of it into the yolks; then fold in the remaining meringue carefully by hand. Fold in sifted flour.

Immediately pipe out on the prepared sheet pans 2 inches (5 cm) long or other appropriate size. Sprinkle with sugar. Pick up each sheet pan, and, holding onto the corner of the paper, carefully shake off the excess sugar. Bake until golden brown, about 10 minutes.

MACAROON PASTE I

about sixty 2-inch (5-cm) cookies

> 2 pounds (910 g) almond paste
> 1 pound (455 g) granulated sugar
> 9 to 10 ounces (2 dl, 7 cl to 3 dl) egg whites

This paste is frequently used as a base for small pastries, but it can also be baked as cookies. Place almond paste and sugar in a mixing bowl; beat in egg whites, one at a time, until creamy and loose but not so loose that it runs when it is piped out. The amount of egg whites you will need depends upon the firmness of the almond paste. Pipe out the cookies, using a no. 8 (16-mm) plain tip, into 2-inch (5-cm) circles, 1 inch (25 mm) apart. This type of macaroon paste should be baked as soon as possible after it has been piped out to prevent a skin from forming. Bake immediately double panned at 410° F (210° C) about 12 minutes.

When macaroons have cooled, they can be frozen. Place them still attached to their papers, on top of each other to save space. Cover them and take them out as needed; they will peel right off the paper. If you must use them immediately, brush the back of the paper with water to eliminate sticking; wait a few minutes and peel off the macaroons.

MACAROON PASTE II

> 2 pounds (910 g) almond paste
> 1 pound (455 g) granulated sugar
> 6 to 7 ounces (1 dl, 8 cl to 2 dl, 1 cl) egg whites

This firm macaroon paste is used only for decorating on cakes and pastries. Follow the same directions for Macaroon Paste I, adding just enough egg whites to make a firm paste that will not spread when it is baked but is soft enough to be piped. If you have the time, refrigerate uncovered overnight to dry it out a little. Bake at 410° F (210° C) until golden.

VANILLA MACAROONS

about 60 cookies   *photograph, p. 197*

> Macaroon Paste I (recipe precedes)
> 1 pound, 14 ounces (855 g) Vanilla Buttercream I or II (see
>   p. 241)
> dark chocolate
> light chocolate

Make the batter for Macaroon Paste. Using a no. 8 (16-mm) plain tip, pipe it into 2-inch (5-cm) circles 1 inch (25 mm) apart. Bake immediately double panned at 410° F (210° C) about 12 minutes.

When cooled, invert macaroons and press them lightly so they do not roll. Smooth buttercream on the bottoms in a dome shape ½ inch (12 mm) thick in the center. Refrigerate until buttercream is firm.

Meanwhile, heat dark chocolate to body temperature; dip the buttercream part of each cookie into the chocolate. Let as much of the chocolate drip from the cookie as possible by waving it up and down above the bowl. Place dipped macaroons in straight lines on a sheet pan, and streak them very lightly with melted light chocolate in both directions.

CHOCOLATE MACAROONS
about 80 cookies   photograph, p. 197

> **Macaroon Paste I (see p. 159)**
> 3½ **pounds (1 kg, 600 g) Chocolate Buttercream (see p. 242)**
> **dark chocolate**
> **roasted whole hazelnuts**

Make Macaroon Paste I. Using a no. 8 (16-mm) plain tip, pipe out cookies, 2¼ inches (6 cm) long and ¾ inch (20 mm) wide, on parchment paper. Bake immediately at 410° F (210° C) about 12 minutes.

When macaroons have cooled, invert them and press lightly so they stay level. Using a no. 7 (14-mm) plain tip, pipe 2 mounds of Chocolate Buttercream on each cookie, covering the whole surface. Refrigerate until buttercream is firm.

Dip the buttercream and the top edge of the macaroon into melted dark chocolate. Before the chocolate sets, place a whole roasted hazelnut between the mounds.

MACAROON COINS
about 70 quarter-size coins

> 6 **ounces (170 g) almond paste**
> 4 **ounces (115 g) sugar**
> 2 **to 3 egg whites**

Mix almond paste and sugar. Beat in enough of the egg whites to make a soft creamy mixture that still holds its shape when piped. Using a no. 3 (6-mm) plain tip, pipe small dots the size of a quarter on a paper-lined sheet pan. Bake immediately, double panned at 425° F (220° C) until golden, about 6 minutes.

MACAROON BANANAS
about 55 cookies   photograph, p. 197

Macaroon Paste I (see p. 159)
Buttercream (see p. 239)
currant jelly
bananas
dark chocolate
light chocolate

Make batter for Macaroon Paste I. Using a no. 8 (16-mm) plain tip, pipe out slightly curved strips 3 inches (7.5 cm) long for buffet servings; for standard servings, use a no. 9 (18-mm) tip and pipe them 4½ inches (11 cm) long. Bake immediately at 410° F (210° C) 12 to 15 minutes.

When macaroons have cooled, invert them and press down lightly so they are level. Using a no. 2 (4-mm) plain tip, pipe a frame around the edge of each macaroon with Buttercream. Pipe a thin line of currant jelly in the middle. Cut bananas lengthwise in half, and cut into pieces to fit the macaroons. Usually cutting each half into thirds for buffet servings and in two for standard servings will work. Place a banana piece, cut side down and bending it slightly if needed to fit, on the Buttercream. Bananas should not protrude outside the cookies. Press softly so they stick. Refrigerate just until the Buttercream is firm (if refrigerated too long, the bananas will discolor).

Line macaroon bananas on cake rack over paper-lined sheet pans. Heat dark chocolate to 100° F (38° C); spoon it over the bananas to cover (bananas must be completely covered in order to not turn dark). Finally, on each top write "banana" or simply streak a thin line back and forth with light chocolate. Serve in paper cups. If properly iced, these will last 4 to 5 days.

COCONUT MACAROONS

sixty-five 2½-inch (6-cm) cookies   *photograph, p. 197*

  9 ounces (255 g) butter
14 ounces (400 g) sugar
    few drops yellow food color
  1 pound, 2 ounces (510 g) finely chopped coconut (macaroon
      coconut)
  5 whole eggs
  9 ounces (255 g) almond paste
  6 egg whites
    Short Dough (see p. 19)
    strawberry jam
    Simple Syrup (see p. 233)
    dark chocolate, optional

Heat butter, sugar, and food color in a saucepan to boil. Pour into the coconut in a mixing bowl; mix at low speed while adding eggs, one at a time. Beat almond paste and egg whites until smooth. Mix almond paste mixture into coconut mixture.

Roll out Short Dough ⅛ inch (3 mm) thick; cut into 2½-inch (6-cm) circles with a fluted cookie cutter. Pipe the coconut mixture onto the cookies in a star shape. If the mixture is difficult to pipe, mix in an additional egg. Make a small indentation in the middle of the coconut mixture, and pipe in a small amount of jam. Bake at 400° F (205° C) until golden brown, about 18 minutes. As soon as cookies come out of the oven, brush on Simple Syrup. Cool completely. Dip the short-dough bottoms into melted chocolate or serve plain.

PIROUETTES

about fifty 3-inch (7½-cm) cookies

12 ounces (340 g) sugar
6½ ounces (185 g) flour
  1 cup (2 dl, 4 cl) whipping cream
½ teaspoon (3 g) vanilla extract
  1 cup (2 dl, 4 cl) egg whites
  9 ounces (255 g) melted butter

Mix sugar and flour; mix in cream and vanilla, a little at a time; mix until smooth. Let rest 30 minutes. Whip egg whites until peaks are soft and fold in. Fold in the melted butter. In the meantime, butter and flour several inverted sheet pans very lightly. Make a 3-inch (7.5-cm) round template from cardboard ⅟₁₆ inch (2 mm) thick. Spread the batter thinly on the sheet pans using the template.

Bake at 400° F (205° C) until golden, about 4 minutes. Immediately roll the hot cookies, one at a time, around a thin dowel. Press the ends together and remove when they have hardened enough to hold their shape. If they are brittle and hard to roll, put them back in the oven to soften them up. Serve unfilled as a cookie or fill with whipped cream just before serving.

BRYSSELKEX

makes 150   photographs, p. 197

>   1 pound, 11 ounces (765 g) butter
>   10 ounces (285 g) powdered sugar
>   2 pounds, 3 ounces (1 kg) flour
>   ½ teaspoon (3 g) vanilla extract
>   1 ounce (30 g) cocoa powder
>   granulated sugar
>   egg wash
>   Short Dough (see p. 19)

Mix butter, sugar, flour, and vanilla until smooth. Divide the dough in half, and add the cocoa powder to one half. Refrigerate, if needed, until dough is a workable consistency.

Many varieties of cookies can be made from this basic dough; the most common ones are plain vanilla, marble, and checkerboard.

Vanilla
For vanilla cookies, omit the cocoa powder. Divide the dough into 3 parts, and roll each part into a string, about 2 inches (5 cm) in diameter. Color granulated sugar light pink, and roll the strings in the sugar. Transfer the strings to a sheet pan; roll each string even and slightly smaller, 1¾ inches (4.5 cm) diameter. Refrigerate until firm. Slice into ¼-inch-thick (6-mm) cookies. Place them 1 inch (25 mm) apart on sheet pans, and bake at 375° F (190° C) until golden brown, about 15 minutes.

Marble
Divide plain and chocolate doughs into 3 pieces each. This can be done by eye as the pieces need not be exactly equal in weight. Roll each piece into a string about 10 inches (25 cm) in length. Arrange them in 3 groups of

one chocolate and one plain; divide each string in each group into 3 pieces; you now have 3 chocolate and 3 plain pieces in each group. Then, alternating chocolate with plain, gently press the pieces into each other, one group at a time. You will now have 3 pieces of dough with equal amounts of plain and chocolate dough. Roll into strings, 2 inches (5 cm) in diameter, twisting at the same time to get an interesting marble pattern. Transfer the strings to a sheet pan or a board and finish rolling them out to 1¾ inches (4.5 cm) in diameter, evening at the same time. (This is done so that they are not disformed by moving them after they are rolled out.) Refrigerate until firm. Finish as directed for Vanilla Brysselkex.

Checkerboard

Roll plain and chocolate doughs into same-size rectangles, ⅝ inch (15 mm) thick. Brush egg wash on one and place the other rectangle on top of it. Refrigerate until firm. Cut into ⅝-inch-wide (15-mm) strips. Lay half the strips on their sides and brush with egg wash. Place remaining strips on top of egg-washed strips, alternating colors to achieve a checkerboard effect. Roll out Short Dough ⅛ inch (3 mm) thick and the same length as the strips. Brush with egg wash, place the cookie strip on top, and roll the dough around all 4 sides of the strip. Cut clean and refrigerate until firm. Cut and bake as directed for Vanilla Brysselkex.

CHOCOLATE CHIP COOKIES

about forty-five 1-ounce (30-g) cookies   *photograph, p. 197*

> 6 ounces (170 g) brown sugar
> 6 ounces (170 g) granulated sugar
> 9 ounces (255 g) butter, softened
> 2 eggs
> 1 teaspoon (6 g) vanilla extract
> 13 ounces (370 g) bread flour
> 1 teaspoon (4 g) salt
> 1 teaspoon (4 g) baking soda
> 6 ounces (170 g) chopped walnuts
> 12 ounces (340 g) large chocolate chips

Mix sugars and butter well, but do not cream. Mix in eggs and vanilla. Sift flour, salt, and baking soda together, and mix into the batter. Stir in walnuts and chocolate chips. Divide the dough into 1-pound (455-g) pieces, roll them into strings, and cut each string into 16 pieces. Place them with a cut side up (there is no reason to roll them round) staggered on sheet pans.

Bake at 375° F (190° C) just until done, about 10 minutes. (They should be somewhat sticky in the middle and not golden brown.)

CHOCOLATE CUTS
120 cookies   *photograph, p. 197*

     1 pound, 5 ounces (595 g) butter, softened
    14 ounces (400 g) granulated sugar
     1 pound, 12 ounces (795 g) flour
     1 ounce (30 g) cocoa powder
    ½ teaspoon (1 g) ammonium carbonate
        egg wash
        AA confectioners' sugar
        thinly sliced almonds

Mix butter and granulated sugar. Sift the dry ingredients together and mix into the butter mixture. Work the dough until smooth. Divide into 8 pieces, about 8 ounces (225 g) each. Roll each piece into a strip a little shorter than the length of a full sheet pan. Space 2 or 3 strips evenly on each pan (they will double in width). Roll the strips even and, at the same time, roll them to the full length of the pan. Flatten each strip to about 1¼ inches (30 mm) wide with the palm of your hand.

   Brush strips with egg wash; sprinkle with a mixture of equal parts AA confectioners' sugar and sliced almonds. Bake at 375° F (190° C) until almonds are light brown, about 12 minutes. Immediately cut at a slight angle into 1½-inch-wide (35-mm) cookies, using a metal scraper. Stagger the baking of the cookies to have time to cut the cookies before they harden.

GINGERBREAD COOKIES
about ninety 3-inch (7.5-cm) cookies   *photograph, p. 198*

    15 ounces (430 g) butter
    15 ounces (430 g) sugar
     1 pound, 2 ounces (510 g) corn syrup
     6 ounces (1 dl, 8 cl) milk
     2 pounds, 10 ounces (1 kg, 195 g) bread flour
    ½ ounce (15 g) baking soda
    ⅔ ounce (20 g) ground cinnamon
    ⅓ ounce (10 g) ground cloves
    ⅓ ounce (10 g) ground ginger

Combine butter, sugar, corn syrup, and milk; heat to 98° F (37° C). Stir in dry ingredients. Spread batter on a floured sheet pan. Refrigerate overnight.

Roll out a piece of the dough very thin, about ¹⁄₁₆ inch (2 mm) thick. Although the dough may feel sticky at first, it is important that you do not use more flour than necessary because too much flour will make the cookies hard and less crispy. If you are having a hard time rolling out the dough, try rolling it out on a piece of cloth. Keep the dough you are not working on in the refrigerator. When you need more dough, mix the fresh piece into the piece you have been working with. Using a plain cookie cutter, cut out 3-inch (7.5-cm) cookies. Place on paper-lined sheet pans. Bake at 400° F (205° C) until dark brown, about 10 minutes.

This dough can be used to make cookies of any size or shape, as well as the traditional gingerbread figures made for Christmas. The dough should be a little thicker, ⅛ inch (3 mm), if you are making figures. Gingerbread cookies can be kept for many weeks if stored in airtight containers or in a dry place.

SPRITZ RINGS
about 90 cookies   *photograph, p. 198*

    1 **pound, 5 ounces (595 g) butter, softened**
    10 **ounces (285 g) sugar**
    3 **egg yolks**
    1 **pound, 11 ounces (765 g) bread flour**

Mix butter, sugar, and egg yolks; mix in flour until the dough is soft and pipable. Using a cookie press fitted with a no. 4 (8-mm) star tip, pipe out long strips next to each other on the table. Push them together with a dowel or ruler, and cut them all at once into 5-inch (12.5-cm) pieces. Fold each piece around your finger into a ring, and place on a sheet pan.

Another method is to pipe the batter, using a pastry bag fitted with a no. 4 (8-mm) star tip, into 2-inch (5-cm) rings. Do not put too much dough in the bag at one time. This method works best for small batches.

Bake cookies at 375° F (190° C) until golden brown, about 15 minutes. You may have to use a second pan underneath to prevent the bottom of the cookies from overbrowning.

VANILLA DREAMS
150 cookies   *photograph, p. 198*

- 1 pound, 11 ounces (765 g) sugar
- 1 pound (455 g) butter
- 1 scant teaspoon (1.5 g) ammonium carbonate
- 1 teaspoon (6 g) vanilla extract
- 1 pound (455 g) flour

Mix sugar, butter, ammonium carbonate, and vanilla. Add the flour and mix until smooth dough. Divide dough into 3 pieces; if the dough is too soft, refrigerate until it can be handled. Roll each piece into a 1-inch-thick (25-mm) strip, and cut into ⅔-ounce (20-g) pieces. Roll the pieces into balls and place, 1 inch (25 mm) apart, on sheet pans. Press them lightly with the palm of your hand just enough so that they do not roll around when you move the sheet pan.

Bake at 300° F (150° C) until golden, but not brown, and dry enough to hold their shape, about 30 minutes. The color should be very slightly deepened.

Dip these cookies into cold water or milk as you eat them. The hollow space left by the ammonium carbonate will instantly fill up with the liquid but the cookie will remain crisp.

HAZELNUT COOKIES
110 cookies   *photograph, p. 198*

- 1 pound, 5 ounces (595 g) butter
- 11 ounces (310 g) sugar
- 12 ounces (340 g) nuts, finely ground
- 1 pound, 5 ounces (595 g) bread flour
- pinch ammonium carbonate
- whole hazelnuts, roasted lightly, skins removed

Mix butter and sugar. Mix dry ingredients, and stir into butter and sugar, just until mixed. Refrigerate until cold. Divide dough into 3 pieces; shape each piece into a rope 1½ inches (37 mm) in diameter. Refrigerate until firm.

Cut ropes into 5/16-inch-thick (8-mm) cookies. Place cookies on sheet pans. When they have softened, place a whole hazelnut in the middle of each cookie, pressing it to the pan. Bake at 375° F (190° C) until light brown, about 12 minutes.

HAZELNUT SQUARES

96 cookies   photograph, p. 198

> 15 ounces (430 g) sugar
> 10 ounces (285 g) butter
> 3 eggs
> 8 ounces (225 g) flour
> ½ ounce (15 g) cocoa powder
> 1 heaping tablespoon (9 g) baking powder
> 6 ounces (170 g) hazelnuts, roasted, skins removed, coarsely
>   crushed
> ½ teaspoon (3 g) vanilla extract
> 1½ ounces (40 g) sliced unroasted almonds

Beat sugar and butter until creamy; beat in eggs. Mix in remaining ingredients except almonds. Spread dough evenly on parchment paper, 24 × 16 inches (60 × 40 cm); then slide paper onto a sheet pan. Sprinkle dough with sliced almonds.

   Bake at 375° F (190° C) about 25 minutes. Immediately cut into 2-inch (5-cm) squares. The pieces left over on the sides can be used for rum balls.

   These cookies must be stored in airtight containers to remain crisp.

HEIDE SAND COOKIES

85 cookies   color photograph, p. C-3

> 1 pound, 10 ounces (740 g) bread flour
> 7 ounces (200 g) powdered sugar
> 1 pound, 5 ounces (595 g) butter, softened
>   few drops lemon juice
>   few drops vanilla extract
>   Decorating Sugar (see p. 236)
>   Apricot Jam (see p. 238), strained

Sift bread flour and powdered sugar together, and add to butter, lemon juice, and vanilla. Mix at low speed until smooth. Refrigerate if necessary. Cut dough into 3 pieces, and roll them into strips, 2½ inches (6 cm) in diameter, pressing the strips together as you roll. Do not use flour when rolling so that the colored sugar will stick. Place the strips in colored sugar and roll them to about 2 inches (5 cm) in diameter. With the palm of your hand, flatten the side nearest you so that the dough is in a smooth teardrop shape. If dough is too soft, refrigerate it until it can be shaped. Refrigerate again until strips are firm.

Slice dough ¼ inch (6 mm) thick, and place on sheet pans. Using your finger, make a small indentation in the middle of the fat part of the cookie, and pipe a small dot of jam in the hollow. Bake at 375° F (190° C) until golden, about 12 minutes. The dough can be refrigerated 1 to 2 weeks and baked as needed.

MACADAMIA NUT COOKIES
about sixty-five 1-ounce (30-g) cookies

>   14 ounces (400 g) granulated sugar
>   3 ounces (85 g) brown sugar
>   12 ounces (340 g) butter
>   3 eggs
>   ⅓ ounce (10 g) salt
>   ½ teaspoon (3 g) vanilla extract
>   1 pound, 3 ounces (540 g) bread flour
>   ½ teaspoon (2 g) baking soda
>   9 ounces (255 g) chopped macadamia nuts
>   9 ounces (255 g) shredded coconut

Cream sugars and butter. Mix in eggs, salt, and vanilla. Sift flour and baking soda together; mix flour, nuts, and coconut into batter. Divide dough into 1-pound (455-g) pieces; roll each piece into a strip 16 inches (40 cm) long; cut 16 cookies out of each strip. Roll cookies to round them and place on sheet pans. Bake at 375° F (190° C) about 12 minutes. You may have to use a second pan underneath to prevent them from overbrowning.

OAT FLAKES
ninety 2½-inch (6-cm) cookies
photograph, p. 198

>   9 ounces (255 g) butter
>   8½ ounces (240 g) rolled oats
>   3 eggs
>   13½ ounces (385 g) granulated sugar
>   1 ounce (30 g) flour
>   1½ ounces (40 g) baking powder
>   1 pound (455 g) Buttercream, optional (see p. 239)
>   melted dark chocolate, optional

The dough should be made one day and rolled out and baked the next so that the oats have time to absorb moisture.

Melt butter, stir in oats, and let stand 30 minutes. Add eggs, sugar, flour, and baking powder and mix well. Refrigerate.

Using as little flour as possible, roll the dough out into strips and cut into ⅓-ounce (10-g) pieces, or pipe out with a pastry bag. Place pieces on parchment paper or lightly greased and floured sheet pans (cookies will spread out to about 2½ inches (6 cm). Bake at 375° F (190° C) until golden brown, about 10 minutes.

The cookies can be served plain or with Buttercream sandwiched between 2 cookies or dipped halfway into dark chocolate. Store them in airtight containers or refrigerate dough and bake as needed.

RAISIN OATMEAL COOKIES
about 65 cookies

> 1 pound, 3 ounces (540 g) butter, softened
> 12 ounces (350 g) sugar
> 9 ounces (240 g) dark raisins
> 8 ounces (225 g) oat flakes
> ½ teaspoon (3 g) vanilla extract
> ½ teaspoon (2 g) baking soda
> 1 pound, 5 ounces (595 g) bread flour

Mix butter and sugar lightly. Add raisins, oat flakes, and vanilla and combine. Sift baking soda and flour together and stir into batter. Refrigerate the dough if necessary.

Divide dough into 10-ounce (285-g) pieces and roll into strips. Cut each strip into 10 pieces. The fastest way to do this is to roll out 3 or 4 strips at one time, place them next to each other, and cut them all at once. Roll each piece until round. (Practice rolling 2 pieces at a time between your hands. It goes twice as fast!) If the dough is so firm that the strips do not flatten when cut, simply place them, cut sides down, on sheet pans. Press the pieces lightly with the palms of your hands. Mark each one by pressing with a fork in the middle. Bake double panned at 350° F (175° C) until light golden, about 20 minutes.

CHOCOLATE TRIANGLES
64 cakes

> Chocolate Sponge I (see p. 93)
> 4 pounds, 10 ounces (2 kg, 105 g) Chocolate Buttercream (see
>   p. 242)
> 1½ pounds (680 g) Marzipan (see p. 255)
> dark chocolate

Make the batter for Chocolate Sponge I, and spread out ¼ inch (6 mm) thick on 2 full-size sheet pans. Bake at 400° F (205° C) about 10 minutes. Slide cakes off hot pans. When cool, refrigerate covered overnight.

Next day, remove skins from the cakes; cut each cake sheet crosswise in half so that there are 4 cakes 16 × 12 inches (40 × 30 cm). Layer the cakes together with 4 pounds (1 kg, 820 g) of the buttercream. Make sure the cake is straight and even-layered. Refrigerate until firm.

Cut cake the long way into 4 strips, 2¾ inches (7 cm) wide, holding the knife at a 90° angle. Place one strip at a time lengthwise at the very edge of a table so the layers run horizontally. With a long serrated knife, cut the strip in half diagonally, thus creating two triangles. Set aside but do not separate the newly cut pieces. Repeat with the remaining three strips. With the layers still running horizontally, transfer the cut strips to two paper-lined, inverted sheet pans, two strips to a pan. Ice the top of each strip with a ⅛-inch (3-mm) layer of buttercream. Handling the pieces carefully, place the two triangles together in such a way so you now have the layers running vertically. The fresh buttercream will act as "glue" in the middle and thus placed will form a new, larger triangle. Spread a thin film of the remaining buttercream on the two top sides.

Roll Marzipan out very thinly and cover the triangle. Finally, melt dark chocolate to 98° to 100° F (37° to 38° C) and spread on top of the Marzipan just thick enough to cover. Smooth the chocolate until it shows signs of setting. Refrigerate until buttercream is firm.

Cut into serving pieces, using a serrated knife or a thin carving knife dipped in hot water.

ALMOND TRUFFLES

77 cookies

> 4 pounds, 10 ounces (2 kg, 105 g) Mazarin Filling (see p. 262)
> 2 ounces (55 g) bread flour
> Short Dough (see p. 17)
> 4½ ounces (130 g) Apricot Jam (see p. 238)
> 1 pound, 6 ounces (625 g) Ganache (see p. 247)
> melted dark chocolate
> light or white chocolate
> pistachios or candied violets, optional

Make Mazarin Filling with an extra 2 ounces (55 g) bread flour to make it easier to slice. Line a paper-lined half-sheet pan, 16 × 12 inches (40 × 30 cm) with Short Dough rolled out ⅛ inch (3 mm) thick. Spread jam on the dough, and top with Mazarin Filling. Bake at 375° F (190° C) about 55 minutes.

When sheet is cooled, preferably the next day, cut off the skin and even the sheet at the same time. Unmold the sheet and place it on a cardboard or inverted sheet pan. Cut lengthwise into 11 strips (they will be slightly less than 1 inch (25 mm) wide). Separate the strips slightly. Using a no. 8 or 9 (16- or 18-mm) plain tip, pipe Ganache on top of the Mazarin down the middle of each strip. If the Ganache gets slightly off-center, move it with a wet knife or spatula. Refrigerate strips just until Ganache is firm.

Cut 3 or 4 strips at a time into 2¼-inch (6-cm) pieces; you should get 7 pieces out of each strip. Refrigerate again until firm.

Dip pieces into dark chocolate and decorate with thin lines of white chocolate using a piping bag with a very small opening. If desired, place a small piece of pistachio or a candied violet on top.

AMANDINE HEARTS

forty-eight 2¼-inch (5.7-cm) hearts

> Short Dough (see p. 19)
> 4½ ounces (130 g) Apricot Jam (see p. 238)
> 4 pounds, 10 ounces (2 kg, 105 g) Mazarin Filling (see p. 262)
> Marzipan (see p. 255)
> Buttercream (see p. 239)
> strawberries
> dark chocolate
> Pectin or Apricot Glaze (see pp. 237, 239)

Roll out Short Dough ⅛ inch (3 mm) thick, and transfer to a paper-lined sheet pan. Spread on jam and top with Mazarin Filling. Bake at 375° F (190° C) about 55 minutes.

When the sheet is cold, preferably the next day, unmold it and turn right side up on a cardboard. Cut off the skin and cut the sheet even, if needed. Using a heart-shaped cutter, about 2¼ inches (5.7 cm), cut out hearts, dipping the cutter lightly into hot water. The sheet is easier to cut if it is first refrigerated. Leftovers can be used for rum balls.

Roll out Marzipan ⅛ inch (3 mm) thick, and mark with the waffle-pattern rolling pin. Cut strips long enough to fit around the edge of the heart and ⅛ inch (3 mm) wider. At the same time, cut out small Marzipan hearts the size of pennies, and set aside. Spread a thin layer of Buttercream on the side of the heart and fasten the Marzipan strip around the heart. Cut small thin slices of strawberry and set aside. Heat dark chocolate to body temperature and pipe it as thinly as possible inside the border of each heart. Place the small heart in the middle and place strawberry slices on the sides without covering the chocolate completely. Finally, coat with Pectin or Apricot Glaze.

ALMOND DELIGHTS
forty-five 2¼-inch (5.7-cm) pastries   *photograph, p. 199*

    Othello Batter (see p. 174)
    Pastry Cream (see p. 242)
    almond paste
    Buttercream (see p. 239)
    Marzipan, colored green (see p. 255)
    powdered sugar

Make the Othello Batter; pipe into circles, 2¼ inches (5.7 cm) in diameter and ¾ inch (2 cm) high. Bake immediately at 400° F (205° C) until puffed and stable, about 10 minutes; reduce heat to 350° F (175° C); bake 10 minutes. Push your thumb into the circle while it is still hot to create a space for the filling.

Gradually mix enough of the Pastry Cream into the almond paste to make a very soft, but not runny, mixture. You will need about 1 pound, 2 ounces (510 g) almond-paste mixture. Fill the hollows in the Othello circles with the almond paste mixture; sandwich the shells together in pairs. Brush Buttercream on the top shell.

Roll out Marzipan 1/16 inch (2 mm) thick. With a plain cookie cutter, cut out circles large enough to cover the tops of the shells; stick the Marzipan to the Buttercream. Shape the Marzipan to a point at one end of the pastry. Sift powdered sugar lightly over the tops. Using a fork, mark 2 sides of the top, following the round shape of the pastry, starting at the point. Place pastries in paper cups. Let stand a few hours so that the filling has time to soften the shells.

OTHELLOS

forty-five 2¼-inch (5.7-cm) pastries
photograph, p. 199

>   Othello Batter (recipe follows)
> 1 pound, 2 ounces (510 g) Pastry Cream (see p. 242)
>   rum
>   Apricot Glaze (see p. 239)
> 2 pounds, 10 ounces (1 kg, 200 g) Chocolate Glaze or Fondant
>   (see pp. 247, 249)
>   dark or light chocolate

Preheat oven to 400° F (205° C) and prepare a pastry bag, fitted with a no. 6 (12-mm) plain tip, and several paper-lined sheet pans. Make Othello Batter. Pipe out batter into mounds, 2¼ inches (5.7 cm) in diameter, and ¾ inch (2 cm) high. Immediately bake at 400° F (205° C) until puffed up, about 10 minutes; reduce heat to 350° F (175° C); bake about 10 minutes, until golden brown.

Make a hollow in each pastry while still warm with your thumb. Place 2 shells together with rum-flavored Pastry Cream in the middle. Brush Apricot Glaze on the top half, and cover with Chocolate Glaze or Fondant. Pipe a spiral on top with dark or light chocolate.

OTHELLO BATTER

> 4½ ounces (130 g) cake flour
> 12 egg yolks
> 2¾ ounces (75 g) water
> 1 pound, 2 ounces (500 g) egg whites
> 11 ounces (310 g) sugar
>   few drops lemon juice
> 6½ ounces (185 g) cornstarch

Mix flour and egg yolks until smooth. Add the water gradually, whipping at high speed. Whip until mixture goes from ribbon to liquid, about 8 minutes. Meanwhile, whip the egg whites to soft peaks. Reserve 2 ounces (55 g) sugar, and gradually whip remaining 9 ounces (255 g) sugar into the whites. Whip to stiff peaks, adding a few drops of lemon juice. Mix the reserved sugar with the cornstarch and fold into whites by hand. Fold the yolk mixture, a little at a time, into the meringue. Do not overmix, but make sure the mixture is completely combined and smooth.

ALMOND DOUBLES
70 cookies   color photograph, p. C-3

> **Short Dough** (see p. 19)
> **Macaroon Paste II** (see p. 159)
> strawberry jam
> **Apricot Jam** (see p. 238)
> **Simple Syrup** (see p. 233)
> melted dark chocolate

Roll out Short Dough ⅛ inch (3 mm) thick, and cut into 2½-inch (6-cm) circles with a plain cookie cutter. Place circles, 1 inch (25 mm) apart, on sheet pans lined with parchment paper. Make Macaroon Paste II. Using a no. 4 (8-mm) plain tip, pipe macaroon paste on each cookie in a frame around the edge and one line straight across, using one continuous motion. Fill one side with strawberry jam and the other with apricot. Bake at 400° F (205° C) until golden brown, about 20 minutes.

As soon as the cookies come out of the oven, brush the macaroon paste with Simple Syrup without disturbing the jam. When cookies have cooled, dip the bottoms in dark chocolate.

KIRSCHWASSER RINGS
85 rings   photograph, p. 199

> 1 pound, 10 ounces (740 g) butter
> 14 ounces (400 g) granulated sugar
> 2 pounds, 13 ounces (1 kg, 285 g) almond paste
> pinch salt
> 12 eggs
> 1½ ounces (4.5 cl) Kirschwasser
> 10 ounces (285 g) flour
> 1 teaspoon (2 g) baking powder
> crushed sliced almonds
> powdered sugar or melted dark chocolate, optional

Gradually beat butter into granulated sugar, almond paste, and salt. Beat in eggs, two at a time; add Kirschwasser. Sift the flour and baking powder and stir in. Do not incorporate too much air by overmixing. Grease 3-inch (7.5-cm) savarin forms and sprinkle with slightly crushed almonds. Using a pastry bag fitted with a no. 6 (12-mm) plain tip, fill each form two-thirds full. Bake at 400° F (205° C) about 20 minutes. Unmold the cakes before they cool completely.

Lightly sift powdered sugar over the tops and serve or cut into halves and dip the cut ends into dark chocolate. Kirschwasser Rings should be served the day they are made.

FLORENTINA I

> 2 pounds, 3 ounces (1 kg) Semper Florentina
> 12 ounces (340 g) crushed sliced almonds
> 5 ounces (140 g) oat flakes
> 1 ounce (30 g) flour

Mix all ingredients. Semper Florentina is a premixed Florentina base, which can be bought at bakery supply houses. If Semper Florentina is not available, Florentina II can be substituted for Florentina I.

FLORENTINA II

> 1 pound (455 g) sugar
> 1 pound, 3 ounces (540 g) butter
> 6 ounces (1 dl, 8 cl) heavy cream
> 5 ounces (140 g) glucose or corn syrup
> 12½ ounces (355 g) sliced almonds
> 12½ ounces (355 g) candied orange peel, finely chopped

Heat sugar, butter, cream, and glucose to boiling, stirring slowly. Add remaining ingredients; cook, stirring constantly, until mixture pulls away from the side of the pan, about 10 minutes.

FLORENTINES

sixty-five 4-inch (10-cm) cookies
photograph, p. 199

> Florentina I or II (recipes precede)
> melted dark chocolate

Make the florentina. If using Florentina I, refrigerate dough until workable and follow this procedure: Divide into 12-ounce (340-g) pieces, and roll them out to strips, 12 inches (30 cm) long. Cut each strip into 12 pieces. Roll them until round, and place no more than 12 on a paper-lined sheet pan. Be sure to use new parchment paper. Flatten them slightly with your palms.

Florentina I is recommended, but if Semper Florentina is not available, use Florentina II and the following procedure: Draw circles on parchment papers, no more than 12 per sheet. Turn the papers over and place on sheet pans. Using a large plain tip, drop florentina about the size of a cherry tomato on each circle. The spreading will vary depending on how dry the batter is; make a test to avoid surprises. Spread batter out inside each circle while it is still warm.

Bake at 375° F (190° C) until golden brown, about 10 minutes. If they are dark around the edge before they have color at the center, the oven is too hot. Slide the cookies on the papers onto cardboard and cut them clean, using a 4-inch (10-cm) cookie cutter. Slide them back onto the pans to cool. If they harden before they can be cut, heat in the oven just until soft. When cookies are cool and brittle, break off the scraps around the sides. Save the scraps for rum balls.

To finish, brush a thick layer of dark chocolate on the bottom side and comb a wavy pattern in the chocolate before it becomes firm, or simply brush on the chocolate and leave it plain.

Variation
Sandwich Buttercream between 2 florentines and dip them halfway into chocolate.

FLORENTINA NOISETTES
about ninety 3-inch (7.5-cm) cookies   photograph, p. 199

> Florentina I or II (see p. 176)
> Short Dough (see p. 19)
> roasted whole hazelnuts
> 2 quarts (1 l, 9 dl, 2 cl) whipped cream
> hazelnut paste (see p. 8)
> roasted hazelnuts, skins removed, finely crushed

Make florentina. If making Florentina I, refrigerate the dough until somewhat firm, if needed. Divide into 11-ounce (310-g) pieces; roll each piece into a 1-inch-thick (25-mm) strip; cut each strip into 20 pieces. Roll pieces into balls and place 18 balls on each paper-lined sheet pan. Bake at 375° F (190° C) until golden brown, about 10 minutes.

Slide cookies on the papers onto cardboard. Using a 3-inch (7.5-cm) plain cookie cutter, cut through the cookies and return to the pans. When they are cool, break off the excess around the edges. Return them to the oven, and heat until soft. Roll each cookie around a dowel thick enough so that the ends meet. Push the ends together against a table or counter. Turn the cookie a half turn so that it will not stick to the dowel as it cools. Let each cookie cool completely before sliding it off the dowel.

Make Short Dough for cookie decorations. Roll out the dough ⅛-inch (3 mm) thick; cut into cookies the size of a quarter using a fluted cutter. Bake at 375° F (190° C) about 10 minutes.

Heat premixed florentina base to boiling and dip the short-dough cookies in it. If premixed florentina is not available, boil a quarter of the sugar, glucose, butter, and heavy cream listed for the Florentina II recipe until slightly thickened. Dip whole hazelnuts in the same way, and place one nut in the middle of each cookie.

Flavor whipped cream with hazelnut paste to taste. Stir in some crushed hazelnuts. Fill the cookie cylinders with cream from both ends, using a no. 6 (12-mm) star tip. Pipe a small dot of whipped cream in the middle on the seam side, and fasten a cookie on the dot. Serve in paper cups. Filled cookies must be served the same day. The shells alone can be stored in an airtight container for several weeks.

Variation
Florentina Noisettes can be served as a dessert if made larger. Serve each one on top of a rosette of whipped cream piped on a plate.

FLORENTINA SURPRISE
about 100 cookies　　photograph, p. 199

> Short Dough (see p. 19)
> Florentina I or II (see p. 176)
> 1 pound, 12 ounces (800 g) Buttercream (see p. 239)
> 2 ounces (55 g) hazelnut paste (see p. 8)
> dark chocolate

Roll out Short Dough ⅛-inch (3-mm) thick; with a 2½-inch (6-cm) cookie cutter, cut out cookies. Place 1 inch (25 mm) apart on sheet pans. Bake at

375° F (190° C) until golden brown, about 10 minutes. Do not remove from pans.

Make Florentina I if possible. If you must use Florentina II, follow directions under Florentines (see Index). Divide into 10-ounce (285-g) pieces. Roll each piece into a strip about 18 inches (45 cm) long; cut each strip into 24 individual pieces. Roll each piece into a ball and place no more than 12 on each paper-lined sheet pan. Flatten them slightly with your hand. Bake at 375° F (190° C) until golden brown, about 10 minutes.

Quickly slide cookies on paper onto cardboard. Using the same size cookie cutter as used for the Short Dough, cut through the florentina by pressing down and twisting at the same time. If the cookies are too brittle, reheat them. Slide back on the sheet pans to cool. When cookies are cool and crisp, break off the scraps around the edge; save the scraps for rum balls.

Flavor the Buttercream with the hazelnut paste; using a no. 5 (10-mm) plain tip, pipe a border on the short-dough cookies. Refrigerate until the Buttercream is set. Meanwhile, heat dark chocolate to body temperature. Dip chilled Buttercream, including the top of the short-dough cookie, into the chocolate. Before the chocolate hardens, place a Florentina cookie level on top. Do not store in the refrigerator.

MÁLAGA COOKIES
48 cookies   *photograph, p. 199*

       Short Dough (see p. 19)
       Florentina I or II (see p. 176)
 1 **pound, 10 ounces (740 g) Buttercream (see p. 239)**
 2 **ounces (6 cl) rum**
       melted dark chocolate
       Raisin Filling (recipe follows)

Roll out Short Dough ⅛ inch (3 mm) thick; cut out 48 cookies, using a plain cookie cutter 2½ inches (6.5 cm) in diameter. Bake at 375° F (190° C) until golden brown, about 10 minutes.

Make the Florentina I or II. If using Florentina I, weigh two 12-ounce (340-g) pieces. Roll them out to strips about ½ inch (12 mm) thick; cut each strip into 24 pieces. Roll the pieces into balls, and place 12 on each paper-lined sheet pan. Bake at 375° F (190° C) until golden brown, about 10 minutes. Pull paper onto a cardboard, and, using a plain cookie cutter, cut out cookies 2½ inches (6.5 cm) in diameter. At the same time, cut a 1-

inch (25-mm) circle from the middle of each cookie to make a doughnut-shaped cookie. Do not attempt to cut them if they cool and harden; if necessary, heat them to soften. Let them harden completely before breaking off the excess from the edges. Remove the center circles carefully.

If using Florentina II, draw 2½-inch (6.5-cm) circles on parchment paper, spread the warm mixture very thinly inside these circles, bake, and finish as for Florentina I.

Flavor Buttercream with rum; using a no. 4 (8-mm), plain tip, pipe a border on the edge of each short-dough cookie. Refrigerate until Buttercream is set. Dip the Buttercream and the top of the cookie into melted dark chocolate. Top with the florentina ring before the chocolate sets.

Brush the bottoms of the 1-inch (25-mm) cutouts with dark chocolate. Fill the center holes with Raisin Filling. Place each 1-inch (25-mm) cutout, chocolate side up, on top at an angle, as if a half-closed lid.

Raisin Filling

      7 ounces (200 g) dark raisins, softened in warm water
      4 ounces (115 g) sugar
  1½ ounces (40 g) glucose or light corn syrup
  4½ ounces (130 g) butter
  1½ ounces (4.5 cl) heavy cream

Drain raisins and pat dry. Place all ingredients except raisins in a saucepan; heat to boiling. Boil slowly 5 minutes. Stir in raisins. Let stand until cool.

MARIE PUFFS

35 to 60 puffs   *color photograph, p. C-3*

      4 ounces (115 g) granulated sugar
    10 ounces (285 g) Short Dough (see p. 19)
    ½ recipe Pâte à Choux (see p. 47)
  2½ pounds (1 kg, 140 g) Bavarian Cream (see p. 261)
        powdered sugar

Knead granulated sugar into Short Dough. Roll out ¹⁄₁₆ inch (2 mm) thick. Cut out 1½-inch (35-mm) cookies for buffet servings or 2-inch (50-mm) cookies for normal servings, using a plain or fluted cookie cutter. Line cookies up on a sheet pan, one partly on top of the other so that they can be picked up easily later.

Make Pâte à Choux. Pipe out mounds ½ inch (12 mm) high and the same size as the cookies on paper-lined sheet pans. The batter expands a great deal when baked, so do not crowd the pan. Immediately place the cookies on top while the batter is still sticky; press down lightly with 2 fingers to make sure the cookie sticks all around. At this point, the puffs can be frozen and baked as needed directly from the freezer. If properly covered, they will keep frozen for weeks.

Bake at 400° F (205° C) until puffed up and just starting to color, about 10 minutes; reduce heat to 375° F (190° C); bake until golden color and dry enough to hold their shape, about 12 minutes.

When puffs have cooled, make a small hole in the bottom of each puff with a paring knife and fill with Bavarian Cream. Dust lightly with powdered sugar on the tops and refrigerate. Marie Puffs and all pastries made of Pâte à Choux are best if served fresh; they should not be used the next day.

MAZARINS

60 mazarins *photograph, p. 199*

> **Short Dough (see p. 19)**
> ¼ **recipe Mazarin Filling (see p. 262)**
> **sugar**
> **Apricot Glaze (see p. 239)**
> **Fondant (see p. 249)**

Roll out Short Dough ⅛ inch (3 mm) thick and line 60 mazarin forms with the dough. Traditional mazarin forms are small round pans that measure 2¾ inches (7 cm) in diameter at the top, 1 inch (25 mm) high at the side, and 1 inch (25 mm) in diameter at the bottom. All the forms or pans used only for short dough do not have to be greased and should not be washed, if at all possible; but simply wiped clean with a rag when still warm. Place no more than 24 to 30 forms of this size, evenly spaced, on 2 full-sized sheet pans.

Using a large plain tube, pipe Mazarin Filling into forms. Bake at 400° F (205° C) until golden brown, about 20 minutes. Sprinkle pastries lightly with sugar, and turn them upside down as soon as they come out of the oven to flatten the tops. This can be done quickly by putting a sheet paper and cardboard on top of the pastries, pressing hard, and turning the whole pan over at one time. Before pastries have cooled completely, turn them right side up again as you remove the forms.

When Mazarins are completely cooled, brush on Apricot Glaze; then ice with a thin layer of white Fondant. Do not heat the Fondant higher than 100° F (38° C) for a shiny finish. Thin Fondant if necessary with egg white. It is easiest and fastest to glaze them by dipping the surface into Fondant and removing the excess with a spatula.

A mixture of water and powdered sugar can be substituted for the Fondant. Heat in the oven 10 to 15 seconds to harden the frosting and give it a shine.

LINZER TARTLETS

about ninety tartlets   *photograph, p. 200*

- ½ recipe Linzer Dough (recipe follows)
- 1 pound, 5 ounces (600 g) raspberry jam, softened
- egg wash
- powdered sugar, optional

Roll out a small piece of Linzer Dough ⅛ inch (3 mm) thick and as square as possible; refrigerate covered and reserve. Line shallow tartlet forms, 2¼ inches (5.7 cm) wide, with Linzer Dough rolled out little thinner than ¼ inch (6 mm). Place the forms, 1 inch (25 mm) apart, on sheet pans.

Using a no. 5 (8-mm) plain tip, pipe a ¼-inch (6-mm) layer of jam into the dough-lined forms. Use a good-quality jam because the raspberry taste is dominant. Do not overfill dough or tartlets will taste too sweet. Using a fluted pastry wheel, cut the reserved dough into ¼-inch (6-mm) strips. Cross 2 strips on each tartlet. Brush tartlets with egg wash. Bake at 350° F (175° C) until golden brown, about 15 minutes.

When tartlets have cooled, place a ring ⅛ to ¼ inch (3 to 6 mm) smaller than the tartlet on top, and sift powdered sugar lightly on top for a contrasting frame. They can also be served plain without the sugar rim.

Linzer Dough

- 1 pound, 5 ounces (595 g) margarine, softened
- 10½ ounces (300 g) butter, softened
- 1½ pounds (680 g) sugar
- 12 egg yolks
- few drops lemon juice
- 2 pounds (910 g) bread flour
- 1 pound, 9 ounces (710 g) hazelnuts, finely ground
- ½ ounce (15 g) ground cinnamon
- ⅙ ounce (5 g) ground cloves

Place margarine, butter, sugar, egg yolks, and lemon juice in a mixing bowl. Using the dough hook, combine them at low speed 1 minute. Add dry ingredients; mix just until combined. Place on a paper-lined sheet pan and refrigerate covered.

DOBOS FOR PETITS FOURS
about two hundred 1-inch (25-mm) petits fours

> 26 eggs
> 1 pound, 14 ounces (855 g) butter
> 2 pounds, 2 ounces (970 g) powdered sugar
> 1½ teaspoons (9 g) vanilla extract
>   juice from a quarter lemon
> 1 pound, 4 ounces (570 g) bread flour

This is the recipe for the Hungarian Dobos Torta created by the famous Hungarian pastry chef Dobos. We use this fairly heavy and compact batter for *petits fours* because it will not crumble and dirty the Fondant when the *petits fours* are iced, which makes it possible to use the Fondant more than once. You can start with a white Fondant, then dye the leftover to a pale yellow, then to green, and so on.

Separate the eggs a few at a time into small containers and then transfer to mixing bowls. Thus, if you break a yolk, you will not ruin the whole batch. Cream butter with half of the sugar. Mix in the yolks two at a time. Mix in vanilla and lemon. Whip the whites and the remaining sugar to stiff peaks. Sift the flour and fold carefully into the whites. Fold the egg white mixture into the egg yolk mixture.

Divide the mixture among 3 paper-lined sheet pans, spreading the batter evenly. It is best to put the parchment paper on a table, spread the batter on the paper, and then pull the paper onto a pan. Bake at 425° F (220° C) about 8 minutes. Transfer cakes to cold pans when they come out of the oven so that they do not dry out.

PETITS FOURS I
about one hundred 1-inch (25-mm) petits fours
color photograph, p. C-4

> 2 ounces (55 g) cake flour
> 4 pounds, 10 ounces (2 kg, 105 g) Mazarin Filling (see p. 262)
> 1 pound, 6 ounces (620 g) Ganache (see p. 247)
>   Buttercream (see p. 239)
>   Marzipan (see p. 255)

Line a full-size sheet pan with parchment paper. Stir the flour into the Mazarin Filling, and spread it evenly on the pan. Bake at 400° F (205° C) or until the sheet springs back when lightly pressed, about 40 minutes. When the sheet is completely cool, preferably the next day, unmold and cut or scrape off any loose skin. Divide the sheet in half crosswise so that each sheet measures 16 × 12 inches (40 × 30 cm). Place one sheet on an inverted sheet pan, and spread with Ganache. Place the second sheet on top, and press lightly with a pan to make sure it is even and adheres to the Ganache. Spread a thin film of Buttercream on top. Roll out Marzipan ¹⁄₁₆ inch (2 mm) thick. Place Marzipan on top of the Buttercream. Turn the sheet upside down and refrigerate until firm. With the Marzipan on the bottom, cut *petits fours* in desired shapes.

PETITS FOURS II
two hundred 1-inch (25-mm) petits fours

> **Dobos for Petits Fours or Petits Fours I (recipes precede)**
> 3 **pounds (1 kg, 365 g) Ganache (see p. 247)**
> **Buttercream (see p. 239)**
> **Marzipan (see p. 255)**
> **Fondant (see p. 249)**
> **Piping Gel or dark chocolate (see p. 248)**

After removing any loose skin, put the Dobos sheets together with ¹⁄₈-inch (3-mm) layers of Ganache in between, keeping the layers even and removing any skin from the Dobos sheets. Spread a very thin layer of Buttercream on top, just enough to make the Marzipan stick. Roll out Marzipan ¹⁄₁₆ inch (2 mm) thick; place on top of the Buttercream. The Marzipan keeps the Fondant from losing its gloss too fast and also adds flavor. Refrigerate until sheet is completely cool.

With the Marzipan side down, cut into desired shapes, but they should not be much bigger than 1 inch (25 mm). Place *petits fours*, marzipan side up, on racks over sheet pans, spacing them at least 1 inch (25 mm) apart.

Warm Fondant to about 98° to 100° F (37° to 38° C). If the Fondant is too hot, it will lose its gloss and have a flat, old-looking, finish (simply cool to the proper temperature before using). If the Fondant is not hot enough, it will take hours for the Fondant to dry, it will form a skin, and the gloss will not last long or be bright. Thin the Fondant, to the consistency that will clearly show the layers on the sides, with egg whites or heavy cream, which will thin the Fondant without sacrificing its gloss. Ice the *petits fours,* using a pastry bag fitted with a no. 2 or 3 (4- or 6-mm) plain tip or by pouring the Fondant from a small plate. If poured from a plate, the Fondant will have to be reheated more often. Start with plain white, dye to yellow, and then green; set the green aside and make pink; then add the green to the pink for a mocha color. For a dark chocolate color, add cocoa powder. Be sure to keep all the colors light.

Decorate with piping gel dyed to a dark chocolate color or dark piping chocolate. Place *petits fours* in paper cups, pushing the paper cups to the shape of the *petits fours* so that the sides are straight around the little cakes.

NOISETTE RINGS
25 rings

> Short Dough (see p. 19)
> 1 pound, 14 ounces (850 g) almond paste
> water
> arrack or rum
> 8 ounces (225 g) hazelnuts
> thinned dark chocolate

Roll out Short Dough ⅛ inch (3 mm) thick; cut into 3- to 3¼-inch (7.5- to 8-cm) circles with a fluted cookie cutter. Place on paper-lined sheet pans. Using a 1-inch (25-mm) fluted cutter, cut a circle out of the middle of each cookie. Return small circles to the dough to be used again. Bake at 375° F (190° C) just until done, without giving them any color, about 10 minutes. Refrigerate cookies without removing them from the pans.

Mix just enough water into the almond paste so that it can be piped easily. Flavor with arrack or rum.

Roast hazelnuts until golden brown. Rub off as much skin with your hands as is possible. If you want all the skin off the hazelnuts, blanch them in water with baking soda, peel off the skin, and roast them. Crush hazelnuts very coarsely.

Using a no. 6 (12-mm) plain tip, pipe the almond paste about ¼ inch (6 mm) thick and slightly less than the width of the cookie in a circle on the cookie. Hold the bag straight above the cookie to avoid putting pressure on the cookie sideways. If the cookie moves as you do this, the almond paste is too firm. Immediately invert cookies in the crushed hazelnuts. If necessary, reshape the circles by hand. Dip the almond paste circles into chocolate that has been thinned enough so that the hazelnuts show through. The chocolate can be thinned with cocoa butter or with a mixture of 10 percent soy oil and 90 percent coconut oil. (The soy oil, though not essential, adds shine to the cookie.)

ORANGE TRUFFLE STRIPS
60 buffet or 36 regular servings   photograph, p. 200

> Chocolate Sponge II (see p. 94)
> ½ recipe Japonaise Batter (see p. 147)
> 3 pounds (1 kg, 365 g) Ganache (see p. 247)
> 2 ounces (6 cl) Grand Marnier
>   cocoa powder
>   Marzipan Oranges (recipe follows)

Make batter for Chocolate Sponge II. Spread the batter evenly on a half-sheet pan 16 × 12 inches (40 × 30 cm) lined with parchment paper. Bake immediately at 400° F (205° C) about 18 minutes.

Make Japonaise Batter, and spread the meringue evenly on a half-sheet paper. Bake at 300° F (150° C) until golden brown and dry, about 35 minutes. If necessary, open the door and turn down the temperature. Do not remove the paper.

Flavor Ganache with Grand Marnier; you will need 1½ pounds (680 g) Ganache to layer the sheet and about 6 ounces (170 g) to finish each strip. Split the spongecake into 2 layers; spread a ⅛-inch (3-mm) layer of Ganache on the bottom layer. Place the Japonaise upside down on the Ganache, and then peel the paper from the back. Spread another ⅛-inch (3-mm) layer of Ganache on the Japonaise. Place the other layer of spongecake on top. Press down to make the sheet as even as possible; refrigerate until the Ganache is firm.

Cut the sheet lengthwise into 3 strips (4 for buffet servings). Spread the top and sides with Ganache just thick enough to cover the cake. Sift cocoa powder on top to cover the Ganache. With the back of a chef's knife, mark small diamonds in the cocoa powder. Using a sharp knife dipped in hot water, cut each strip into 12 slices about 1¼ inches (30 mm) wide (15 slices about 1 inch (25 mm) wide for buffet servings). Place a Marzipan Orange in the middle, scraping away some cocoa powder with a small knife so that it sticks to the Ganache.

Marzipan Oranges

Color a small amount of Marzipan orange. If you lack orange color, mix red and yellow in appropriate amounts. Roll into a ½-inch-thick (12-mm) strip; cut into pieces the size of cherries. Keeping the rest of the Marzipan covered at all times, roll one piece at a time into a ball; then roll it lightly over a fine grater to make the typical peel markings. Place the "orange" in your hand and make a hole in one end with a toothpick. If you want shiny oranges, coat them with a thin layer of cocoa butter.

FRUIT BARRELS

25 barrels   color photograph, p. C-4

> Almond Decorating Paste (see p. 257)
> ½ recipe Spongecake II (see p. 93)
> cocoa powder
> 1 pound, 9 ounces (710 g) whipped cream
> 4 ounces (115 g) crushed raspberries
> whole raspberries

Make the Almond Decorating Paste. While it is resting, make spongecakes. Cut templates out of crescent board to make small barrels with handles. The template will be an outline of the shape to be filled in with the almond paste. Butter and flour several sheet pans.

Color a small amount of the almond paste dark brown (this can be done with cocoa powder) and set aside. Using the template, spread remaining hippen on the pans, taking care not to spread it out too thick. With the brown hippen, pipe out 2 lines the long way and pipe 2 dots in the handles. Bake at 400° F (205° C) until the hippen starts browning in spots, about 8 minutes. Use the cardboard piece cut from the inside of the template to make a barrel, securing the two ends with some tape. Take the pans of almond paste out of the oven one at a time so they do not harden too fast, and immediately bend the almond paste around the cardboard barrel.

Cut out ½-inch-thick (12-mm) pieces of light sponge the same size as the inside of the barrels and place one in the bottom of each barrel. Flavor the whipped cream with the crushed raspberries and pipe in the barrels almost to the top. Fill barrels with raspberries. Any small berry, such as blackberries, blueberries, and wild strawberries can be substituted for the raspberries.

DIPLOMAT STRIPS

20 regular or 40 buffet-size servings   *photograph, p. 201*

> Spongecake I (see p. 92)
> 9½ ounces (155 g) strawberry jam
> 3 pounds, 12 ounces (1 kg, 800 g) Pastry Cream (see p. 242)
> sliced raw almonds
> 1 pound, 4 ounces (570 g) Macaroon Paste II (see p. 159)
> 8 ounces (225 g) Apricot Jam (see p. 238)
> red food color
> Simple Syrup (see p. 233)

Make the batter for Spongecake I. Line a half-sheet pan 16 × 12 inches (40 × 30 cm) with parchment paper, fill evenly with the batter, and bake at 375° F (190° C) until done, about 18 minutes. Cut spongecake into strips, three 4-inch (10-cm) strips for regular servings and four 3-inch (7½-cm) strips for buffet servings. Cut off the skin and slice each strip into 3 layers. Spread the bottom piece with a thin layer of strawberry jam (reserve half of the strawberry jam for topping); then add the second layer. Spread second layer with ¼-inch (6-mm) layer of Pastry Cream; add the top layer. Cover with Pastry Cream, and put sliced raw almonds, crushed slightly by hand, on the sides.

Make Macaroon Paste II, making it as stiff as possible, but soft enough to pipe out smoothly. Using a pastry bag with a no. 4 (8-mm) star or plain tip, pipe 4 evenly spaced lines down the length of the sponge strips. Fill in spaces between lines with Apricot and strawberry jam tinted red. Bake double panned at 425° F (220° C) about 15 minutes. Brush strips lightly with Simple Syrup when they come out of the oven. Cool and cut into 1½-inch (35-mm) pieces.

Variation

Omit piping straight lines; instead, mark off 1½-inch (35-mm) slices on the Pastry Cream. Using a no. 3 (6-mm) plain tip, pipe a figure 8 on each piece and fill with strawberry and Apricot jams. Alternately, bake the pastry plain and decorate with fresh fruit when cool. Glaze the fruit with Apricot or Pectin Glaze. Cut at the markings.

SMALL DIPLOMATS

about 48 cookies   *photograph, p. 200*

Spongecake II (see p. 93)
strawberry jam
Pastry Cream (see p. 242)
crushed unroasted almonds
Macaroon Paste II (see p. 159)
small strawberries, thinly sliced
Pectin or Apricot Glaze (see pp. 237, 239)

Make batter for Spongecake II, and spread evenly in a paper-lined half-sheet pan. Bake at 375° F (190° C) until golden brown, about 15 minutes. Let cool completely before cutting the cake from the pan. Remove the skin and slice into 2 layers.

Spread a thin layer of jam on the bottom layer and top with the second layer. Cut into 2-inch (5-cm) circles with a plain cookie cutter; save the leftovers for rum balls. Spread a thin layer of Pastry Cream on the sides of the cookies, and roll them in crushed almonds. Place on lined sheet pans. Using a no. 3 (6-mm) plain tip, pipe a circle of macaroon paste on the edge of each cookie. Make sure the macaroon paste is firm and will not run and look sloppy. Pipe Pastry Cream in the middle to cover only the sponge. Bake double panned at 400° F (205° C) until golden brown, about 10 minutes. Cool. Place a small slice of strawberry in the middle and glaze with Pectin Glaze.

SMALL PRINCESS CAKES

about 48 pastries   *photograph, p. 200*

Spongecake II (see p. 93)
6 **ounces (170 g) strawberry jam**
Marzipan, colored green (see p. 255)
Buttercream (see p. 239)
Pastry Cream (see p. 242)
whipped cream
strawberries
chocolate wedges

This pastry is usually baked in small 2½- to 3-inch (6- to 7.5-cm) rings. For buffet servings, the sponge circles should be no larger than 1¾ inches (4.5 cm).

Make the batter for Spongecake II, and spread it evenly on a half-sheet pan. Bake at 375° F (190° C) until cake springs back when lightly pressed, about 20 minutes. The spongecake will be easier to cut if the cake is baked the day before.

When the cake has cooled, cut the skin off the sheet and slice the cake into 2 layers. Spread the jam on the bottom layer, and place the second layer on top. With a plain 1¾-inch (4.5-cm) cookie cutter, cut out circles from the cake; stagger the cuts for minimum waste.

Roll out Marzipan ⅛ inch (3 mm) thick. Mark with a waffle roller, turn upside down, and cut into strips 6 × 1½ inches (15 × 4 cm). While the strips are still together, spread a thin film of Buttercream on top. Roll the Marzipan strips around sides of cakes. The edges should overlap ⅛ inch (3 mm); you may have to stretch it slightly. Press with a knife so the seam sticks.

Pipe Pastry Cream ¼ inch (6 mm) thick on top of the cakes. Using a no. 3 (6-mm) star tip, decorate the tops in an 8-pointed pattern with whipped cream. Put a thin slice of strawberry and a wedge of chocolate in the middle.

SACHER CUTS
sixty-six small cake rectangles
photograph, p. 200

> Sacher Sponge (see p. 121)
> 2 recipes Apricot Glaze (see p. 239)
> Buttercream (see p. 239)
> Marzipan (see p. 255)
> 1 pound, 12 ounces (795 g) Chocolate Glaze (see p. 247)
> light chocolate
> dark chocolate

Make Sacher Sponge, and spread it evenly on a full-size paper-lined sheet pan. Bake at 375° F (190° C) 20 minutes.

When the cake has cooled, cut it in half into two sheets 16 × 12 inches (40 × 30 cm). With a sharp knife, cut the skin off the sheets and at the same time even them. Heat the Apricot Glaze to the thread stage. Spread it on 1 cake sheet, forcing the glaze into the cake. Do not leave a layer thicker than 1/16 inch (2 mm) on top. Immediately place the other cake sheet on top, and press down firmly so that the sheets stick together.

Spread a thin film of Buttercream on the top, just enough to make the top sticky. (Apricot Glaze would make the Marzipan wet.) Roll out Marzipan 1/16 inch (2 mm) thick, and place on top of the Buttercream. Turn the cake upside down, and refrigerate for a few minutes.

Cut the cake lengthwise into 11 strips; cut each strip into 6 pieces. It is important that you cut at exactly a 90° angle on high pastry as Sacher Sponge. Turn pieces right side up and place them 1½ inches (4 cm) apart on a screen placed over a sheet pan. Cover them with Chocolate Glaze piped from a no. 4 (8-mm) plain tip. Decorate by piping an "S" in chocolate directly on the glaze, by placing a small round of light chocolate in the middle and piping an "S" in contrasting chocolate on top; or by piping the word "Sacher" in chocolate.

POLYNEES
about 55 pastries   photograph, p. 200

    Short Dough (see p. 19)
    strawberry jam
  1 **pound (455 g) sugar**
  2 **pounds (910 g) almond paste**
12 **ounces (3 dl, 6 cl) egg whites**

Line mazarin forms (see Index) with Short Dough rolled out ⅛ inch (3 mm) thick (other forms of similar size can be used). Pipe a small amount of strawberry jam in the bottom. Beat sugar, almond paste, and enough of the egg whites to obtain a soft, creamy consistency. Pipe into the forms almost to the top. Roll out a small piece of Short Dough; cut into strips ¼ inch (6 mm) wide, and cross 2 strips on top of the almond paste in each form.

Bake at 380° F (195° C) until golden brown, about 22 minutes. They will puff up and crack in the middle.

POTATOES
48 small cakes   photograph, p. 200

    Spongecake I (see p. 92)
14 **ounces (400 g) Pastry Cream** (see p. 242)
 1 **pound, 12 ounces (800 g) Buttercream** (see p. 239)
    arrack or rum
    Marzipan (see p. 255)
    cocoa powder

Make the batter for Spongecake I, and spread it on a half-sheet pan. Bake at 375° F (190° C) about 20 minutes. Let cool completely.

Remove the skin, and cut a ¼-inch (6-mm) layer from the top. Keeping the layers together, cut out ovals with a cutter, 2 × 1½ inches (5 × 3.7 cm) (you can easily make one by bending a 2-inch (5-cm) round cookie cutter). Remove the thin ovals; using a no. 3 (6-mm) plain tip, pipe Pastry Cream on top of the thicker cake ovals. Flavor the buttercream with arrack. Using a large plain tube, pipe a 1-inch (25-mm) oval mound of Buttercream on top of the Pastry Cream.

Cut the thin sponge ovals the long way into halves; place both halves on top of the Buttercream, leaving a ¼-inch (6-mm) gap between the halves. Roll out Marzipan ¹⁄₁₆ inch (2 mm) thick; cut into ovals large enough to fit over the whole pastry, or cut circles of Marzipan and stretch them to fit the ovals; arrange Marzipan over the cakes. Make indentations with your fingers to make the cakes look like potatoes. With a straw, punch the Marzipan to make a few eyes. Sift cocoa powder on top of finished potatoes and brush off the excess.

PRETZELS
photograph, p. 200

> **Puff Paste (see p. 36)**
> **Short Dough (see p. 19)**
> **egg wash**
> **AA confectioners' sugar**
> **crushed sliced almonds**
> **Simple Syrup (see p. 233)**

Scrap puff paste should be used for this recipe, but, if that is not available, give fresh dough a half turn (fold in half) and prick well before placing the Short Dough on top.

Roll puff paste into a rectangle 16 inches (40 cm) long and ⅛ inch (3 mm) thick. Place on parchment paper on the back of a sheet pan. Roll out Short Dough to the same size. Brush the puff paste with egg wash, and carefully roll the Short Dough on top. Refrigerate until firm, 15 to 20 minutes.

Using a dowel and a sharp knife, cut into strips ¼ inch (6 mm) wide and 16 inches (40 cm) long. This can be done with a plain pastry wheel but a knife will give a sharper cut. Twist each strip into an even spiral by turning the ends in opposite directions; do not twist too tightly or the strip will break. Shape the twisted strip into a pretzel 4½ inches (11 cm) long. If the dough becomes too soft to handle, refrigerate the strips for a short time; if the strips are too firm, they will break when you twist them.

Invert pretzels into a mixture of equal amounts of AA confectioners' sugar and crushed almonds, pressing gently to be sure the mixture sticks to the dough. Place pretzels, sugar sides up, on a paper-lined sheet pan. They can be frozen at this point and baked directly from the freezer. Bake at 375° F (190° C) until golden, about 15 minutes. Make sure the puff paste has been thoroughly baked. Brush pretzels with Simple Syrup as soon as they come out of the oven to give them a shine.

BABAS AU RHUM

about 35 babas   *photograph, p. 201*

    1 cup (2 dl, 4 cl) milk
    1 ounce (30 g) yeast
   11 ounces (310 g) bread flour
    8 eggs (400 g)
  2½ ounces (70 g) sugar
    1 teaspoon (3.5 g) salt
   12 ounces (340 g) soft butter
   15 ounces (430 g) cake flour
    5 ounces (140 g) raisins
      Rum Syrup (recipe follows)
      Apricot Glaze (see p. 239)
      maraschino cherry, halves
      whipped cream

Heat milk to 105° F (41° C). Dissolve yeast in milk. Stir in 8 ounces (225 g) of the bread flour and knead until smooth. Let rise covered in a warm place just until the sponge starts to fall.

Meanwhile, grease classic baba forms, about 3 inches deep and 1¾ inches wide (7.5 × 4.5 cm). Place forms on 2 sheet pans and set aside.

When the sponge is ready, mix in eggs, sugar, salt, butter, cake flour, and the remaining bread flour. Mix until the dough is smooth and quite loose. Mix in raisins. Using a pastry bag with a no. 7 (14-mm) plain tip, pipe filling into forms, filling each half full. Let batter rise to the top of the forms. Bake at 400° F (205° C) until done and golden brown, about 20 minutes.

When babas are cool enough to handle, remove from the forms, cut off the crusts on top, and, at the same time, cut the tops even because they will be served upside down. Make Rum Syrup and reserve one-third of it for serving. Heat the remaining syrup to scalding temperature; place the babas in the syrup until thoroughly saturated. To make sure they are soaked all the way through, keep them submerged until there are no more bubbles; babas will increase in volume quite a bit. When they have absorbed as much syrup as possible, remove them and place them on a rack to cool. Keep the syrup hot while soaking the babas.

Coat the top of each cake with Apricot Glaze, and place a maraschino half in the middle. To serve, pour about 2 ounces (6 cl) of the reserved Rum Syrup on a plate and place a baba, cut side down, in the middle. Decorate with a rosette of whipped cream piped on the plate.

Rum Syrup

    1 orange
    3 pounds (1 kg, 356 g) sugar
    5 cups (1 liter, 2 dl) water
    2 cups (4 dl, 8 cl) rum

Cut the orange in half and add to the sugar and water. Heat to boiling and boil for a few minutes. Remove from heat, strain, and stir in the rum.

RUM-BALL MIXTURE

Because Rum Balls recycle good leftover end pieces and scraps of dough and other preparations, there is no set recipe. However, the rum-ball bucket should not be mistaken for a garbage can. Only those scraps that will not spoil within a week or so should be added. No pastry cream or whipped cream can be used; Buttercream can only be used if it is freshly made. Puff paste, Danish, or other yeast dough should not be used in a quality rum-ball mix; they should be put in their own special bucket and used in Danish filling.

Soak raisins in water overnight to soften. Place the week's scraps in a mixer bowl with a paddle, making sure you do not add any that should not be in because you will not be able to tell once the scraps are mixed. Depending on how many dry items you have, add just enough water so that the mixture starts to cake and the lumps are broken down. Crush roasted hazelnuts or any other kind of nut coarsely and add to the mixture. This is also a good time to get rid of any small amounts of nuts that have accumulated during the week. Add Buttercream, Ganache, chocolate scraps (if you do not already have too many chocolate items in the mix), and Apricot Jam. Add raisins to taste last so that they will not be crushed. The mix should be soft enough so that you can easily roll it into balls without it crumbling. Remember that the nuts absorb fat as the dough rests.

RUM BALLS
photograph, p. 201

> **Rum-ball Mixture (recipe precedes)**
> **light chocolate**
> **Short Dough (see p. 19)**
> **melted dark chocolate**

Make Rum-ball Mixture, refrigerate until firm, and divide into 1-pound (455-g) portions. Roll each piece into an 18-inch (45-cm) log and cut into 18 pieces. Roll the pieces into balls and refrigerate until cold.

Melt light chocolate, and let it cool, stirring occasionally, until it is as thick as mayonnaise. Using your hands, roll the balls into chocolate; the chocolate must be thick enough to leave ridges and points when the balls are rolled. Be sure not to roll them too long because the warmth of your hands will thin the chocolate.

Roll out Short Dough ⅛ inch (3 mm) thick; cut out 1¼-inch (30-mm) cookies with a fluted cutter. Bake at 375° F (190° C) about 10 minutes; let cool completely. Dip the cookies into dark chocolate, and, before the chocolate becomes firm, place a Rum Ball on top.

RUM-BALL PORCUPINES
photograph, p. 201

> **Rum-ball Mixture (see p. 194)**
> **blanched soft whole almonds**
> **melted dark chocolate**
> **Royal Icing (see p. 251)**

Make Rum-ball Mixture; refrigerate until firm. Divide Rum-ball Mixture into 1-pound (455-g) pieces, roll each piece into a 14-inch (35-cm) log, and cut each log into 14 pieces. Roll each piece into a ball, and refrigerate until firm.

Meanwhile, cut blanched almonds into pointed strips, and dry them in the oven until hard.

Push 6 to 8 almond pieces, pointed ends out, into the back two-thirds of each cone. Dip porcupines into chocolate. With Royal Icing, pipe on eyes large enough so that you can pipe pupils with dark chocolate.

RUM-BALL SPOOLS

photograph, p. 201

> **Rum-ball Mixture (see p. 194)**
> **Marzipan (see p. 255)**
> **Buttercream (see p. 239)**
> **powdered sugar**
> **dark chocolate**

Make Rum-ball Mixture; refrigerate until firm. Divide into 12-ounce (340-g) pieces and set aside. Roll out Marzipan into a rectangle, 20 inches (50-cm) long and ⅛ inch (3 mm) thick. Turn Marzipan upside down, and spread on a thin film of Buttercream on top.

Roll each rum-ball piece in powdered sugar into a log the length of the Marzipan. If the rum-ball mix is crumbling and dry, add some Ganache or jam. Roll the log in the Marzipan one full turn and cut. The edges of the Marzipan should not overlap but line up next to each other. Move the logs onto a cardboard or sheet pan. Roll them even and at the same time stretch them to the length of the sheet pan, 24 inches (60 cm). Refrigerate until firm.

Cut each log into 9 pieces, about 2¾ inches (7 cm) long each. Cut 3 or 4 strips together to save time. Dip the ends no more than ⅛ inch (3 mm) into dark chocolate, and pipe a small dot of chocolate in the middle.

Vanilla Macaroon

Chocolate Macaroon

Macaroon Bananas

Coconut Macaroons

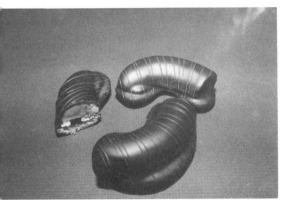

Brysselkex

Vanilla Brysselkex

Chocolate Chip Cookies

Chocolate Cuts

Gingerbread Cookies

Spritz Rings

Vanilla Dreams

Hazelnut Cookies

Hazelnut Squares

Oat Flakes

Almond Truffles

Amandine Hearts

Almond Delights

Othellos

Kirschwasser Rings

Florentines

Florentina Noisettes

Florentina Surprise

Málaga Cookies

Mazarins

Linzer Tartlet

Orange Truffle Strips

Small Diplomats

Small Princess Cakes

Sacher Cuts

Polynees

Potatoes

Pretzels

Baba au Rhum

Rum Balls

Rum-ball Porcupines

Rum-ball Spools

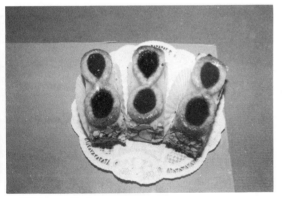

Diplomat Strips

7

Custards, Mousses, and Soufflés

MOUSSE AU GRAND MARNIER

fifteen 5-ounce (140-g) portions

16 egg yolks
5 ounces (140 g) sugar
2 cups (4 dl, 8 cl) milk
6 ounces (170 g) white chocolate
½ ounce (15 g) unflavored gelatin
1 ounce (3 cl) water
2 ounces (6 cl) Grand Marnier
2 cups (4 dl, 8 cl) heavy cream
   whipped cream
   sliced roasted almonds

Beat egg yolks and sugar lightly. Scald milk, and pour into the egg-yolk mixture with one hand while stirring with the other. Chop the white chocolate into small pieces; and add chocolate to hot milk mixture. Stir until chocolate is completely melted and cooled to body temperature. Dissolve gelatin in water and Grand Marnier, heat to 150° F (65° C), and add to the milk mixture. Whip the heavy cream to soft peaks; gradually fold the cooled mixture into the whipped cream.

Using a medium-size tip on a pastry bag, pipe the mousse into champagne glasses. Refrigerate for at least 4 hours. Because of the small amount of gelatin, this mousse will take a little longer than normal to become firm but will also remain soft and smooth the next day.

Using a no. 7 (14-mm) star tip, pipe a whipped cream rosette in the middle of each mousse. Sprinkle sliced almonds lightly on top. Serve cold with a cookie on the plate. Any liqueur of good quality can be substituted for the Grand Marnier. If you change the amount of liqueur in the recipe, also change the amount of milk to make up for the increased or decreased liquid.

RASPBERRY CHOCOLATE MOUSSE
twelve 3½-ounce (100-g) servings   photograph, p. 216

      1 ounce (28 g) pectin powder
      9 ounces (255 g) sugar
    10 ounces (3 cl) egg whites
    ½ ounce (15 g) unflavored gelatin
      4 ounces (1 dl, 2 cl) water
    11 ounces (310 g) white chocolate
      2 pounds, 3 ounces (1 kg) strained raspberry purée
      4 ounces (1 dl, 2 cl) lemon juice
      1 quart, 1½ ounces (1 l) heavy cream
          whipped cream
          shaved dark chocolate
          about 100 raspberries

Mix the pectin and sugar in a bowl; add egg whites. Heat to about 150° F (65° C), whipping the mixture to a foam at the same time. Dissolve gelatin in water and mix into egg whites. Chop white chocolate into small chunks and stir into the warm batter. When all the chocolate is melted, stir in raspberry purée and lemon juice. If the mixture is still warm, cool it to body temperature.

Whip heavy cream to soft peaks and fold into the batter by hand. Pipe into champagne glasses or another desired glass. Refrigerate at least 2 hours.

Decorate each mousse with a rosette of whipped cream piped with a no. 6 (12-mm) star tip. Sprinkle dark chocolate lightly on top of the whipped cream. Place fresh raspberries in a ring around the cream. Serve with macaroons. If raspberries are out of season but you still want that wonderful flavor, simply omit them from the decoration.

CRÊPES VIENNA

25 servings   *color photograph, p. C-4*

> Crêpes (recipe follows)
> fresh oranges, peeled
> Orange Sauce (see p. 260)
> fresh raspberries
> whipped cream

Make the crêpe batter. While the batter is resting, section the oranges (save any juice for the sauce). Make Orange Sauce.

Place crêpe so that the golden brown side will show when it is rolled. Fill the crêpes with equal amounts of raspberries and orange wedges cut to the size of raspberries, four or five of each. To serve, place 2 filled crêpes on a dessert plate and cover with enough Orange Sauce so that it spills around the crêpes. Decorate with a whipped cream rosette.

If raspberries are out of season, use fresh strawberries, cut into quarters.

Crêpes

45 to 50 crêpes

> 6 ounces (170 g) cake flour
> 6 ounces (170 g) bread flour
> 2½ ounces (70 g) sugar
> ⅓ ounce (10 g) salt
> 6 whole eggs (300 g)
> 7 extra egg yolks (140 g)
> 6 ounces (170 g) butter, melted
> 3 cups (7 dl, 2 cl) lukewarm milk
> 3 ounces (9 cl) brandy
> clarified butter

Combine dry ingredients in a mixing bowl. Beat the whole eggs and extra egg yolks lightly; stir gradually into the dry ingredients. Add butter, milk, and brandy; mix until smooth. Let batter rest 1 hour.

Heat a 6- to 7-inch (15- to 17.5-cm) crêpe pan, and brush with clarified butter (do not use a nylon brush unless you have an inexpensive source for brushes). Cover the bottom of the pan with the batter by quickly tilting and rotating the pan; return excess batter to the bowl. The crêpes should be very thin, but if big bubbles develop as they are baked, add a little flour (bubbles may also appear if the pan is too hot). If the crêpes are too thick, add some milk (unless you are pouring too much batter into the pan). If you are cooking many crêpes, do not try to turn them with a spatula; it is faster to flip them over into a heated big skillet and cook a few seconds longer. The second side only has to cook until it is no longer sticky; if you cook it long enough to color it, the crêpe will be too dry.

When crêpes are finished, stack them so that the second one almost covers the first one, and so on, to prevent them drying and make it easier to pick them up later.

Do not wash the crêpe pan, but just wipe it off with a rag.

PEARS CALIFORNIA
photograph, p. 216

> pears
> lemon juice
> Poaching Syrup (see p. 233)
> Chocolate Leaves (see p. 245)
> Apricot Sauce (see p. 239)
> almond paste
> honey
> whipped cream

Try to use small pears (such as Bartlett) of the same size and ripeness. If necessary, trim larger pears down to a smaller size. Peel pears evenly, but leave the stems intact. When they are peeled, place them in acidulated water. Poach pears in Poaching Syrup until tender; you should be able to stick a fork into the pear with no effort. Cool pears in syrup. In the meantime, make Chocolate Leaves and Apricot Sauce.

When pears are cool, make a horizontal cut ½ inch (12 mm) below the stem, but do not cut all the way through; core the pears up to the cut, leaving the stems intact. Soften almond paste with water and flavor it with honey; fill the hollows of the pears with almond paste. Refrigerate until ready to serve.

Place a pear on a dessert plate. Pour enough Apricot Sauce (about 3 ounces/9 cl) on top of each pear so that it runs down and covers the plate. Make a cut ¼ inch (6 mm) below the stem and place a Chocolate Leaf in the cut. Put a whipped cream rosette on the plate and serve immediately.

CHARLOTTE WITH PEARS AND CARAMEL SAUCE

30 servings   *color photograph, p. C-4*

> 5 to 6 medium-size pears
> Poaching Syrup (see p. 233)
> 1 pound (455 g) granulated sugar
> 14 ounces (4 dl, 2 cl) water
> Bavarois (recipe follows)
> Caramel Sauce (see p. 235)
> whipped cream
> strawberry wedges

Preferably the day before serving but no less than 4 hours before serving, peel, halve, and core the pears. Poach them in Poaching Syrup. Cut them lengthwise into thin slices. Caramelize the granulated sugar (see Index); stir in the water and cook out the lumps. Add the sliced pears and soak in the syrup. Make Bavarois.

Remove the pear slices from the syrup, and pat them dry on a towel. Line the sides of *pot de crème* cups or coffee cups, 2½ inches (6.2 cm) wide and 3 inches (7.5 cm) deep, with 4 or 5 pear slices evenly spaced and standing up in a tulip pattern. Fill cups three-quarters full with Bavarois. Refrigerate until set, at least 2 hours. Meanwhile make Caramel Sauce.

To serve, unmold the charlotte onto a serving plate by first placing the cup briefly in warm water. Pour 1 ounce (3 cl) Caramel Sauce around the charlotte; garnish with a rosette of whipped cream and a strawberry wedge.

Bavarois

> 8 ounces (225 g) egg yolks
> 4 ounces (115 g) sugar
> 1 quart (9 dl, 6 cl) milk
> 1 vanilla bean or 1 teaspoon (6 g) vanilla extract
> 1½ ounces (40 g) unflavored gelatin
> 1½ cups (3 dl, 6 cl) water
> 1 quart (9 dl, 6 cl) heavy cream
> ½ recipe Italian Meringue (see p. 143)

Beat egg yolks with the sugar. Scald milk with a vanilla bean or extract, and pour slowly over yolks, beating constantly. Dissolve gelatin in water and stir into egg-yolk mixture. In this case, you do not have to heat the gelatin, since the milk is hot. Refrigerate the mixture or hold at room temperature, stirring occasionally. If necessary, cool over ice water. If lumps form, reheat the mixture, stirring constantly, and cool again.

Whip cream to soft peaks. When egg-yolk mixture is cooled to room temperature fold it into the cream. When mixture is just starting to set, fold in the Italian Meringue. It is important to incorporate the meringue after the Bavarois starts to set so that the pudding and the meringue do not separate.

CHARLOTTE CHARENTE

thirty 3-inch (7.5-cm) servings   photograph, p. 216

       4 ounces (115 g) dried currants or raisins
      ½ recipe Ladyfingers (see p. 158)
      15 ounces (3 dl, 9 cl) port
     2½ ounces (7.5 cl) Cognac
      ⅚ ounces (24 g) unflavored gelatin
       6 ounces (170 g) egg yolks
    13½ ounces (4 dl) syrup, at 30° Baumé
     9½ ounces (270 g) sugar
     2½ ounces (7.5 cl) water
     4⅓ ounces (125 g) egg whites
     2½ cups (6 dl) whipping cream
         whipped cream
         Chocolate Rounds (see p. 245)
         orange wedges and strawberry slices

Soak currants or raisins in 2 ounces (6 cl) warm port and set aside. Using a no. 3 (6-mm) plain tip, pipe out Ladyfingers 2 inches (5 cm) long and close enough to each other so that they will just barely bake together. Bake at 410° F (210° C) about 8 minutes. You should be able to pick up a row of 6 or 7 cakes all at once. If Ladyfingers are too dry to bend into a circle without breaking, place a wet towel on a sheet pan and place the Ladyfingers (still on the baking paper) on top; invert another sheet pan over the Ladyfingers, using it as a lid, and steam them at 375° F (190° C) about 5 minutes. If there is no hurry to soften them, just place them in the refrigerator prepared the same way. Line straight-sided molds, such as 3-inch (7.5-cm) soufflé ramekins with Ladyfingers. (You may, instead of using ramekins, simply staple together plastic strips to the correct size, since the molds do not require a base; just make sure you place them on a pan lined with baking paper.)

Cut the bottoms if cakes are taller than 2 inches (5 cm). Dissolve the gelatin in the remaining 13 ounces (3 dl, 9 cl) port and the Cognac; heat to 150° F (65° C).

Whip egg yolks and syrup to the ribbon stage; beat in the gelatin mixture. Make Italian Meringue. Boil sugar and water to 235° F (108° C). When the sugar reaches 180° F (82° C), start whipping the egg whites. Slowly whip syrup into the egg whites; whip until mixture is cold. Whip the whipping cream to soft peaks. Fold the egg whites into the yolk mixture; fold in the whipped cream. Finally, fold in the currants. Make sure the mixture is just starting to set before piping it into the prepared molds so that the currants do not sink to the bottom. Using a large plain tube, pipe into the prepared molds. Refrigerate until set, at least 2 hours.

Unmold the charlottes, and, using a no. 4 (8-mm) plain tip, decorate with whipped cream in a pearl-drop shape around the sides. Put 1 small mound of cream on top. Place a Chocolate Round on top and orange wedges and strawberry slices around the plate.

PERSIMMON PUDDING
16 to 18 servings

> 10 ounces (285 g) raisins, mixed dark and light or all dark
> 1 cup (2 dl, 4 cl) brandy
> 2 cups (2 dl, 4 cl) strained puréed ripe persimmons
> 1 pound, 4 ounces (570 g) sugar
> 2 teaspoons (8 g) oil
> 1 teaspoon (3 g) vanilla extract
> 8 ounces (225 g) bread flour
> 2 teaspoons (8 g) baking soda
> 1 teaspoon (4 g) salt
> pinch ground cloves
> pinch grated nutmeg
> 7½ ounces (215 g) walnuts, chopped to the size of raisins
> 1 cup (2 dl, 4 cl) milk
> Brandied Whipped Cream (recipe follows)
> fresh strawberry wedges
> grated nutmeg

Make sure the persimmons are ripe. If they are not, you can speed up the process by freezing them. When they have thawed, they will be soft, but you will still have to watch for the dry unripe taste. If possible, use fruits of the Japanese variety (*fuyu*), which do not have the dry taste and can be used not fully ripe if they are soft enough to purée.

Soak raisins in brandy while preparing batter. Mix persimmon purée, sugar, oil, and vanilla. Combine dry ingredients, including walnuts, and combine with the persimmon mixture. Slowly stir in the milk. Stir in raisins and brandy. Grease an angel-cake pan; line the bottom with parchment paper. Pour batter into pan. Bake at 325° F (165° C) 1¼ to 1½ hours. Let pudding cool completely before unmolding.

Cut into serving slices and place on plates. Spoon Brandied Whipped Cream over half. Place a small strawberry wedge on the side for some color. Sprinkle nutmeg on top of the whipped cream.

If the pudding is served whole, place it on a serving platter. Heat 3 ounces (9 cl) brandy to scalding, 170° F (77° C), but do not boil. Pour brandy into a small flame-proof cup, and place it in the middle of the ring. Turn down room lights, ignite the hot brandy, and spoon it flaming around the pudding. Serve Brandied Whipped Cream on the side.

Brandied Whipped Cream

>   2 cups (4 dl, 8 cl) whipping cream
>   brandy
>   grated nutmeg
>   sugar

Whip cream to the consistency of a sauce; flavor with brandy, nutmeg, and sugar to taste.

CRÈME BRULÉE
about 20 4½-ounce (1-dl, 3-cl) servings
photograph, p. 216

>   24 egg yolks (480 g)
>   12 ounces (340 g) brown sugar
>   4½ pints (2 l, 1 dl, 6 cl) whipping cream
>   pinch salt
>   1 teaspoon (6 g) vanilla extract
>   brown sugar

Mix egg yolks and 12 ounces (340 g) brown sugar lightly. Scald cream; whisk into egg mixture. Whisk in salt and vanilla. Pour custard into small individual forms, such as individual soufflé dishes, 3½ inches (8.5 cm) wide.

Place forms in a hot water bath with water halfway up the forms. Bake at 350° F (175° C) until custards just start to gel; they will set more as they cool. Store in the refrigerator.

Before serving, lightly sift dry brown sugar over the tops (dry brown sugar slightly in the oven). Wipe the edges of the forms clean. Caramelize the sugar in a salamander or under a broiler. Serve chilled.

POTS DE CRÈME À LA VANILLE
26 5-ounce (1-dl, 5-cl) servings

> 3 quarts (2 l, 8 dl, 8 cl) light cream
> 1 vanilla bean or 1 teaspoon (6 g) vanilla extract
> 10 whole eggs (500 g)
> 14 egg yolks (280 g)
> 15 ounces (430 g) sugar

Scald cream with the vanilla bean or extract until a skin forms on top, about 160° F (71° C). Mix eggs, egg yolks, and sugar just until mixed. Stir cream slowly into egg mixture. Mix thoroughly, strain, and pour into *pots de crème* cups or other desired forms at least 2 inches (5 cm) deep. Skim off any foam before baking.

Place forms in water bath filled to one-third of the height of the forms with cold water. If you are not using *pots de crème* cups with individual covers, cover the entire pan of water with a lid or aluminum foil, leaving an opening to allow steam to escape. Bake at 350° F (175° C) until custard starts to set in the middle, 30 to 35 minutes. Remove from hot water immediately and cool completely. Serve chilled.

POTS DE CRÈME AU CHOCOLAT
16 5-ounce (1-dl, 5-cl) servings

> 3 pints (1 l, 4 dl, 4 cl) milk
> 1 vanilla bean or 1 teaspoon (6 g) vanilla extract
> 1½ ounces (40 g) dark chocolate, chopped
> 6 ounces (170 g) cocoa powder
> 4 eggs (200 g)
> 16 egg yolks (320 g)
> 1 pound (455 g) sugar

Scald the milk with the vanilla bean or extract until a skin forms, about 160° F (71° C). Remove from heat and stir in chopped dark chocolate and cocoa powder. Follow the procedure for Pots de Crème à la Vanille.

BASIC SOUFFLÉ
photograph, p. 216

24 portions
3½ ounces (100 g) flour
3½ ounces (100 g) butter
1 quart, 1½ ounces (1 liter) milk
15 egg yolks (300 g)
pinch salt
½ teaspoon (3 g) vanilla extract
19 egg whites (540 g)
9 ounces (255 g) granulated sugar
3 ounces (85 g) cornstarch
powdered sugar

4 portions
⅔ ounce (20 g) flour
⅔ ounce (20 g) butter
5½ ounces (1 dl, 6½ cl) milk
3 egg yolks (60 g)
pinch salt
1 drop vanilla extract
3 egg whites (90 g)
1½ ounces (40 g) sugar
½ ounce (15 g) cornstarch
powdered sugar

Mix flour and butter. Heat milk to scalding. Stir flour mixture into milk. Stir a third of the egg yolks. Cook, stirring constantly, over low heat until thick and boiling. Remove from heat but keep stirring. Stir in salt, vanilla, and the remaining egg yolks. Place a paper on the surface and set aside.

Prepare 3-inch (7.5-cm) individual soufflé cups by brushing with soft butter and sprinkling with granulated sugar.

About 40 minutes before the soufflés are to be served, start whipping the egg whites. Mix one-fifth of the sugar with the cornstarch, and add to yolk mixture. Whip remaining sugar into the whites as directed for French Meringue (see Index). Beat egg whites to stiff peaks. Fold whites carefully into the yolk mixture. Fill each soufflé form to the top, smooth the top with a spatula, and clean the rim with your thumb. Place soufflés evenly spaced on a sheet pan; do not crowd. Bake immediately at 375° F (190° C) 25 to 30 minutes. If soufflés will not be served immediately, do not use sheet pans. Instead, bake them in a hot-water bath, with water to half the height of the form. This prevents the soufflés from drying at the bottom or becoming too dark on top. With this method, your soufflé will not be quite as high, but it does allow you to delay serving for 15 minutes. For maximum height remove the soufflés from the water bath—but do *not* remove from oven—and bake directly on a sheet pan for 3 to 4 minutes before serving.

Dust lightly with powdered sugar and serve immediately with a separate sauce.

Liqueur Soufflé
Add ½ ounce (1.5 cl) desired liqueur for every 4 servings. To add more flavor, soak Ladyfingers (see Index) in liqueur, fill half the form with soufflé batter, place Ladyfingers in the middle, and fill with remaining batter.

Chocolate Soufflé
Add 3 ounces (85 g) cocoa powder, 2 ounces (6 cl) water, 2 ounces (6 cl) Simple Syrup (see Index), 2 egg whites, ½ ounce (15 g) cornstarch for 24 servings. Use ½ ounce (15 g) cocoa powder, ⅓ ounce (1 cl) water, ⅓ ounce (1 cl) Simple Syrup, but no extra eggs or cornstarch for 4 servings. Add water and Simple Syrup to the cocoa powder and mix to a smooth paste. Combine this with the soufflé batter before folding in the stiffened egg whites.

Harlequin Soufflé
Place a precut piece of cardboard down the middle of each soufflé cup. Divide the recipe in half before adding the egg whites. Use additional 1½ ounces (40 g) cocoa powder, 1 ounce (3 cl) water, 1 ounce (3 cl) Simple Syrup, 1 egg white, and ⅓ ounce cornstarch to half of the soufflé batter for 24 servings. Add ⅓ ounce (10 g) cocoa powder, ¼ ounce (½ cl) water, ½ ounce Simple Syrup, but no extra egg or cornstarch for 4 servings. Make paste by adding water and Simple Syrup to cocoa powder. Combine with souffle batter before adding egg whites. Fill one side of each cup with vanilla and the other side with chocolate; then pull the cardboard straight up and out.

SOUFFLÉ WITH CRÊPES

about 16 servings   photograph, p. 216

½ recipe Crêpes (see p. 206)
1¾ ounces (50 g) flour
1¾ ounces (50 g) butter
 2 cups (4 dl, 8 cl) milk
 8 egg yolks (160 g)
   pinch salt
1½ ounces (4.5 cl) liqueur
   vanilla extract
   Melba Sauce (see p. 260)
 9 egg whites (255 g)
4½ ounces (130 g) granulated sugar
1½ ounces (40 g) cornstarch
   powdered sugar

Make Crêpes and set aside. Mix flour and butter. Heat milk to boiling; stir gradually into the batter mixture. Stir in 3 of the egg yolks (60 g). Cook, stirring constantly, over low heat until thick and boiling. Remove from heat and keep stirring. Stir in salt, liqueur, vanilla, and the remaining egg yolks. Cover the surface with paper and set aside.

Line 3-inch (7.5-cm) ramekins with Crêpes, brown side facing out, pushing them down halfway into the forms.

Make Melba Sauce.

About 25 minutes before serving, start whipping the egg whites. Mix 1 ounce (30 g) of the granulated sugar with the cornstarch. Whip remaining sugar and the whites as directed for French Meringue (see Index); whip to stiff peaks. Stir cornstarch mixture into the custard by hand; fold meringue carefully into prepared custard. Pipe batter up to the tops of the prepared ramekins. Bake immediately at 400° F (205° C) about 15 minutes. If the soufflés are not to be served immediately when done, bake instead in an oversized pan filled with water to half the height of the ramekins. This will prevent the soufflés from drying out for up to 15 minutes. Your soufflé will not be quite as high using this method; for maximum height, remove from water bath—but not from oven—and bake for 3 to 4 minutes on a sheet pan.

While soufflés are baking, spoon 1 to 2 ounces (3 to 6 cl) of Melba Sauce on each dessert plate. Dust soufflés lightly with powdered sugar, remove from ramekins, and place on the sauce. Serve immediately.

Raspberry Chocolate Mousse

Pears California

Charlotte Charente

Crème Brulée

Basic Soufflé

Soufflé with Crêpes

8

Frozen Desserts

Ice creams and other frozen desserts of different shapes and combinations have always been favorites of guests and chefs alike. Ice cream seems to bring out the child in us, making it almost impossible to resist. The taste is refreshing, which is especially appreciated in summer, and the light consistency makes it easy to digest. This is one dessert that truly melts in the mouth. Ice cream is also an ideal dessert for chefs to prepare because it can be made days in advance. Today even the home cook can make wonderful ice creams with the small electric ice-cream freezers now available at a reasonable cost. Churning ice cream by hand is almost obsolete.

For a finished product of high quality, absolute cleanliness and sanitation is a must. Because the ice-cream mixture is a perfect breeding ground for bacteria, the equipment and utensils that come in contact with the ice cream must be stainless steel or other noncorrosive material and must be cleaned thoroughly after each use. The warm ice-cream mixture must not be poured directly into the ice-cream freezer; the mixture should cool slowly and then be refrigerated for a few hours or overnight. The extra time in cooling the mixture will result in a smoother finished product. When the ice cream has churned to the desired consistency, turn off the freezer unit of the ice-cream maker but keep the churner on for a few minutes.

The amount of air incorporated into the ice cream while it is churning is what determines the volume and lightness of the finished product. As a rule, the higher quality ice creams have the least volume. Because an ice cream made with heavy cream is more compact in its composition, it yields a lesser amount than an ice cream made with milk or half-and-half, but it is also richer and smoother.

Custard ice cream is the most commmon and is usually what is meant by ice cream. It is really nothing more than a frozen vanilla sauce in which the egg yolks and sugar have been adjusted to suit a particular flavor. The gelato type, which is gaining in popularity, is a richer, creamier version. In an emergency, thawed vanilla ice cream can be used as a sauce.

Sorbets, also known as fruit and water ices, are made of fruit purée and/or juice combined with a simple syrup at a density of 18° to 22° Baumé. Sorbets are also made from liqueurs and wines. Sometimes a small amount of Italian meringue is added to give the sorbet a smoother texture, but the meringue takes away some of the flavor. When a large amount of Italian meringue is added to a sorbet, it is called a spoom. A granité is a water ice that is not churned during freezing but frozen in a hotel pan or other shallow container. The sugar density is only 14° Baumé, which produces a somewhat grainy texture, as the name suggests. Both sorbets and granités are served as palate cleansers in between courses of large dinners.

A parfait is a delicate dessert made of a mixture of egg yolks and sugar whipped to a ribbon, whipped cream, and flavoring. To achieve the distinctive light texture of this dessert, it is of utmost importance that the ingredients be combined very carefully to preserve the whipped-in air. The mixture is then poured into molds and frozen. Parfaits are also combined with ice creams in ice bombes; the inside of the mold is lined with ice cream, which is then frozen until hard, and filled with the parfait mixture. Parfait mixtures are also used in frozen cakes. Another delicious variation is soufflé glacé, which is made by mixing Italian meringue, ice cream, and the parfait mixture and freezing in soufflé cups. Many of the different frozen desserts were created years ago and are now classics, such as, Meringue Glacé, Vacherin, and Peach Melba, but there is still plenty of room for your particular taste and imagination.

Sorbets and some ice creams taste best when freshly made and still soft, but it is possible to store ice cream for three to four weeks without any loss of volume or quality if it is stored in airtight containers. Sorbets and parfaits, however, cannot be kept longer than one or two weeks at the most. Ice cream should be frozen at $-6°$ F ($-25°$ C) to harden quickly and stored at a temperature between 14° F ($-10°$ C) and 6° F ($-15°$ C). They should be served at a lower temperature, however, so that they are soft enough to be pleasant to eat and easy to serve (the temperature depends on the type of ice cream or sorbet used). The ice cream desserts can be unmolded or scooped into serving glasses one to two hours in advance, but final touches must be applied at the last moment.

VANILLA ICE CREAM
1½ quarts (1 l, 4 dl, 4 cl)

> 2 cups (4 dl, 8 cl) milk
> 2 cups (4 dl, 8 cl) heavy cream
> 1 vanilla bean or vanilla extract
> 10 egg yolks (200 g)
> 10 ounces (285 g) sugar

Heat milk, cream, and vanilla bean to boiling. Meanwhile beat egg yolks and sugar to the ribbon stage. Slowly pour milk mixture into the eggs, whisking rapidly. Place a wet towel under the bowl to keep it from turning as you whisk. Cook over hot water until the mixture coats a spoon. The eggs will coagulate if heated above this point. To keep the mixture from coagulating, keep stirring for 30 seconds after removing it from heat or immediately transfer it to another bowl. If the mixture coagulates anyway, add a few ounces of heavy cream and blend until smooth. The mixture will lose some volume, but it can be used.

Cool the mixture completely before freezing to prevent ice crystals from forming as the cream freezes. Make the mixture 10 to 12 hours before it is to be frozen and refrigerate it for a creamier, less icy ice cream. Place a container in the freezer to chill at the same time the mixture is put in the ice-cream freezer.

MANGO OR PAPAYA ICE CREAM
1½ quarts (1 l, 4 dl, 4 cl)   *photograph, p. 229*

> 2 egg yolks (40 g)
> 4 ounces (115 g) sugar
> 2 cups (4 dl, 8 cl) milk
> 2 cups (4 dl, 8 cl) mangoes or papayas
> 1 cup (2 dl, 4 cl) whipping cream
> 2 egg whites (60 g)
> Chocolate Tulips (recipe follows)
> blanched, skinned, and crushed pistachios

Beat egg yolks and half the sugar. Heat milk to boiling, pour into egg mixture, whisking rapidly, and heat to boiling again. Cool completely. While mixture is cooling, purée the mangoes or papayas, leaving a third of the fruit in small chunks. Stir into the cooled cream mixture and freeze in ice-cream freezer.

Whip cream to soft peaks. Whip egg whites and the remaining sugar and fold into the whipped cream. When the ice cream is halfway frozen, add the whipped cream mixture and finish freezing.

Serve in Chocolate Tulips with a sprinkle of crushed pistachios on top.

Chocolate Tulips
25 to 30 tulips

```
  7  ounces (200 g) sugar
8½  ounces (240 g) egg whites
5½  ounces (160 g) bread flour
  ½  ounce (15 g) cocoa powder
  7  ounces (200 g) clarified butter
```

Mix sugar and egg whites well, about 1 minute. Sift flour with cocoa powder and fold in. Fold in clarified butter. Butter and lightly flour the back of 3 sheet pans thoroughly. Using a 5- to 6-inch (12.5- to 15-cm) plain cookie cutter, mark 9 circles on the pan; spread the batter in a thin layer inside the circles. The circles will get slightly larger when baked. Bake at 400° F (205° C) about 5 minutes. Working quickly and gently, place each warm cookie circle over an upside-down custard cup or other form, 1¾ inches (4.5 cm) at the bottom and 3 inches (7.5 cm) at the top. Place a ramekin or soup cup over the cookie and shape it using the form. Make sure the tulips can hold their shapes before removing the forms.

Variation
Use recipe above with the following changes: replace cocoa powder with ½ ounce (15 g) bread flour. Reserve 3 ounces (85 g) of the batter before spreading on circles. Color batter with a small amount of cocoa powder. Before baking, pipe brown batter onto circles in a thin spiral. Using the back of a small knife or spatula, fan the spiral out from the center all around to form a spider web pattern.

BANANA POPPY-SEED ICE CREAM

2 quarts (1 l, 9 dl, 2 cl)   *color photograph, p. C-4*

>   3 cups (7 dl, 2 cl) milk
>   2 cups (4 dl, 8 cl) cream
>   9 ounces (255 g) sugar
>   10 egg yolks
> 1½ cups (3 dl, 6 cl) puréed ripe bananas
>   2 ounces (55 g) dried poppy seeds
>   3 ounces (9 cl) Frangelico
>   Strawberry Sauce (see p. 260)
>   whipped cream

Scald milk and cream mixed. Whip sugar and egg yolks lightly. Whipping constantly, pour the hot liquid into the egg mixture. Place in a hot-water bath and, stirring constantly, heat until the mixture thickens enough to coat the spoon; be careful not to overheat. Cool the mixture, and refrigerate covered at least 8 hours. Before freezing, stir in bananas, poppy seeds, and liqueur.

Serve with Strawberry Sauce and decorate with whipped cream rosettes.

CARAMEL ICE CREAM IN CAGE

2¼ quarts (2 l, 4 dl)   *photograph, p. 229*

>   ½ recipe Caramel Sauce I (see p. 235)
>   1 quart (9 dl, 6 cl) milk
>   10 egg yolks (200 g)
>   2 ounces (55 g) sugar
>   2 cups (4 dl, 8 cl) whipping cream
>   7 ounces (200 g) Nougatine Crunch (recipe follows)
>   whipped cream
>   shaved dark chocolate
>   Caramel Cages (procedure follows)

Make Caramel Sauce I. Add the milk and heat to scalding. Whip egg yolks and sugar to the ribbon stage. Gradually add caramel mixture to yolk mixture, whisking rapidly. Heat over hot water, stirring constantly, or until the mixture coats a wooden spoon. Remove from heat and stir in whipping cream. Cool and refrigerate covered. Just before freezing, stir in Nougatine Crunch. Freeze in ice-cream freezer.

To serve, scoop ice cream into prechilled glasses. Using a no. 4 (8-mm) plain tip, pipe whipped cream in a pearl pattern around the bottom of each scoop. Shave dark chocolate over the ice cream and put the cages on top. Serve immediately.

Nougatine Crunch

3½ ounces (100 g) blanched almonds, finely chopped
4½ ounces (130 g) sugar
    juice of a quarter lemon

Roast almonds until golden brown. Place sugar and lemon juice in a saucepan, and caramelize to a light golden color. Stir in almonds, and pour immediately onto an oiled marble slab or sheet pan. When crunch is cooled, crush into small pieces in a food processor or by hand. Nougatine Crunch can be made in large batches and stored in airtight containers.

Caramel Cages

Caramelize enough sugar so you can afford to break a few cages. Start with a light golden caramel so that it can be reheated a few times without getting too dark. Find a ladle that fits just inside the rim of the serving glass you are using. Holding the ladle upside down, brush the back of the ladle with oil and streak the caramel across in lines about ½ inch (12 mm) apart. Turn the ladle and repeat, making a dome that has about ½-inch (12-mm) square openings. If the caramel streaks are too thin, wait a few minutes for the caramel to thicken before making the cages. Leave the cage on the ladle about 30 seconds; remove and repeat the process. If the cage is left on the ladle too long, it will stick. Working with 2 ladles speeds up the process. When the caramel gets too thick, heat it without stirring so that no air is mixed in.

SORBET AU CHAMPAGNE

20 servings

3½ cups (8 dl, 4 cl) dry champagne
2½ cups (6 dl) Simple Syrup at 28° Baumé (see p. 233)
1½ cups (3 dl, 6 cl) noneffervescent mineral water
    juice of 2 lemons
    Champagne Sabayon Sauce (recipe follows)
    Ganache (see p. 247)
    Simple Syrup or Chocolate Sauce (see pp. 233, 248)

Mix champagne, Simple Syrup, the mineral water, and lemon juice; freeze in an ice-cream freezer.

To serve, ladle 1 to 2 ounces (3 to 6 cl) Champagne Sabayon Sauce on a prechilled serving plate. Thin Ganache with Simple Syrup or Chocolate Sauce and place in a piping cone; pipe a spiral of Ganache on top of the sauce. Using the back of a knife, streak the sauce every 1 inch (25 mm) all around to create a spider's web effect. Place a scoop of sorbet in the middle and serve immediately.

Champagne Sabayon Sauce

    10 egg yolks (200 g)
     1 ounce (30 g) maraschino liqueur
     2 cups (4 dl, 8 cl) dry champagne
    10 ounces (285 g) sugar

This sauce must be served within a half hour of its making. Place egg yolks, liqueur, and champagne in pan over hot water; whip 6 to 8 minutes, keeping the temperature between 110° and 115° F (42° and 46° C) at all times; you may have to remove the saucepan from the hot water a few times to maintain the temperature. Remove from heat; add the sugar gradually, whipping at a medium pace 5 minutes. Whip at a slow pace over crushed ice 5 minutes.

Variation

For a very colorful presentation, omit the Champagne Sabayon Sauce and serve instead with Melba Sauce (see Index) and blackberry sauce. To make blackberry sauce, follow the procedure for Melba Sauce but replace the raspberries with blackberries.

Chill the serving plates. Pour the Melba Sauce on one-half of the plate and the blackberry sauce on the other half. Be sure the two sauces are thick enough to stay separate from each other. To keep them separated, pipe a ⅛-inch (3-mm) line of Piping Gel (see Index) between the two sauces. Freeze the sauced plates to prevent the sorbet from melting into the sauces while you decorate each serving.

Place a medium-sized scoop of Sorbet au Champagne in the middle of the plate. Arrange 3 fresh raspberries in the blackberry sauce and 3 fresh blackberries in the Melba Sauce. Top the sorbet with a small sprig of fresh mint. Serve immediately.

WHITE-CHOCOLATE ICE CREAM

1½ quarts (1 l, 4 dl, 4 cl)   *photograph, p. 229*

> 2 cups (4 dl, 8 cl) whipping cream
> 2 cups (4 dl, 8 cl) half-and-half
> 8 egg yolks (160 g)
> 5 ounces (140 g) sugar
> 10 ounces (285 g) white chocolate, melted
>   whipped cream
>   Chocolate Tulips variation (see p. 221)
>   light and white chocolate curls

Mix cream and half-and-half; heat to boiling. Beat egg yolks and sugar until frothy. Pour hot cream slowly into egg yolks, stirring rapidly. Place a wet towel underneath the bowl to keep it from turning as you stir. Place the custard in a *bain marie* and heat, stirring constantly, until the mixture is thick enough to coat the spoon. Remove from heat. Stir in melted white chocolate. Cool the mixture completely.

For a smoother ice cream, make the custard the day before it is to be frozen and refrigerate it to mature. Freeze in an ice-cream freezer.

To serve, pipe a small dot of whipped cream in the middle of a chilled plate to prevent tulip from sliding; place a Chocolate Tulip on the whipped cream. Scoop ice cream into the tulip, and decorate with chocolate curls.

ICE-CREAM CAKE JAMAICA

two 10-inch (25-cm) cakes   *color photograph, p. C-4*

> 6 ounces (1 dl, 8 cl) egg whites
> 1 drop tartaric acid
> 12 ounces (340 g) sugar
> 1½ ounces (40 g) cocoa powder
>   dark chocolate
>   Rum Parfait (recipe follows)
>   whipped cream
>   small slice of fresh fruit

Draw four 10-inch (25-cm) circles on 2 transparent sheets of parchment paper, and turn papers over. Whip egg whites and tartaric acid until foamy. Add 10 ounces (285 g) of the sugar over 3 minutes, whipping constantly, until peaks are stiff. Mix remaining sugar with cocoa powder, and fold in by hand.

Using a no. 3 (6-mm) plain tip, pipe a 1-inch (25-mm) meringue frame around all 4 circles. Divide the remaining meringue among the circles, and spread it evenly with a spatula. Bake meringues at 200° F (90° C) until completely dry, 1 to 1½ hours.

Brush a thin layer of melted dark chocolate on the cooled meringue layers. Place them on cardboards and cut them, if necessary, to exactly 10 inches (25 cm). Place an adjustable cake ring lined with parchment paper around two of them. Make Rum Parfait; divide it equally between the meringue bases. Place remaining meringue layers, chocolate sides down, on top. Freeze until hard, 3 to 4 hours.

Remove cake rings and paper. Spread cakes with a thin layer of whipped cream. Cut into serving pieces. Sprinkle dark chocolate 6-inch (15-cm) circle in the middle, and return to the freezer. Chill serving plates in the refrigerator.

To serve, pipe whipped cream on the side of each serving with a no. 4 (8-mm) plain tip, and pipe a rosette at the edge with a no. 6 (12-mm) star tip. (Put the bigger tip inside the bag and hold the smaller tip, when you need it, on top outside the bag.) Decorate with a thin slice of fresh fruit, such as orange, strawberry, or kiwi. Serve immediately.

Rum Parfait

> 5 ounces (140 g) golden raisins
> 5 ounces (1 dl, 5 cl) dark rum
> 7 eggs (350 g)
> 7 ounces (200 g) sugar
> 3 cups (7 dl, 2 cl) whipping cream

Macerate raisins in rum preferably overnight. Whip eggs and sugar over hot water to about 120° F (48° C). Remove pan from heat; whip until eggs are cold and frothy. Whip cream to soft peaks; fold cream, rum and raisins into the egg mixture. The mixture should be thick enough for the raisins not to sink to the bottom.

MERINGUE GLACÉ LEDA

about 30 servings   *photograph, p. 229*

> French Meringue (see p. 143)
> Vanilla Ice Cream (see p. 220)
> Almond Decorating Paste (see p. 257)
> cocoa powder
> whipped cream
> Spun Sugar (see p. 234)

Make French Meringue; using a no. 7 (14-mm) star tip, pipe out cone-shaped shells 3 inches (7.5 cm) long. Bake at 200° to 212° F (90° to 100° C) 3 to 4 hours. Make Vanilla Ice Cream, preferably the day before it is to be served to make sure the ice cream is hard.

Make Almond Decorating Paste. While it is resting, make templates for the wings and necks of the swan, using cardboard ¹⁄₁₆ inch (2 mm) thick. The wings should be 2 inches (5 cm) high and 3½ inches (8.7 cm) long at the top, tapering to 2½ inches (6.2 cm) at the base. The necks should be 4 inches (10 cm) high. Grease and flour sheet pans; do not use baking paper. Color a little of the paste brown with cocoa powder and pipe on for the eyes. Spread the remaining paste flat and even in the templates. Be sure to make a left and a right wing for each swan. Bake paste at 375° F (190° C) until the color turns spotty brown, about 10 minutes. Immediately remove pieces from pans. Make Spun Sugar.

Swans must be assembled as rapidly as possible just before serving. Place a meringue shell on a chilled serving dish. Place a scoop of ice cream slightly wider than the shell on top of the meringue. Stick the wings to the ice cream and put the neck between the ice cream and the shell. Pipe whipped cream at the tail of the swan. Finally, place Spun Sugar loosely around the swan. Serve immediately.

PEARS WITH TWO SAUCES

Vanilla Ice Cream (see p. 220)
Spongecake II (see p. 93)
pears
lemon juice
Poaching Syrup (see p. 233)
Melba Sauce (see p. 260)
Romanoff Sauce (recipe follows)
marzipan leaves (see p. 255)
crushed pistachios
ginger-flavored almond paste

Make custard for Vanilla Ice Cream 10 to 12 hours before it is to be frozen, refrigerate it to mature, and then freeze it in an ice-cream freezer. Make Spongecake II.

Peel and core pears of the same size and ripeness. Place peeled pears in acidulated water . Poach pears in Poaching Syrup flavored with vanilla extract and lemon zest until tender; test carefully—you should be able to insert a fork with no effort. Cool them in syrup.

While pears are cooling, chill serving plates in the refrigerator. Make the Melba and Romanoff Sauces; make Marzipan Leaves. Finally, cut out thin circles of spongecake no wider than the pears. When pears are cool, cut them in half. Fill the centers with ginger-flavored almond paste, pat the pears dry, and place them on a sheet pan until ready to serve.

To serve, put a cake circle on a chilled plate, a small scoop of Vanilla Ice Cream on top, and one prepared pear half on top of the ice cream, pressing it in place with your hand. Cover the stem half of the pear with Melba Sauce and the thicker half with Romanoff Sauce (some sauce should run down on the plate). Sprinkle crushed nuts in the center where the two sauces meet. Put the marzipan leaf at the top narrow part of the pear. Serve immediately.

Romanoff Sauce

Mix 1 part sour cream and 4 parts whipping cream, first mixing a small amount of whipping cream into the sour cream and then adding the remaining cream. Whip until the cream will cover the pear but, at the same time, is still slightly runny.

Mango Ice Cream

Caramel Ice Cream in Cage

Sorbet au Champagne

White-chocolate Ice Cream

Meringue Glacé Leda

9

Decorations
and Sauces

Decorating

Making decorations by hand is becoming a vanishing art because of today's high labor costs and the pressure to get more done in less time. More and more decorations on cakes and pastries are being made in factories. There are also piping machines that pipe the same preselected pattern on cake after cake, plastic animals and cars for children's birthday cakes, living or plastic flowers for anniversary and wedding cakes—all in colors too many and too bright.

I do believe decorations should not only be edible but also add to the taste. A birthday or wedding cake decorated with dried ornaments made out of royal icing or flowers and leaves made of pulled sugar may look great and technically be completely edible, but the decorations do not add flavor and are next to impossible to eat.

The key to decorating in the pastry kitchen is to make the finished pastry look as if you expended great effort for just this one customer, while doing it fast enough to be economically feasible. In this chaper, I will explain the materials, the techniques, and some tricks of the trade. On the following pages you will find recipes for apricot jam, buttercream, chocolate coveture, fondant, marzipan, *pâte à choux,* piping gel, royal icing, and gum paste, to mention a few, and the methods for working with these decorating materials.

SIMPLE SYRUP

28 to 30 Baumé

 1½ pounds (680 g) corn syrup
  3 pounds (1 kg, 356 g) granulated sugar
 1½ quarts (1 l, 4 dl, 4 cl) water

Pour the corn syrup on top of the sugar, first making a well in the sugar. Place all ingredients in a saucepan; heat to boiling and boil for a few minutes. Skim off the scum on the surface. The corn syrup keeps the syrup from crystallizing. If the syrup must keep longer than a week, refrigerate it.

POACHING SYRUP

 ½ lemon
  1 quart (9 dl, 6 cl) water
  1 pound (455 g) granulated sugar
 ⅓ teaspoon (2 g) vanilla extract
  6 whole cloves
  1 small cinnamon stick

Cut the zest from the lemon and juice it, or slice it. Place lemon, water, and sugar in a saucepan. Heat to boiling while you measure the remaining ingredients. Add spices and the fruit you are poaching. Place a plate that fits inside the saucepan on top of the fruit to submerge it. Boil over medium heat 5 minutes. Simmer until fruit is tender. If the fruit is easily pierced with a fork, it is done. For a plain poaching syrup use water, sugar, and lemon only.

CARAMEL

There are two methods of caramelizing sugar—with water or dry. Using water is easier because you do not have to stir the whole time, but then you have to cook away the water, which takes more time. The dry or direct method is faster but requires your constant attention. In either case, it is best to use a copper pan.

Caramelizing Sugar with Water

Stir just enough water into sugar to get a porridgelike consistency. Boil slowly, brushing down the side of the saucepan with water every 2 or 3 minutes until the desired color. When caramel is done, dip the pan into cool water for a few seconds to stop the cooking process.

Caramelizing Sugar Dry

Place part of the sugar in a preheated saucepan. Heat, stirring constantly, until melted; stir in more sugar and a few drops of lemon juice, which will help to prevent the already melted sugar from getting too dark before all the sugar is melted. Continue cooking and adding sugar until it is all melted and the desired color is reached. Dip pan into cool water to stop the cooking process.

SPUN SUGAR

Nothing sets off an ice-cream dessert like spun sugar. It looks showy and is not as hard to make as it appears. Just remember to use very clean sugar and be precise in measuring and cooking. As a rule, the wetter or more humid the weather, the more difficult it is to work with sugar. A drafty working area can also present problems. Spun Sugar can be made well ahead of serving and stored in airtight containers in a warm dry place. If you want to add color, use light pink or light green. Brown or yellow will look as if you burned the sugar or almost had. You have to add a little bit more color than for fondant because the color shows less in these thin airy strings.

The basic recipe for spun sugar is simply 5 percent thick corn syrup (as thick a corn syrup as you can find), of the weight of the sugar, and enough water to make a thick paste. Remember, the more water you add the longer it will take for the sugar to reach the hard crack stage. It is also important to use the largest size sugar possible, such as cube sugar or AA confectioners' sugar, because it is purer and cleaner.

The following proportions are a good combination for one batch of spun sugar:

> 1 pound (455 g) sugar
> ⅔ ounce (20 g) heavy or light corn syrup
> 4 ounces (1 dl, 2 cl) water

Use a copper pan, or, if one is not available, a thick-bottomed saucepan.

Boil sugar, corn syrup, and water together, brushing down the sugar crystals on the side of the pan with clean water every 2 minutes or so. When the sugar reaches 270° F (132° C), add color if desired and stop brushing but continue boiling until the syrup reaches 318° F (154° C). Dip the pan briefly into cold water to stop the cooking. If you stir at this point, you will add cold air to the syrup, causing it to crystallize. Place the pan back on the heat; heat to boiling, and dip the pan into cold water again for 1 second.

Put 2 sheet pans on edge about 25 inches (64 cm) apart and a sheet pan flat on the floor between them. Cut the rounded ends evenly off an old whip so that it looks like an odd-shaped metal brush. Dip the end of the whip ¼ inch (6 mm) into the sugar; shake off excess sugar lightly. Do not lift the whip too high above the sugar when shaking it so that the drops do not cool off too much and crystallize the sugar. Spin the sugar with quick swinging motions between the sheet pans. It is important that this be done in a dry and draft-free room. If the sugar becomes too thick, heat it briefly but do not stir. Store the finished sugar in a dry airtight container.

SUGAR BOILING CONVERSION

Stage	Fahrenheit	Celsius
gloss	214°	101°
small thread	217°	103°
long thread	223°	106°
blow	228°–234°	110°
soft ball	239°	115°
firm ball	244°	118°
hard ball	257°–275°	125°–135°
light crack	277°–286°	136°–141°
hard crack	293°–302°	145°–157°
very hard crack	311°–315°	155°–157°
light caramel	320°	160°

CARAMEL SAUCE I

2 cups, 5 ounces (6 dl, 3cl) sauce

    1 **pound (455 g) granulated sugar**
      juice of ½ lemon
   12 **ounces (3 dl, 6 cl) water**

Follow the same procedure as given for caramel, but add most of the water when the caramel has reached the right color. The syrup will lump because of the difference in temperatures. Cook out the lumps, and let cool, adding more water if needed. You cannot determine whether the sauce has the correct consistency until it is completely cool because the caramel will continue to thicken as it cools.

CARAMEL SAUCE II

2 cups, 2 ounces (5 dl, 4 cl) sauce

    8 ounces (225 g) granulated sugar
       few drops lemon juice
    1 ounce (3 cl) water
 1½ cups (3 dl, 6 cl) heavy cream
    1 ounce (30 g) soft butter

Caramelize the sugar with the lemon juice until golden. Remove from heat and add the water. Return to heat and cook out the lumps. Remove from heat; stir in the cream and butter slowly (do not whip). Stir until sauce is smooth. The sauce should be just thin enough to be transparent. Serve hot.

DECORATING SUGAR

Put granulated sugar on a sheet pan lined with parchment paper. Add a few drops of the desired color (yellow with a touch of brown in it makes a perfect sand color) and a few drops of vanilla extract, and rub the sugar in your hands. Keep adding color until the sugar is colored to your satisfaction, but do not overcolor. Spread the sugar out flat so that it can dry.

CARAMELIZING NUTS

Blanch and remove skin from almonds, pistachios, or hazelnuts (use some baking soda in the water for the hazelnuts to remove the skins more easily). Walnuts or pecans are caramelized as is. Caramelize sugar to a golden color and remove from heat. Add the nuts to coat with caramel, but do not stir, as you will incorporate cold air and the sugar will crystalize. Pick up the nuts with two forks and place on an oiled marble slab or sheet pans. If the sugar cools too much and gets too thick, reheat but do not stir.

If the nuts are to be crushed, add as many to the saucepan as can be coated with the caramel (in this case you may stir since you are removing and cooling the caramel all at once). Pour onto an oiled marble slab or sheet pan. When cold, crush to the desired coarseness. Alternatively, for denser caramelization, crush the nuts first, caramelize, cool, and crush to desired size.

HAZELNUT PRALINE

3½ ounces (100 g) granulated sugar
3½ ounces (100 g) roasted hazelnuts

Remove as much skin as possible from the hazelnuts by rubbing them between your hands. Crush them finely and set aside. If you wish all the skin removed, blanch them in water with baking soda, and peel them before roasting. Caramelize the sugar in a saucepan to golden brown. Add the crushed hazelnuts, stir to mix, and quickly pour out on an oiled marble slab; if marble is not available, use a sheet pan. When praline is cold, crush to currant-size pieces. This can be made up in large quantities and stored in air-tight containers.

PECTIN GLAZE

5¼ cups (1 l, 3 dl) water
¾ ounce (22 g) pectin powder
3 pounds (1 kg 60 g) sugar
tartaric acid

It is very important that the recipe is followed precisely or the pectin glaze will either gel too fast to be spreadable or will not gel at all.

In a saucepan large enough to hold all the ingredients, heat the water until it starts to steam, about 175° F (80° C). In the meantime, mix pectin powder and 6 ounces (170 g) of the sugar. Mix thoroughly into the hot water. Heat to boiling and add the remaining sugar. Heat again to boiling, but this time watch for the precise moment when it starts to boil (reduce the heat a bit so that it does not boil too heavily) and boil for 5 minutes. Remove from heat and let cool. Skim off any skin or dirt on the surface and pour into a container with a lid. Store in the refrigerator. It will keep for months if it is kept clean. If the Pectin Glaze gels too fast when you are using it, thin it down with some water. If it does not gel, boil it for another minute or two.

Commercial pectin is usually extracted from apples and can be purchased in a powder or liquid form. Unfortunately the proper strength of pectin powder is not available in this country, as far as I know. But I am including the recipe for the glaze and referring to it in recipes throughout the book. I expect it will not be long before this type of pectin powder is available in this country. The reader should certainly not miss the opportunity to purchase some on a trip to Europe. It is very inexpensive, has years of shelf life as long as it is kept dry, and a little goes a long way. Pectin Glaze with the addition of tartaric acid, which is a catalyst to make it gel, tastes slightly tart and is especially good in combination with fruit. It also has the advantage of gelling when you want it to gel by adding the tartaric acid to the amount of glaze you need at that time. The quick gelling prevents the glaze from soaking into the fruit, making only a thin shiny coat on top.

To use Pectin Glaze: Pour as much as you need into a small cup and add about 2 drops tartaric acid (see Index) to every 1 ounce (3 cl) Pectin Glaze. The flavor must be definitely tart but not too "puckery." Stir the tartaric acid rapidly into the Pectin Glaze and use immediately. Keep the glaze from hardening by stirring it every few seconds. Be sure to add tartaric acid only to as much glaze as you need immediately because, once the tartaric acid sets the glaze, it cannot be applied.

APRICOT JAM

        2 pounds (910 g) apricot pulp, fresh or canned
        1 pound (455 g) sugar
        2 ounces (6 cl) water

Combine in a saucepan, and boil over medium heat, stirring occasionally until the mixture has reduced to a jam consistency. Strain or use as is when cold.

Apricot Jam is not used as much today for decoration when so many ready-made mixtures are available, but it is very easy to make and use and has a very distinctive look. If you have the time, make your own jam; then you know the quality will be the same every time. Any good apricot jam can be used, but it must be reduced as follows: To each 1 pound (453 g) jam add 4 ounces (115 g) granulated sugar and 8 ounces (225 g) water. Place in a saucepan and boil to 230° F (108° C).

When you are ready to use the jam for decorating, press it through a fine sieve and heat to boiling, preferably in a stainless-steel bowl. Cool the jam to just above body temperature, about 100° F (38° C) and use.

Apricot jam is very effective when used with chocolate, especially to fill loops and patterns of piped-out chocolate on *petits fours* and pastries. If the jam seems too thick to fill in patterns, thin it with Simple Syrup (see Index) to the right consistency. Jam can be colored, but keep in mind that it already is an amber color; if you add red, for example, it will end up orange.

APRICOT GLAZE

> 8 ounces (225 g) apricot jam
> 2 ounces (55 g) sugar
> 1 ounce (3 cl) water

Place jam, sugar, and water in a saucepan. Heat to boiling, and boil over low heat until you can pull a thread ¼ inch (6 mm) long between your fingers. Be careful not to reduce the glaze too much or it will be impossible to work with; if this happens, thin with hot water. Strain and brush on tarts immediately.

APRICOT SAUCE

Because apricots are in season for only a short time, canned apricots will be used more often. If you have fresh apricots, they must be overripe to use for a sauce. Blanch and peel fresh apricots. Force the fruit, fresh or canned, through a firm sieve, or purée in a food processor or a blender. If the purée is overprocessed, the sauce will be full of bubbles and look cloudy. Strain if necessary. Thin the purée with Simple Syrup (see Index) or water if necessary. Flavor the sauce with kirsch or another suitable liqueur.

BUTTERCREAM

Although buttercream is mostly known as an icing, it is a convenient and easy-to-work-with decorating material. It can be colored to achieve the color contrast you want, but be careful not to mix too many or too bright colors.

Any buttercream that has been set aside for more than a short while should be mixed again to make sure it is smooth and free of any air bubbles. Do this, if at all possible, with your hand because you need to add heat to the buttercream in most cases. You can place the buttercream over hot water, being careful not to overheat it. Remember the bowl will keep on heating (melting) the buttercream for some time after you remove it from the heat. If you have to store buttercream in the refrigerator or freezer, let it soften to room temperature before using it. If you soften buttercream over hot water, you will lose the airy consistency and get a heavy, compact icing.

Buttercream Roses

It is easier than it looks to make a buttercream rose. You need a very smooth buttercream that is not too soft, a decorating nail (it looks like a nail with a very large head, about 1½ inches (37 mm) in diameter), and a special rose-petal tip for the pastry bag (no. 124 for a medium-size rose). Both decorating nail and tip can be purchased at a cookware store.

Hold the stem of the decorating nail in your left hand between thumb and forefinger. Turn flower nail counterclockwise while forming flower petals clockwise. Hold piping bag so that the larger opening of the tip is facing down towards the nail.

To make the base of the rose: Start by holding the bag perpendicular to the top of the nail and at the right side of the nail. Place bottom of tip directly on the head of the nail and slightly outside of the middle with the small end of tip raised a bit higher. Turn the nail one complete turn while piping to create a short dome or cone. Using the same procedure, make a second smaller and steeper dome on top of the first.

To make the inside of the rose: Start close to the top of the cone. Pipe a long ribbon and draw tube away while turning the nail to wrap the ribbon around the top of the cone.

To make the first row of petals: Place wide end of tip at base of inside bud. Pipe 3 overlapping petals turning nail 120 degrees for each. Lift tip up for middle of petal and down to finish.

To make the second row of petals: Start second row of petals directly underneath first row. Point narrow end of tip out further so petals begin to curve outward. Pipe 4 overlapping petals using the same up, around, and down motion.

To remove the rose, simply cut it off with a thin knife. This is easier to do if you refrigerate the rose first until firm.

Buttercream leaves are piped directly on the place where you want them, using a leaf tip.

VANILLA BUTTERCREAM I

10 pounds, 8 ounces (4 kg, 775 g) buttercream

>   1 quart (9 dl, 6 cl) egg whites
>   4 pounds (1 kg, 820 g) sugar
>   ¼ ounce (7 g) salt
>   4 pounds (1 kg, 820 g) sweet butter softened
>   1 pound, 4 ounces (570 g) margarine or shortening, softened
>   2 teaspoons (12 g) vanilla extract

¼ recipe

2 pounds, 10 ounces (1 kg, 195 g) buttercream

>   1 cup (2 dl, 4 cl) egg whites
>   1 pound (455 g) sugar
>   pinch of salt
>   1 pound (455 g) sweet butter, softened
>   5 ounces (140 g) margarine or shortening, softened
>   ½ teaspoon (3 g) vanilla extract

Heat egg whites, sugar, and salt in a pan over hot water; heat until sugar and salt are dissolved, about 130° F (54° C). Whip egg whites to stiff peaks. Gradually whip in butter, margarine, and vanilla. Store covered at room temperature.

VANILLA BUTTERCREAM II

9 pounds, 2 ounces (4 kg, 150 g) buttercream

>   4 pounds (1 kg, 820 g) unsalted butter, softened
>   1½ pounds (680 g) margarine, softened
>   2 pounds, 12 ounces (1 kg, 250 g) sugar
>   12 ounces (3 dl, 6 cl) water
>   1 pint (4 dl, 8 cl) eggs
>   2 teaspoons (12 g) vanilla extract

¼ recipe

2 pounds, 4½ ounces (2 kg, 75 g) buttercream

>   1 pound (455 g) sweet butter, softened
>   6 ounces (170 g) margarine, softened
>   1 pound, 3 ounces (540 g) sugar
>   11 ounces (3 dl, 3 cl) water
>   4 ounces (1 dl, 1 cl) eggs
>   ½ teaspoon (3 g) vanilla extract

Cream butter, margarine, and vanilla until light and fluffy. Place sugar and water in a saucepan; heat to boiling and reduce heat. Boil until syrup reaches a temperature of 275° F (135° C). If you do not have a sugar thermometer, simply watch for a change in the size of the bubbles—they get smaller as the mixture gets hotter. In the meantime, put eggs in a mixing bowl, and whip just for a few minutes to break them up. When the syrup is ready, remove from heat, wait a few seconds, and, with the mixer at medium speed, pour the syrup into the eggs in a slow steady stream between the whip and the side of the mixing bowl. Whip at full speed until mixture is cooled.

Mix egg mixture and butter mixture. Store in a covered container, but do not refrigerate.

CHOCOLATE BUTTERCREAM
4 pounds, 8 ounces (2 kg, 55 g) buttercream

> 10 ounces (3 dl) egg whites
> 1 pound, 4 ounces (570 g) sugar
> pinch of salt
> vanilla extract
> 1 pound, 4 ounces (570 g) butter, softened
> 5 ounces (140 g) shortening or margarine, softened
> 1 pound, 1 ounce (485 g) dark chocolate

Heat egg whites, sugar, salt, and vanilla to taste over hot water until sugar and salt are dissolved and the mixture reaches about 140° F (60° C). Whip egg whites to stiff peaks; at medium speed, add butter and shortening, a little at a time; the mixture must be cool enough not to melt the butter.

Heat chocolate to 130° F (54° C). Mix a small amount (1 or 2 handfuls) of the buttercream into the chocolate rapidly by hand or with a small whisk; then mix into the remaining buttercream.

PASTRY CREAM
10 pounds, 4 ounces (4 kg, 665 g) pastry cream

> 1 gallon (3 liters, 8 dl, 4 cl) milk
> 3 teaspoons (18 g) vanilla extract
> 10 ounces (285 g) cornstarch
> 2 pounds (910 g) sugar
> 12 eggs
> 1 teaspoon (4 g) salt

¼ **recipe**
2 pounds, 9 ounces (1 kg, 165 g) pastry cream

> 1 **quart (9 dl, 6 cl) milk**
> 1 **teaspoon (2 g) vanilla extract**
> 2½ **ounces (70 g) cornstarch**
> 8 **ounces (225 g) sugar**
> 4 **eggs (200 g)**
> **pinch of salt**

Heat milk and vanilla just until boiling. Meanwhile, mix cornstarch and sugar; gradually mix in the eggs; mix until smooth, about 1 minute. Add about a third of the hot milk gradually to the egg mixture, whisking constantly. Mix egg mixture, remaining milk, and salt in a saucepan; cook, stirring constantly with a wooden spoon, until cream thickens, several minutes. If the cream burns, which usually happens at the last moment when the cream is getting thick and hard to stir, you can save the flavor by straining the cream into a container without the burnt cream at the bottom.

CHOCOLATE

Chocolate is the classic decorating material. Today, when there is so much "non-temp" chocolate on the market (as explained later, this type may not legally be called chocolate), there is no reason to use real chocolate and go through the time-consuming procedure of tempering. However, when you want something to look really special, real chocolate is the most elegant and satisfying ingredient to use. It can be piped directly onto a coated cake, pastry, or *petits fours,* or you can use the same tracing method as for *pâte à choux* and fondant decorations by placing a transparent paper on top of your design. Be sure the paper is as thick as possible, or better yet use clear plastic sheets, approximately ¹⁄₁₆ inch (2 mm) thickness. If the surface allows it and if the chocolate is spread thin enough, chocolate will curl slightly when it hardens.

To obtain a satin shine on pure chocolate, you have to go through the procedure of tempering it. One way of doing this is to heat the chocolate to about 115° F (42° C) and let it slowly cool to 86° F (30° C). Add 1 ounce (30 g) finely grated chocolate to cool the larger mass to slightly below 86° F (30° C). Then rewarm the chocolate to 86° F (30° C), stirring out any lumps at the same time. Be careful not to go more than 1° or 2° above the 86° F (30° C); if the chocolate gets any warmer than that, you have to start all over again. Do not stir too fast when tempering so that the chocolate does not get unwanted air bubbles. The room temperature is also important. It is impossible to cool the chocolate to below 86° F (30° C) if the temperature in the kitchen is 90° F (32° C). The ideal temperature for tempering or any chocolate work is 65° F (18° C). If, because of incorrect tempering or too warm working conditions, the chocolate takes too long to harden, the cocoa butter (pure chocolate has 20 to 30% cocoa butter) has time to float to the surface and gives the finished product an unwanted grey or streaked grey look.

When filling in decorations or when you want the chocolate to settle or float out lightly, use it as is. When you want the chocolate in precise lines, as for piping, mix in Simple Syrup, a drop at a time, until the chocolate holds its shape or has the typical ribbon consistency. If you add too much liquid, the chocolate will cake and be useless. Adding Simple Syrup works fine with both tempered real chocolate and the non-temp, or coating, chocolate.

If you are not tempering chocolate anyway, an easier and more sensible method is to use non-temp chocolate (coating), which cannot legally be called chocolate because it does not have a large enough percentage of cocoa butter. To use non-temp chocolate, simply melt it down to 98° to 100° F (37° to 38° C) and add Simple Syrup, a drop at a time, until you have the required consistency. Different brands of non-temp coatings require different amounts of syrup.

If you should get the chocolate too hot, cool it to the specified temperature before using it to keep it from graying as it hardens. It will also take a few more drops of Simple Syrup to thicken; consequently when it cools down, it will be too thick to work with. The same thing will happen if it drops too many degrees below 98° to 100° F (37° to 38° C), but simply warm it up again. To prevent cooling, you can keep the chocolate in a hot-water bath.

To loosen chocolate decorations, refrigerate them for a few minutes, and then carefully remove them with a knife or slide the plastic sheet over a sharp edge. Designs can be used upside down, if the top side does not look quite right.

Dark and light chocolate combined in one design look especially nice, for example, in a flower, small simple animals, or signs. Make the frame from dark chocolate prepared for piping; after it has set, fill with light chocolate without any syrup added. Let designs harden and remove them as explained previously.

It is important when piping chocolate that no foreign matter, such as crumbs, is mixed in, because such particles clog the small opening of the piping cone.

Another and much simpler way to make decorations from chocolate is to spread the chocolate on parchment paper or waxed paper, just thick enough to cover the paper. If the chocolate gets too thick, the decorations will look clumsy. Make sure the chocolate is 98° to 100° F (37° to 38° C). Keep spreading the chocolate back and forth, using a 10 to 12 inch (25 to 30 cm) spatula, until the chocolate just starts to set. Pick up the sheet by 2 diagonal corners, and place it on a full sheet of cardboard. Do not refrigerate. When chocolate has set completely, you can cut it into the shapes you want, for example, squares for Black Forest Cake or rectangles for Swedish Chocolate Cake. Use a knife with not too much pressure so that the paper underneath is not cut with the chocolate. A multiple pastry wheel, if you have it, is much faster. If you want a round shape, use a plain or fluted cookie cutter. Dip it into hot water to warm it, shake it off quickly on a towel to remove any water, and simply melt through the chocolate, stamping out 2 or 3 rounds before warming the cutter again.

Chocolate Rectangles

Melt dark non-tempered chocolate to about 100° F (38° C) and spread it out. When chocolate is firm, cut it into rectangles 3½ inches × ¾ inch (8.5 × 2 cm) for standard servings, 2½ inches × ¾ inch (6 × 2 cm) for buffet servings. Refrigerate until chocolate is completely hard. Put one hand underneath the paper to push off the rectangles without breaking them.

Chocolate Squares

Follow the same procedure as for rectangles. Cut 2-inch (5-cm) squares for standard servings, a little smaller for buffet size.

Chocolate Rounds

Follow the same procedure as for rectangles. Cut 1- to 1¼-inch (25- to 30-mm) rounds with a fluted cookie cutter heated in hot water.

Chocolate Leaves

You can also cut leaves from chocolate sheets; using a small paring knife, make the veins by just scraping on top. A more eye-catching leaf is made by painting chocolate that has been melted to 98° to 100° F (37° to 38° C) on top of a rose leaf, or any thin leaf with an oily surface, thick enough so that you cannot see the rose leaf anymore. Place coated leaves in the refrigerator or freezer for a few seconds; then carefully peel off the real leaf or separate the 2 leaves. You should be able to make at least 3 leaves before all the oil is gone from the rose leaf.

Another simple way of giving pastries, cakes, or *petits fours* a special effect is to pipe out lines with as small an opening as possible in a piping cone, as in Vanilla Macaroons and Macaroon Bananas. The lines can be done with a contrasting chocolate or with the same kind the pastry has been coated with. But the same rules apply. Chocolate has to be at 98° to 100° F (37° to 38° C), and you should use new clean chocolate without lumps or crumbs. Also important in using this technique is to move with even, determined strokes and only as fast as you can press out chocolate; if the cone gets clogged, stop immediately and find out why.

Dark Chocolate Figures

Draw one figure on a piece of transparent baking paper. It should be about 1¾ inches (45 mm) high and 1½ inches (37 mm) wide. Many different figures may be used: a simple one is created by drawing one small oval. Beginning at one tip of the oval, draw a second, slightly larger oval around the first; beginning at the same tip, draw an even larger oval around the second. The result will be three ovals, each beginning at the same point but progressively larger. Draw a horizontal line at the midpoint of the narrow width of the largest oval. The line should protrude slightly from either side of the oval. Connect each end of the line with the starting point of the ovals to make a triangle. Trace as many times as necessary. Invert the paper.

Melt 2 to 3 ounces (55 to 85 g) of chocolate to 100° F (38° C); thicken with Simple Syrup (see Index); add one drop at a time until chocolate is just thick enough to stay in your piping bag. Keeping the chocolate warm, pipe over your lines; as a rule, the thinner the lines, the more elegant the figure looks, but be careful not to pipe too thinly, or the figures will break when you move them. Refrigerate for a few seconds. Remove from paper with a small metal spatula. Place the figures on the pastry or onto a tray for later use. Avoid handling them directly, or the chocolate will melt.

Chocolate Cigars

Melt dark non-temp chocolate to about 100° F (38° C). Spread on a marble slab in a narrow, thin strip, close to the edge of the slab. The slab is used as a straightedge to keep the edges of the strip perfectly straight. Continue spreading with a metal spatula until the chocolate has haredened. Cut the strip the long way to the exact width of the cigars you are making (for Mocha Meringue, 1½ inches—37 mm wide). Hold a chef's knife or a metal scraper at a 45° angle to the slab. Pushing away from you, cut off and curl up about 1 inch (25 mm) of the chocolate; repeat along the length of the strip. If the chocolate is too cold and breaks, put your hand on top of it to warm. If the chocolate cakes or sticks to the knife, it is too soft; wait a few minutes for it to harden, or place a cold sheet pan on top of it for a few seconds.

CHOCOLATE GLAZE
3½ pints (1 l, 6 dl, 8 cl) glaze

- 13 ounces (3 dl, 9 cl) water
- 1 pound, 1 ounce (485 g) granulated sugar
- 9 ounces (255 g) corn syrup
- 6 ounces (170 g) cocoa powder
- 14 ounces (400 g) dark chocolate, melted
  Simple Syrup (see p. 233)

Heat water, sugar, and corn syrup to boiling. Stir in the cocoa powder, and heat again to boiling. Remove from heat and stir in the dark chocolate. Use when slightly cooled.

Store leftover glaze in a covered container or pour a little water on top. The idea is to protect the glaze from air. When ready to use it again, pour off the water and heat glaze to boiling. If the glaze needs to be thinned, add a few drops of Simple Syrup.

GANACHE
7 pounds, 3 ounces (3 kg, 270 g) ganache

- 4 pounds (1 kg, 820 g) dark chocolate
- 1 quart, 2 ounces (1 l, 2 cl) whipping cream
- 10 egg yolks
- 10 ounces (285 g) sugar
- 1 teaspoon (6 g) vanilla extract

¼ recipe
1 pound, 13 ounces (825 g) ganache

- 1 pound (455 g) dark chocolate
- 8½ ounces (2 dl, 6 cl) whipping cream
- 3 egg yolks
- 2½ ounces (70 g) sugar
  few drops vanilla extract

Chop the chocolate into small pieces; place chocolate, cream, and vanilla in a saucepan. Heat to 150° F (65° C), stirring constantly. Meanwhile, whip egg yolks and sugar to stiff peaks. Stir in hot chocolate-cream mixture, and stir slowly until cold.

Store in an airtight container. If Ganache forms a skin anyway, pour some hot water on top and wait 1 minute before pouring it off. When using Ganache, make sure it has a soft and smooth consistency. Do not overmix it; if you incorporate too much air into it, the Ganache will develop a light color and lose its dark satin shine.

CHOCOLATE SAUCE (HOT OR COLD)
about 2 quarts (1 l, 9 cl, 2 cl)

> 3 cups (7 dl, 2 cl) water
> 17 ounces (485 g) granulated sugar
> 9 ounces (2 dl, 7 cl) corn syrup
> 6 ounces (170 g) cocoa powder
> 1 pound (455 g) dark chocolate, chopped into small pieces

Heat water, sugar, and corn syrup to boiling. Stir in cocoa powder, and heat again to boiling. Remove from heat, add the chocolate, and stir until chocolate is melted. Strain and use.

For a cold sauce, cool completely before using and thin with additional water if necessary. This recipe makes a fairly thick sauce.

PIPING GEL

Piping gel is made of a mixture of sugar, corn syrup solids, and vegetable gum, such as gum arabic. It is very sweet and not very pleasant to eat by itself, but it is one of the most practical decoration materials in today's pastry shop. It looks a little "plastic" next to a chocolate decoration, but it is ready-made, in neutral and in colors, is inexpensive, and simple to work with. It is very practical to use for everyday decorating, but for something special, a showpiece or *petits fours,* I do not recommend it. If you take the time to cut out *petits fours* and ice them with fondant, it does not make sense to decorate them with piping gel. Piping gel takes a long time to dry and, when it finally dries, it gets dull. It is also easily smeared or otherwise damaged.

FONDANT

Fondant is widely used in the pastry shop for glazing and decorating. It is quite easy to make your own fondant, but it is time-consuming for most bakers today. However, here is the procedure.

> 2 cups (4 dl, 8 cl) water
> 2 pounds, 3 ounces (1 kg) AA confectioners' sugar
> 7 ounces (200 g) glucose or corn syrup

Boil water and sugar in a saucepan, taking care to brush down the sugar particles that accumulate on the side with clean water about every 2 minutes. When the sugar reaches 230° F (110° C), add glucose and continue boiling to 238° F (115° C). Immediately pour out on a preoiled marble table or slab. Sprinkle a little water on top to keep a crust from forming, which would make the Fondant grimy. After the sugar has cooled down to about 65° F (18° C), start to incorporate air using a wide spatula or metal scraper and moving the sugar back and forth until it is white and smooth and properly called fondant.

Store in an airtight container with just enough water on top to cover the surface to keep a skin from forming.

Glazing or Icing with Fondant

Warm fondant to 98° to 100° F (37° to 38° C). If fondant gets too warm, it will lose the distinctive shine, making the pastry or *petits fours* look dull and old. On the other hand, not warming the fondant enough will prevent a skin from forming soon enough. It will be hard to move and work with and, when it does dry, the shine will not be as good or last as long. Thin fondant with egg whites or heavy cream so that the gloss is not lost; this will happen if you added too much Simple Syrup. The fondant should be thinned to the point where the contour of the *petit fours* or pastry can clearly be seen. If, however, the fondant is too thin, the pastries or *petits fours* will look as if they have been exposed to heat and will not hold their shine long.

Fondant can be piped on, using a small plain tip, starting in the middle and working towards the edges; keep in mind that the corners need a little extra fondant for total coverage. This is a practical way to apply fondant if you are making only a dozen or so of each type or color, because you have more control of the amount of fondant you are using. If you are icing many pastries or *petits fours,* a much faster way is to apply the fondant with a dessert plate. Line up the pastries or *petits fours* about ½ inch (12 mm) apart on a rack with a sheet pan underneath. Holding the bowl of fondant in one hand and the plate in the other, scoop up the fondant with the plate and move it at a slow even pace 1 inch (25 mm) or so above the *petits fours* or pastries. The flatter the object you pour from, the wider the area the fondant will cover. You may be able to cover 2 or 3 rows with one stroke of the plate. The only drawback to this method is that one needs to be working with a lot of fondant for it to be practical.

Decorating with Fondant

Fondant should be fairly cold, 85° to 90° F (30° to 34° C), for piping. Add just enough egg white for the fondant to be easily pipable but still hold its shape when piped out. Use fondant slightly warmer for filling in designs so that it spreads out just a little bit.

Method I: Place a perfectly flat transparent plastic sheet, about ¹⁄₁₆ inch (2 mm) thick, on top of your drawings. Pipe out a thin frame of fondant and then fill in with the slightly warmer fondant, moving the piping bag back and forth to get a smooth surface and at the same time build up the pattern. Take care not to disturb the piped frame. Let the design dry overnight, and then loosen it by moving the plastic sheet over a sharp edge, bending it down lightly. Place the finished decoration on top of your pastry or cake, but do not loosen the design before you are ready to use it.

Method II: You can also pipe a fondant decoration directly on top of marzipan. If you have a cookie cutter of the shape and size you want, simply press lightly into the marzipan so it leaves a slight mark. Then trace the mark with the fondant, using a paper cone with an opening just big enough so it covers the mark. Nobody will know that you had any help in making the design. The decorations will come out looking almost the same with just enough variation to make them look hand-made, which they certainly are.

If you do not have a marker, make your own this way: Draw your design on paper and turn the paper upside down; if it does not matter that the drawing is reversed on the cake, you need not invert the paper. Place a small piece of Plexiglas or basic window glass on top, but make sure the corners and edges of the glass have been sanded dull. Using fondant in a paper cone with a small opening, trace your drawing on top of the Plexiglas or glass.

It is important that the Plexiglas be inflexible and clean and free from fingerprints and that the fondant is not too dry (hard) so that the fondant does not fall off or get stuck in the marzipan. Let the fondant design dry overnight; then, turning the glass upside down, simply press the design into the marzipan all the way to the glass. Trace the design on the marzipan and fill in, or just trace. In this manner, you can make up whole cake decorations when you anticipate that you will need many, for example, for Christmas or Mother's Day. In such cases, coat the marzipan with a thin layer of cocoa butter before you stamp out and decorate your patterns to protect the marzipan from drying out. You can also have patterns permanently traced on top of the glass. The decoration is certainly handmade but with a little help from a friend.

ROYAL ICING

Royal icing is the best material with which to practice decorating. It is fast to make, inexpensive, and has the same basic qualities as chocolate. Royal icing is used as part of the eye on marzipan figurines. Around Christmas time, it is used in making gingerbread houses and writing on gingerbread cookies because it looks like snow. Royal icing can be used to pipe on a Plexiglas or glass template for decorating marzipan (as described for fondant). Finally, it can be used to make ornaments for wedding and other special-occasion cakes and to make showpieces. Pipe royal icing on a plastic sheet or thin baking paper placed flat on top of a blueprint or a drawing. Bend the plastic sheet around something if the design is to be round. Let it dry overnight, and fasten the pieces together with some more royal icing. Although it is all edible, I would limit its use to showpieces.

The proportions for royal icing are 3½ ounces (100 g) sifted powdered sugar to ⅔ ounce (20 g) egg white. Add sugar to the egg whites until it is a thick, smooth paste. Stir rapidly until thickened to a white fluffy consistency. Adjust with more egg white or sugar until, when making a peak in the icing or on a spoon, the peak bends down slightly. It should be thick enough so that it will not spread but not so thick that it is brittle or falls off easily when dried. Add 1 drop tartaric acid to keep the icing from yellowing if it is to be kept for a few days. Also, make sure that you cover royal icing and clean off any icing on the side of your cup or bowl because it dries very quickly and the small lumps will interfere with piping. A wet towel is a fine temporary cover as you work, but use plastic wrapping or some water on top for longer storage.

GUM PASTE (PASTILLAGE)

Gum paste is practical for making display or showpieces. It can be molded around any object and cut or pressed into any shape and form you want. Before making up the gum paste, have all your templates ready. Use thick enough paper so that you can cut around the template with a sharp paring knife. The cutting has to be done very precisely and at the same time quickly. If you want to mark or texture the gum paste, do it immediately after it is rolled out. When you are not working with the dough, cover it with a wet towel to prevent a crust from forming. Roll out one small piece at a time, using cornstarch to keep it from sticking, to the desired thickness, and rapidly cut out the design, using templates, molds, or presses. Be sure to use as much as possible of each rolled-out piece because it cannot be rolled again. Place the cutouts on an even surface to dry for 12 to 24 hours, depending on the thickness. Because moisture in the paste tends to sink to the bottom when drying, keep turning the pieces over from time to time; this will also prevent the ends from curling. Once dry, the cutouts can be filed and sanded to make them fit better. The gum paste can be either colored before you roll it out or painted when it is finished. Assemble the pieces with royal icing. Gum paste display pieces will keep forever if they are kept away from moisture. Theoretically, gum paste is edible, but I do not recommend it even if you have strong teeth, a ravenous appetite, and good insurance. When properly made and dried, gum paste is as hard as glass.

Gum Paste

- 1½ ounces (40 g) unflavored gelatin
- 15 ounces (4 dl, 5 cl) lukewarm water
- 6 pounds, 3 ounces (2 kg, 815 g) powdered sugar
- 1 pound (455 g) cornstarch
  pinch cream of tartar

Be sure to weigh all ingredients precisely. Dissolve gelatin in water and heat to 150° F (65° C). Sift powdered sugar, cornstarch, and cream of tartar together, and place in a mixing bowl with a paddle. Gradually add the gelatin mixture and mix at medium speed until it is a smooth elastic paste of rolling consistency. Cover with a wet towel and wrap airtight in plastic. Use immediately or refrigerate for later use.

MARZIPAN

Marzipan is widely used in the pastry industry, especially in Scandinavian countries, Germany, Austria, and Switzerland. It is used as decoration, icing, to make all kinds of figures, as candy, and in pastries. It consists basically of almonds and sugar in proportions of approximately 2 parts sugar to 1 part almonds. When made from almond paste, the proportions are equal parts of almond paste and sugar because almond paste is 50% sugar and 50% almonds; a small amount of corn syrup or egg white is added to make it less short and more pliable. However, just like almond paste, marzipan is hardly ever made from scratch today but usually bought ready-made. Due to the large amount of sugar, marzipan dries very quickly when exposed to air and should be covered at all times. Marzipan made with egg white has a shorter shelf life than that made with corn syrup.

As explained in the pages on fondant and royal icing, marzipan is imprinted for cake decorations; it is also used on *petits fours* and pastries that are to be coated with fondant or chocolate to keep the coating from soaking into the sponge and to achieve an even surface. Also, a thin layer of marzipan on a *bûche de Noël* or chocolate roulade prevents the thin layer of chocolate from mixing with the cake. Not only does marzipan make a smooth finish possible, but it also gives the pastry a very special and distinctive flavor.

The use of marzipan in candies and figurines would take a book all by itself.

Marzipan Roses

A marzipan rose is, in my opinion, just as elegant as the famed pulled sugar rose and much more practical because it can be made in minutes and, in addition, can be eaten. Although a rose made for a special occasion should have 6 to 8 petals, a nice-looking production rose can be made from only 4 petals. A 4-petal rose is quicker, easier, and is less likely to take the shape of a cabbage head.

To make a marzipan rose, first make sure the marzipan has just the right consistency. If the marzipan is too hard or too dry, it will be impossible to shape the petals nicely; if the marzipan is too soft, the rose will not hold its shape after it has been made. Make the marzipan soft and pliable with the warmth of your hand. Roll it out into a strip about 1 inch (25 mm) thick and cut into even pieces, according to the size of rose you plan to make. Cover the pieces to keep them from drying. Use a marble slab or wooden table, and make sure it is clean; oil the edge very lightly. Roll out another piece of marzipan to about ½ inch (12 mm) in diameter; place it at the edge of the table. Using the palm of your hand, flatten this piece somewhat to make sure it sticks to the table. At the same time, keep the marzipan in a straight line. Oil a knife or spatula lightly; with long even strokes and with the knife tilted toward you and the table, apply enough pressure so that you flatten the strip to about 1 inch (25 mm) wide, ⅛ inch (3 mm) thick on the far side, and a sharp thin edge on the side next to you. Cut this strip into about 1½-inch (37-mm) pieces. Roll up each piece at an angle so that it forms a cone. Push out the end piece slightly so that it looks like a bud about to break open. Place the bud in front of you when you finish making all the buds. Take the precut petal pieces, oil the edge of the table lightly, and place them in a row approximately 10 inches (25 cm) apart to provide working space. With the palm of your hand, flatten them, so they are uneven, sloping toward you. At the same time, make sure they stick to the table; you may have to put some powdered sugar on your palm to keep the marzipan from sticking at the wrong place (your palm) as you do this. Then, using an oiled knife or plastic scraper, make petals round and razor thin on the side sloping toward you and approximately 1½ inch (37 mm) in diameter. Cut petals loose with a chef's knife. Bend them to petal shape and fasten three of them evenly around each bud. Cut away the unnecessary marzipan underneath, and the production rose is done.

Take care not to flatten too many petals at one time for they dry quickly and become difficult to bend and form. You can, however, make up the complete roses days in advance; they will dry and the thin edges will turn lighter, but that makes them look so much more real.

For a rose stem, roll light green marzipan to a thin string. Make the thorns by cutting stems here and there with scissors; as on the real flower, thorns should point upward. Make leaves by rolling out green marzipan 1/16 inch (2 mm) thick. Using a sharp paring knife, cut out leaves of the appropriate size. Make veins with the back side of the knife. Place leaves on top of a dowel so that they dry slightly bent, but place a small piece of marzipan under each end of the dowel so that the dowel does not suddenly roll, throwing all the leaves off. Because the marzipan is thin, the leaves will dry enough to hold their shape in just a few hours.

You can also make daffodils and other simple petal flowers, including fantasy flowers, by rolling out the marzipan quite thin and cutting out petals with a plain or fluted cookie cutter. Put a 1-inch (25-mm) layer of AA confectioners' sugar in a pan, fasten the petals with some egg white, and push them into the sugar so that they form the typical flower shape. By forming them in the AA confectioners' sugar, they will be exposed to the air from both sides and will dry much faster than if you were to put them in a metal or plastic form.

Marzipan

14 pounds (6 kg, 370 g) almond paste
4 pounds (1 kg, 820 g) corn syrup
1 cup (2 dl, 4 cl) water
15 pounds (6 kg, 825 g) powdered sugar

⅛ recipe

1 pound, 12 ounces (795 g) almond paste
8 ounces (225 g) corn syrup
1 ounce (3 cl) water
1 pound, 14 ounces (855 g) powdered sugar

Place almond paste in a large mixing bowl and attach a dough hook. The bowl should be stainless steel so that the marzipan does not gray. Add corn syrup. A very thick corn syrup can be messy. The easiest way to handle it is to wet your hand and pick up a chunk the size of a tennis ball, which will weigh about 1 pound. If you are weighing it, weigh it on top of some powdered sugar so that it does not stick to the scale. With machine on low speed, start adding the powdered sugar, scraping the bowl as necessary, until the marzipan is off-white in color and firm enough to handle.

The large amount of powdered sugar makes the marzipan dry very quickly. Store the marzipan in an airtight container at all times, and, if stored for any length of time, refrigerate it. If making a large amount, wrap the marzipan in convenient size pieces within the container so that the whole batch is not exposed to the air when removing a small amount.

PÂTE À CHOUX FOR DECORATION

Pâte à choux is little known as a decorating material and, therefore, is little used. You can use the basic *pâte à choux* recipe if you force it through a fine sieve. Because you normally need a very small amount, it will save time if you take a few ounces of the pastry when you make eclairs or cream puffs and freeze it until needed. However, if there is none in the freezer and you need some right away, use the following recipe.

1½ ounces (4.5 cl) milk
1⅙ ounces (35 g) flour
    pinch salt
½ ounce (15 g) butter
1 small egg

Proceed as directed for Pâte à Choux (see Index) and pass the dough through a fine sieve.

Draw patterns on transparent parchment paper with a heavy pencil. Remember that the pattern will eventually be reversed. Turn the paper upside down so that the *pâte à choux* does not pick up the lead. Make a piping cone of paper, cut an appropriate opening with scissors, and follow the lines. Place the paper on a sheet pan, and bake at 375° F (190° C) until golden brown. But beware, it does not take long. If you need many decorations or make the same one from time to time, draw patterns to fill the paper, and place another transparent paper on top. Secure the corners so that the paper will not move as you pipe. Before parchment paper was available, ovenproof transparent glass was used, which had its disadvantages—it was easily broken. The baked decorations can be placed on top of *petits fours,* pastries, cakes, and ice-cream desserts to create very unusual effects. It looks especially elegant if designs are placed on top of buttercream piped out in the same pattern, using a small plain tube.

You can also partially or fully fill in the *pâte à choux* patterns with a slightly modified Almond Decorating Paste: Add 1 ounce (28 g) powdered sugar to ¹/₁₀ of Almond Decorating Paste (see Index). Adjust the amount of milk so the almond paste just barely runs smooth when piped into the pattern. Paste can be colored with cocoa powder or food color to contrast with the golden *pâte à choux,* for example, a New Year's bell fully filled with cocoa almond decorating paste or an oak leaf filled halfway with pale green almond decorating paste. However, because you cannot use almond paste on top of baking paper that is thin enough to see through; you must use the ovenproof glass method, which is time-consuming in today's run-and-rush pastry shop but for a special occasion, well worth it. Lightly wax the glass with beeswax or other natural wax. It is best to work with a small piece, 24 × 16 inches (60 × 40 cm) maximum, which can easily be placed inside a full sheet pan for baking. Place the glass on top of your pattern, trace, and bake. Pick off the designs with a small paring knife as they get finished.

WEAVERS' DOUGH

This dough is used to make decoration pieces and ornaments.

    1 quart (9 dl, 6 cl) water
    2 eggs
    2 ounces (55 g) salt
    1 ounce (30 g) sugar
    2 ounces (6 cl) vegetable oil
    5 pounds (2 kg, 275 g) bread flour
      egg wash

Mix water and eggs; mix in salt, sugar, and oil. Incorporate enough of the flour to make a medium-stiff dough. Knead until smooth and elastic. Cover and let rise 1 hour. Keep the dough covered at all times to prevent a skin forming, which makes the dough slide when rolling it out and gives the finished product a wrinkled, uneven appearance. Because there is no yeast in this dough, the ornaments made from it will look exactly as you shape them, except for the color, when they are baked. Carefully brush with egg wash. Bake at 325° F (165° C) until brown, 25 to 45 minutes, depending on the size and/or thickness of the ornament. As long as you do not overbrown it, bake it long enough to be sure it is hard and dry (after all it is not supposed to be eaten).

ALMOND DECORATING PASTE

    8 to 10 egg whites
  18 ounces (510 g) almond paste
    2 ounces (55 g) flour
    1 drop lemon juice
      small pinch ground cinnamon
      pinch salt
      milk
      cocoa powder, optional

Mix 8 egg whites, one at a time, into the almond paste; mix until smooth. Mix in flour, lemon juice, cinnamon, and salt. The paste should be thin enough to spread easily. If it is not, add the remaining egg whites. The number of egg whites necessary depends on the firmness of the original almond paste. Let it rest 30 minutes before using it because almond paste tends to absorb liquid. If it needs to be thinned more before using, add milk.

You can add cocoa powder to all or part of the paste; simply add proportionally less flour. Almond Decorating Paste is very versatile. It can be bent 360 degrees if needed and can be prepared well ahead of time, as long as it is stored in an airtight container. If making a flat design, you want the paste to be just thin enough so that it spreads easily. If you are to bend the design, add as much milk as you can and still have the design hold its shape when you remove the template.

Making a Template and Baking Designs

If you do not have and cannot buy the template you need, you can easily make your own by drawing the design on crescent board, which is the right $\frac{1}{16}$-inch (2-mm) thickness, and cutting it out with a sharp X-acto knife. If you want the template to last a long time, soak it in varnish and let it dry. For a permanent template, take a bit more time and cut it out of Plexiglas. Do not forget to include a handle which should be bent slightly upwards. Also, remember not to make too wide a frame; the wider the frame, the fewer designs you can fit on a sheet pan.

Use even sheet pans, greased lightly with a mixture of 1 part flour to 4 parts melted butter or lined with waxed paper. You cannot use parchment paper because it gets uneven from the moisture. Bake the designs at 375° F (190° C), a little hotter if you plan to bend them, until they start to get light brown in places, 5 to 8 minutes. Baking time depends totally on the size of the design, but they should become hard and dry as they cool. Pick each design off the sheet pan as it is done. If they are to be bent, it has to be done right away or they will break.

SAUCE ANGLAISE (VANILLA CUSTARD SAUCE)
5 cups (1 l, 2 dl)

  1 quart (9 dl, 6 cl) half-and-half
     vanilla bean or 1 teaspoon (6 g) vanilla extract
 12 egg yolks (240 g)
  8 ounces (225 g) sugar

Vanilla sauce is made basically the same way as basic custard for vanilla ice cream; in an emergency the two are interchangeable. You can freeze the sauce to make vanilla ice cream, or you can thaw vanilla ice cream to use as sauce.

Place the half-and-half and vanilla in a saucepan; heat to boiling. Whip egg yolks and sugar to the ribbon stage; then strain the half-and-half gradually into the yolk mixture, stirring rapidly. Place the mixture over hot water; heat, stirring constantly, until the mixture coats a spoon (at the very moment you pull a wooden spoon out of the sauce, you will not be able to see the wood). Pour into another container immediately or continue stirring for about 30 seconds. Use the sauce hot or cold.

The sauce can also be cooked directly over heat, but it is a little trickier. If you overheat the mixture and the yolks coagulate, you can save the sauce by adding 1 ounce (3 cl) heavy cream and processing it in a blender until smooth. Some volume will be lost, but the sauce will be saved.

SAUCE SABAYON
2 quarts (1 l, 9 dl, 2 cl)

> 10 egg yolks (200 g)
>   7 ounces (200 g) granulated sugar
>   2 cups (4 cl, 8 cl) Marsala, light or dark

This sauce can be served as a light dessert by itself, sprinkled lightly with nutmeg, or poured over fresh strawberries, and it is a perfect sauce for a liqueur soufflé. For the best results, it should be made just before serving because it loses some of its lightness and fluffiness and tends to separate after a few minutes. After some practice, it takes only 3 to 5 minutes to make.

Beat egg yolks and sugar over hot water until thick and fluffy. Add Marsala; continue whipping until the sauce coats a spoon. If the sauce is overheated, the eggs will coagulate and break the sauce. It is important to remove the sauce from the hot bowl as soon as it is done. Pour into the serving dishes and serve immediately, or if you need the sauce cold, stir it carefully over ice water until cool.

ORANGE SAUCE
about 6 cups (1 l, 4 dl, 4 cl)

> 2½ cups (6 dl) water
> 2 ounces (55 g) potato starch or cornstarch
> 2½ cups (6 dl) fresh orange juice
> few drops lemon juice
> 12 ounces (340 g) sugar
> 1 drop yellow food color
> tartaric acid
> Simple Syrup (see Index), optional
> 6 ounces (170 g) dark raisins, soaked

Mix enough water into the starch to make it pourable. Place the remaining water, the orange juice, lemon juice, sugar, and food color in a saucepan. Heat to boiling; stir in the starch solution. Heat again to a boil and cook for 2 to 3 minutes to remove the starch flavor. Let cool. Add tartaric acid to taste and, if needed, dilute with Simple Syrup. Lastly, stir in the raisins.

If potato starch is not available, use cornstarch. However, potato starch will make the sauce clearer, and it will last longer before it starts to break down.

STRAWBERRY SAUCE

Purée ripe or overripe strawberries and strain out some of the seeds; it is not necessary to strain out all of them because strawberry seeds are quite soft and look good in the sauce. Sweeten with Simple Syrup (see Index) to taste and add red food color if necessary.

Freeze strawberries that are getting too old or overripe to use for other things. Thaw them and use for sauces or sorbets.

MELBA SAUCE

Purée and strain fresh or frozen raspberries. Sweeten to taste. As a second choice only, force a good raspberry jam through a sieve fine enough to strain out the seeds and thin with lemon juice.

KIWI SAUCE

Purée ripe kiwis through a sieve by hand. If you use a food processor, be careful that you do not break some of the seeds, giving the sauce a muddy appearance. Thin and sweeten to taste with Simple Syrup (see Index).

LEMON CREAM

   12 eggs (600 g)
    1 pound, 2 ounces (510 g) granulated sugar
    6 ounces (170 g) butter
    6 ounces (1 dl, 8 cl) heavy cream
 1½ cups (3 dl, 6 cl) lemon juice
    3 ounces (9 cl) orange juice

Place eggs in a saucepan and beat them lightly. Add remaining ingredients; heat, stirring constantly, until mixture coats a spoon, about 155° F (68° C).

LEMON CURD AND SAUCE

     juice and finely grated zest of 16 to 18 lemons
  18 eggs
   1 pound, 9 ounces (710 g) butter
   3 pounds, 5 ounces (1 kg, 500 g) sugar

This recipe makes an excellent flavoring or filling, and it will keep for a long time in the refrigerator. Mix all ingredients in a saucepan; heat to boiling. Boil for a few seconds, stirring constantly, until the sauce thickens. Strain and let cool. To use for sauce, thin with more lemon juice.

BAVARIAN CREAM

   heavy cream, whipped stiff
   Pastry Cream (see p. 242)

This is a very uncomplicated version of bavarian cream that uses no gelatin. It is therefore important that the Pastry Cream is firm and free from lumps, or the final cream will be runny, hard to work with, and unpleasant and messy to eat.

Combine equal parts (by weight) of whipped cream and Pastry Cream. Mix only as much as you need at a time, since whipped cream starts to get a little soft after only a half hour, and you cannot bring it back to peak because of the addition of the Pastry Cream.

APPLE FILLING
4 cups (9 dl, 6 cl) filling

> 3 pounds (1 kg, 360 g) tart cooking apples (Gravenstein, pippin, or Jonathan)
> acidulated water
> 10 ounces (285 g) sugar
> 1 to 2 ounces (3 to 6 cl) water
> juice of ½ lemon

Peel and core the apples (4 cups). Place them in acidulated water to prevent them from turning brown. Chop two-thirds of the apples into ½-inch (12-mm) chunks. Place together apple chunks, sugar, water, and lemon juice in a saucepan. Adjust sugar and water according to the tartness and ripeness of the fruit. Cook over medium heat. In the meantime, chop remaining apples into ¼-inch (6-mm) chunks; add to the apple mixture when it starts to thicken. Finish cooking, but do not overcook; you want to have soft chunks in the filling. Cool and use, or store in the refrigerator until needed.

MAZARIN FILLING
12 pounds, 6 ounces (5 kg, 630 g) filling

> 5 pounds (2 kg, 270 g) almond paste
> 15 ounces (430 g) sugar
> 2½ pounds (1 kg, 135 g) butter
> 6 cups (1 l, 4 dl, 4 cl) eggs
> 9 ounces (255 g) flour

Place almond paste and sugar in a bowl; mix in butter gradually. Mix just until smooth. Mix in eggs, a few at a time. Stir in the flour.

Mazarin Filling can be stored in the refrigerator, but as with anything that contains a large number of eggs, it is best freshly made. Therefore, it is a good idea to use it all. Freeze the pastries or sheets you do not need and bake them later.

STREUSEL
3 pounds, 1 ounce (1 kg, 190 g)

  6 ounces (170 g) brown sugar
  6 ounces (170 g) granulated sugar
11 ounces (310 g) butter
½ ounce (15 g) ground cinnamon
½ tablespoon (6 g) salt
½ teaspoon (3 g) vanilla extract
  1 pound, 5 ounces (595 g) bread flour, approximately

Mix both sugars, butter, cinnamon, salt, and vanilla, and stir in the flour. The mixture should not come together but be crumbly; so adjust the amount of flour accordingly. Store on a paper-lined sheet pan in the refrigerator.

Index